S0-CVF-033

The economic ideal
in British government

Phyllis Colvin

The economic ideal in British government

Calculating costs and benefits in the 1970s

Manchester University Press

Published by Manchester University Press
Oxford Road, Manchester M13 9PL, UK
and 51 Washington Street, Dover, New Hampshire 03820, USA

British Library cataloguing in publication data
Colvin, Phyllis
The economic ideal in British government
1. Government spending policy—Great Britain
2. Great Britain—Appropriations and expenditures
I. Title
336.3'9'0941 HJ7766

Library of Congress cataloging in publication data
Colvin, Phyllis
The economic ideal in British Government.
1. Great Britain—Economic policy—1945– —Cost effectiveness. 2. Great Britain—Social policy—Cost effectiveness. 3. Cost effectiveness. 4. Policy sciences—Cost effectiveness. I. Title.
HC256.6.C617 1985 338.941 85-2978

ISBN 0-7190-1744-0 (cased)

Printed and bound in Great Britain by
Biddles Ltd, Guildford and King's Lynn

Contents

List of figures

Figures

Tables

Acknowledgements

A great number of people very kindly provided assistance and advice to me during the research and writing of this book. First, I would like to thank the many civil servants, both in Whitehall and the provinces, who gave generously of their time in interviews explaining many of the intricacies of the application of cost–benefit analysis in government and the role which economists play in the policy-making process. A number of them also commented on drafts of several of the chapters that follow, and helped me avoid many of the pitfalls one encounters when probing the process of policy-making in British government. One of the conditions of access, however, is guaranteeing the anonymity of civil service sources, so while their contribution is acknowledged here, and in many of the chapter notes, they, of necessity, must remain anonymous.

I also owe a debt of gratitude to the Commonwealth Scholarship Commission in the United Kingdom and the Social Sciences and Humanities Research Council of Canada for providing the financial support that allowed me to conduct the research for this book. Special thanks are also due to Professors Michael Gibbons and Roger Williams of the Department of Science and Technology Policy at Manchester University who read and commented upon earlier drafts of this book. I would also like to express my appreciation to Richard Whitley, Dean of the Manchester Business School, who introduced me to the philosophy and sociology of the social sciences and encouraged me to pursue this work.

Christine Dubois and Line Daigle typed several of the drafts of the manuscript with care and good humour, and made the production of the final manuscript a much more pleasant task. My final thanks go to my husband, who has coped with all of the hardships associated with a manuscript in preparation and who has always been a fund of wit, wisdom and good humour. Naturally, any remaining weaknesses in argument and content in this book are my responsibility.

Ottawa,
April 1984

P.C.

1

The microeconomic worldview and public policy

The collectivist era

Since the late nineteenth century, and especially since the Second World War, one of the most distinctive features of modern life has been the emergence of public values and public administration in areas of existence that were once largely private. Many activities that originally centred on the marketplace, the family, or community and religious groups are now part of the public realm. The late 1970s and the 1980s brought a major debate about public 'intrusion' into the private sector. Concerns with low growth and public sector inefficiency, especially in the nationalized industries, precipitated demands for privatization and deregulation, and these have found expression in many of the policies of the Thatcher Government. However, the scale of modern-day economic activity, the pace of technological change, the new emphasis on individual rights, and continuing widespread commitments to social equity have in large measure precluded a return to a minimalist state. In many fields reliance on private sector initiative is constrained because of problems with market failure, the same problems that earlier led to public intervention. Moreover, the traditional pillars of private social action – the family and organized religion – have been weakened, and no alternatives have emerged to replace them. Thus, the interpretation of public values, and the administration of the public sector, offer a continuing challenge, both for those employed in the public domain and for society as a whole.

So extensive has the advent of public culture been that the twentieth century may legitimately be described as a collectivist era. Many of the most important decisions that affect people's lives are taken in the political or public arena. Consequently, the views politicians and civil servants hold about the development and implementation of public policy have assumed major significance. Traditionally, these have arisen from a complex interplay of forces ranging from commitments that have grown up within the civil service about the appropriate role for government action to the party political or ideological preferences that Ministers bring to their portfolios. In recent decades, however, a major new influence has come into play within the public sector, one that has its roots outside the political and administrative milieu of British central government. This is the economic worldview, and, in particular, the tendency to see public action in terms of its economic costs and benefits.

Since the last war, in Britain, as elsewhere in the industrialized world, public policy questions have increasingly come to be construed in explicitly economic terms. Whether in the social or the industrial sphere, government policy has been effected mainly through economic instruments. In the wake of the assimilation of Keynes's work within government circles in the years immediately after the War, maintaining high and stable levels of employment through the promotion of sustained economic expansion became a major priority.[1] Keynes's active conception of the state also brought rising levels of public expenditure, notably a major expansion of the welfare state and substantial provision of new industrial infrastructure in the form of roads, ports, telecommunications facilities and research laboratories.

The main beneficiary of this meshing of economics and public policy both in Britain and elsewhere has been the economics profession. Economists first assumed an important profile within the public sector as a result of the Keynsian revolution and their expertise in demand management. Gradually, however, economists broadened their sphere of policy interests. Rising levels of public expenditure brought the question of how best to allocate public moneys to the fore, and this question became all the more urgent as economic debate came to focus on the costs of economic growth.[2] This expansion of interest was accompanied by growth in the numbers of government economists. During the 1950s and 1960s economic expertise was largely confined to the Cabinet Office, the Treasury and macroeconomic pursuits. However, beginning in the mid-1960s the number of professional economists within central government increased dramatically (from less than 25 in 1964 to more than 350 in 1975).[3] By the end of the 1970s the economics profession had come to be represented in virtually all parts of Whitehall, and government economists were engaged in work ranging across all aspects of the discipline: macroeconomic and microeconomic, positive and normative.

One of the most important symbols of the economic profession's new status in the public sector has been the analytical and evaluative technique called cost–benefit analysis (CBA). Based in the welfare economics of Pareto, Pigou and their followers, this technique held out the promise of a viable 'technology' for the optimal allocation of public resources, thereby giving public sector investment analysis a framework comparable to that which apparently obtained in the private sector. Like many potent symbols, CBA is essentially an empty vessel that has given shape to a variety of aspirations. For the economist, it is a vehicle for structuring questions about policy problems and lending these an arithmetic cast. Just as importantly, the apparent simplicity of the cost–benefit terminology has meant that it has gained wide currency with non-economists. Few politicians, for example, can resist giving weight to their positions with arguments such as 'the benefits exceed the costs'. The result has been that discussions about policy are saturated with the methodology's logic, whether those involved acknowledge this to be the case or not.[4] On occasion, as well, CBA has been at the centre of heated, but often unfocused, debates about technocracy in public life, as was the case with the Third London Airport and the Channel Tunnel proposals. The acrimony surrounding such debates has frequently lingered for years, a dull reminder of deep conflicts that have seldom been fully articulated, much more rarely resolved.

This book explores the worldview that the economics profession brought into public life as it is represented in the application of cost–benefit analysis to public sector investment. As such, it is a study of the outlook that structures economic analysis, and the various types of knowledge that follow from that outlook and their implications for the way in which work is organized and carried out in the public sector. Gaining an understanding of the role that an economic technique such as CBA plays within the public sector is sometimes difficult, in part because of the closed nature of the Whitehall policy process, and in part because of the wide variety of issues and subject areas that have been affected by the advent of microeconomic perspectives, each in a slightly different way. Nevertheless, the study of the application of CBA in central government provides an important window on what happens when economics and policy come together. Where, for example, does the economic perspective on policy come from? What are the origins of the cost–benefit grammar that now pervades public debate? How did a technique such as CBA become so rapidly integrated into the policy development process? Finally, and perhaps most importantly, how has the economic perspective on policy, and CBA in particular, affected the way in which policy issues are conceived and handled within Whitehall?

The book falls into four parts, although these have not been labelled explicitly. The first, comprising this chapter and the next, looks at the conceptual underpinnings of economic analysis as it is applied to public policy, and especially at the relationship between theory and practice in the use of cost–benefit analysis. The second part of the book, consisting of Chapter 3, provides an analysis of the process whereby economists and economic methodologies came to be integrated into the various branches of central government during the 1960s and 1970s. There then follows the third part of the book – three case studies of the application of CBA to particular policy issues. The focus is on the 1970s, when the enthusiasm for cost–benefit analysis was at its height. The case studies cover three very diverse topics: transport, manpower and health policy. They were chosen because together they serve to indicate the breadth of the policy domain in which economics plays a part and because they display different aspects of the way CBA has been integrated into the policy arena. Finally, the concluding chapter offers an assessment of the implications the economic worldview has for public policy in the UK and where its application may be leading us as a society.

The remainder of this chapter focuses on the conceptual roots of cost–benefit analysis and the distinctive analytical framework that economics brings to public policy. It explores the multipolar view of the market at the core of economic theory and the role this has played in the development of a scientific and, later, a professional ethos within the economics discipline. The key to this process was the emergence of the Neoclassical synthesis in the years after 1870. This chapter examines how the mechanistic assumptions at the centre of Neoclassical economics gave rise to a new definition of behaviour – that which economists call rational – and the implications of this for the development within economics of a 'technology' of business and latterly politics and public administration.

The market and the foundations of economic theory

The discipline of economics is a product of Western economic and intellectual development. Therefore, from whatever perspective it derives, economic reasoning must contend with the dominance of capitalism in Western societies. There are many approaches to the conceptualization of capitalist economic relations, but the majority elevate the market to the position of the most prominent and most characteristic capitalist economic formation. Moreover, although theories of monopoly and oligopoly have assumed an important place in economics in this century, the traditional and still most widely used reconstruction of the market stresses its multipolarity.[5]

The Classical version of this reconstruction, developed in the writings of Smith, Ricardo and Mill, portrays the market as a self-adjusting system founded upon individual initiative and governed by free competition. Market participants pursue their individual interests. Their intent is to enlarge and make best use of their incomes. Producers and consumers translate their intentions into action by continuously adjusting the terms of exchange for goods and services, with the result that the system as a whole moves rapidly and smoothly towards equilibrium. In the process, individuals enhance their own interests, and raise the collective wealth of the nation. Competition precludes unequal levels of accumulation leading to monopoly or oligopoly, and liberty is thereby preserved.[6]

The Classical reconstruction of the market is based upon an understanding of economic relations that stresses the individualistic, the atomistic and the discrete, but it was originally intended to explain the nature and development of aggregate features of the market such as the pricing shorthand. Later in the model's development, specifically following the emergence of marginalism, questions concerning the nature of the efficiency guaranteed by the market came to the fore, and it was employed to elucidate, on the producer side, 'the extent to which market prices reflect real opportunity costs' and, on the consumer side, 'the extent to which competitive equilibrium is a Pareto optimum'.[7] Yet aggregate properties of markets such as price and equilibrium have never been obvious derivatives of the freely competitive chaos of the multipolar representation of the market.

> The emphasis is placed upon the profusion of decentralized individual decisions which are juxtaposed and not integrated. Overall equilibrium is their necessary but fortuitous consequence because it is not one of their motivations.[8]

This contrast between the necessary and the fortuitous epitomizes the difficulties that have traditionally been associated with specifying the type of order characteristic of the market.

The problem of order in this case of model-building derives in the first instance from the properties of individuals postulated in the model. The subjects of the model are discrete, self-contained, self-interested individuals. They are continuously involved in the exchange of commodities, but this process lacks an interpersonal, and, therefore, a social and historical dimension. Market actors are not engaged in expanding their familiarity with the market and the manner in which it is evolving by comparing their preferences with those of others and then, on that basis, elaborating or restricting particular wants. Rather, in the Classical description, and more emphatically in the later development of the multipolar model, perfect knowledge of the market in its entirety is given for all subjects. Concomitantly, the Classical description is not concerned with the way in which certain understandings of the market affect the articulation of wants, and, therefore, while all subjects are self-motivated and have perfect knowledge, the nature of their wants remains undifferentiated. In later, specifically Neoclassical, versions of the model, it is quite explicit that individual tastes are taken as given.

Just as their wants are undifferentiated, so are the subjects themselves. The collection of individuals that comprises the multipolar reconstruction of the market is amorphous in a number of senses. For example, distinctions involving form and scale are not part of the model. An 'economy' can range from a single firm and a single household to all firms and households in some geographic universe. There is no ordering principle that permits distinctions between 'one' and 'some', or between 'some' and 'many'. These differences rest upon simple enumeration, and are, therefore, meaningless to further analysis under the terms established by the model. In addition, the relations between subjects in the multipolar reconstruction are such that structure and organization are minimized. Competition, for example, is an integral feature of the reconstruction. It ensures that market participants cannot be constrained to any necessary postures within the market, and is the guarantee that they have latitude of choice and decision. For precisely these reasons, however, competition plays no role in the description of the market as a collective. Indeed, with the later development of the model it has become apparent that competition is best described as a guarantee for the colourlessness of the model's subjects. Competition ensures that no individual producer or consumer acquires sufficient influence so as to have an impact upon price levels, and this guarantee permits the resolution of a number of model-induced problems:

> . . . first, the sumultaneous determination of price and quantity by the intersection of mutually independent demand and supply curves; secondly, the solution of the problem of the exact exhaustion of the product by the aggregate of the factor bills . . ., and thirdly, the formal description of production at minimum unit cost.[9]

Thus, the properties attributed to the subjects of the multipolar model are not such as to make the solution to the problem of order obvious. Nevertheless, a solution did emerge in the years after 1870 when Walras and others introduced an economic calculus based on rational self-interest. The Walrasian or Neoclassical variation of the multipolar model has since constituted the dominant reconstruction of the market and the foundation of a variety of microeconomic theories.

The Neoclassical synthesis

Economics is a social science in that it addresses the most basic activities of mankind, namely the production and distribution of values, however defined. Yet it differs from other social sciences in the traditional strength of its practitioners' commitment to modes of explanation drawn from the physical sciences. Indeed, economics can be regarded as an eclectic discipline[10] in that it has assimilated models, methodologies and techniques from physical sciences and engineering specialities with which its affiliations in terms of subject matter are less than immediate. For example, the Quantity Theory of Money, upon which modern monetarism has been erected, is hydraulic in character. Business cycle theories have frequently been founded upon the assumption that the market behaves in the same manner as a mechanical device like a steam engine with regularly repeated cycles as measured by clock time. However, the most striking manifestation of the dependence of economics upon the exact sciences is the Walrasian mechanics of self-interest.[11]

The founders of much of modern microeconomics and in particular general equilibrium theory, most notably Walras, Jevons, Menger and Pareto, were preoccupied with enhancing the exactitude, consistency and completeness of the Classical multipolar model, primarily by emphasizing the application of physical models and mathematical notation to economics.[12] Implicit in their work was the recognition that the manner in which the attributes of market subjects had been conceived under the Classical reconstruction paralleled stances about the nature of reality inherent to theories in the physical sciences. In particular, the attributes of the self-interested subjects of the Classical model are potentially consistent with the rigours of theoretical reasoning because they belong to a class of concepts which Georgescu-Roegen has called 'arithmomorphic'. As the name implies, concepts of this type are discretely distinct in the way that a single number is distinct from the infinity of all other numbers.[13] This attribute of discrete distinctness stems from the subordination of quality (in the sense of form, scale, configuration and temporal variation). Such conceptual simplicity has important advantages, for arithmomorphic concepts constitute the foundation of logic, computation and axiomatically-based theoretical sciences.[14] It was this consideration that informed the work of Walras and his contemporaries.

Like their Classical predecessors, the architects of Neoclassical economics focused upon exchange, and specifically the individual valuations inherent to this process, with the difference that in the Neoclassical framework exchange possesses a much more general significance than it has in Classical economics. Thus, from the Neoclassical standpoint, the economic system consists of a general market composed of a number of specialized markets in which individuals buy and sell. The task was to establish the laws of exchange, whether for two-party two-commodity barter, multi-commodity exchange, production, or the capital and money markets. The result of the Neoclassicals' efforts in this direction was a mathematical elaboration of the theory of rational self-interest, a calculus that lends coherence to the economic explanation of market relations.

Neoclassical economics as developed by Walras and his contemporaries involves a conservation principle and a maximization rule, and is, therefore, a mechanical analogue.[15] It is assumed that at any particular instant in time the means at the disposal of every economic actor are given (the conservation principle). Given too are the ends of each economic actor, and, therefore, the object of economic analysis is to determine the *allocation* of the given means that most fulfils the given ends of the market participants. Prereconciliation of choice (the Walrasian *tâtonnement* or groping) constitutes an important precondition for this type of analysis. The latter is founded, however, upon the nineteenth century discovery of the maximization rule at the centre of marginal utility theory and other marginal doctrines. Diminishing marginal rates of substitution allow a state(s) of maximum satisfaction for all market participants, or 'competitive equilibrium', to be defined and analysed.[16] Thus, in the Neoclassical reconstruction, the ordering principles integrating market subjects with the market system, components with the whole, are explicit, if only for the static case.

This mechanical synthesis has had immense implications for the conceptualization of man and of thought in the twentieth century. In particular, it is premised on a view of the economic actor that is as spare as possible given the limits of plausibility. One aspect of this was the tendency to exclude the individual from economic analysis by reducing the economic actor either to his mental states or to his actions:

> As Pareto overtly claimed, once we have determined the means at the disposal of the individual and obtained 'a photograph of his tastes . . . the individual may disappear'.[17]

Another was the tendency to restrict the economic actor's cognitive capacities to a particular type – that which economists call rational.

Before the advent of Neoclassical economics rationality was a term with a rich and varied history derived from Western man's inclination to apply reason to his situation and in the wake of the Enlightenment his increasing doubts about divine revelation. However, in this century rationality has generally assumed a more limited meaning as a result of the influence of the Neoclassical synthesis both within economics and outside. To be precise, in order for market participants to conform to the conservation principle and the maximization rule of the Neoclassical mechanical analogue their mental processes must be of a specific kind – that which economists call rational. Perfect knowledge ensures that thought and action are determinate. The ability to prereconcile one's choices with the choices of others guarantees that all market subjects contribute equally to the exchange process and, at the same time, permits actions in the market to be simultaneous. This last point is important, for to be rational is to orient individual thought and action towards the attainment of a specific 'public' standard, namely the demonstrably optimal. If prereconciliation of choice, and hence, simultaneity were not integral parts of the Neoclassical model, the march of time would prevent the full fusion of individual action and the optimality standard upon which rationality rests.[18]

To be sure, aggregate properties of the Neoclassical model cannot be reduced to the properties of individuals. Therefore, in the course of prereconciling his choices with those of others the rational actor does not know the prices characteristic of equilibrium. What he does know are his own preferences, the resources that he has at his disposal and the environment he faces. His problem is to allocate his resources in such a way that his well-being is enhanced to the greatest degree possible, and given that the maximization rule applies to all (as evident in the universal convexity of indifference curves), this problem has a solution. In responding to the signals latent in his situation, in groping towards this solution, the market participant is said to behave rationally. By doing so, he practises economy at his own level, and ensures that equilibrium and, hence, efficiency are characteristics of the market as a whole.

An important facet of rationality, and one that is of great significance in the remainder of this book, is the practice of resolving all economic questions into problems of *counterpoint*.[19] Economics has traditionally, and quite naturally, been preoccupied with the realization of human desires in an environment that presents both opportunities and constraints. However, with the development of the mechanics of self-interest the treatment of this subject became limited to the consideration of a single issue. Rational behaviour in the Neoclassical sense is centred upon given ends and given means.[20] It is this pair of concepts, this counterpoint, that is fundamental to the structure of microeconomic theory, so much so that economics is replete with pairs of concepts that in varying degrees reproduce the symmetry of the ends–means dyad: demand and supply, needs and satisfactions, outputs and inputs, *benefits and costs*.

The ends–means counterpoint of Neoclassical economics has two aspects. On the one hand, the integrity of general equilibrium theory requires that ends and means be viewed as complementary. Thus, for example, in Walras's system demand is the mirror image of supply.[21] On the other hand, means place limits on the achievement of ends, and, therefore, means and ends may be regarded as juxtaposed. Moreover, it is this interpretation of the ends–means counterpoint that is most prominent in the development of economic thought. In the main, the explanation for this lies with the lack of concern for the *nature* of ends and means characteristic of Neoclassical economics. The mechanics of self-interest portrays ends and means as discretely distinct. As a result, it has no answers to offer to questions focused on whether and in what degree means are appropriate to ends. Thus, beyond stating its existence, economists operating within this framework have not concerned themselves with the complementarity of ends and means. Instead, they have tended to focus their attention upon the arithmetic character of the

Neoclassical synthesis and, hence, upon the separation or juxtaposition of ends and means.

Economic analysis in the Neoclassical sense is not concerned with the reasons why particular ends and means come to be juxtaposed, nor can it suggest how ends and means are reconciled during economic processes. Nevertheless, the juxtaposition of ends and means has had important consequences for economic methodology. Specifically, this structure has served to extend what Shackle calls 'the additive or scalar character of economic theory':

> When there are 'two sides' the natural and inevitable question is: Which is the stronger? Which is the greater?[22]

Questions of this type allow arithmetic answers, and they are at the centre of input–output theory, cost-effectiveness and cost–benefit analysis and many other vehicles employed by the economics profession at the present time. Moreover, the juxtaposition of ends and means has been instrumental in extending the range of microeconomics. As will become evident during the course of this book, the problems of many fields can be construed in terms of a pair of juxtaposed opposites.

The elaboration of the mechanics of rational self-interest in the thirty to forty years after 1870 had a radical impact on the discipline of economics. In particular, it consitutes the historical foundation for the economics profession. By adopting and elaborating a model of the market in which arithmomorphic concepts are central, economics enhanced its claims to special and, in many presentations, scientific knowledge of the social order. The mathematical character and generality of the Neoclassical model, especially as espoused by Walras in the course of his voluminous correspondence, was central to the emergence of a common approach and a common language within the discipline.[23] The Neoclassical model allowed particular problems to be viewed as specific manifestations of a general scheme, and, therefore, served to unify economic debate and to cement intellectual and social relationships between economists in different institutional and national settings.

This consolidation process meant, in turn, that the economics discipline became committed to reproducing the Neoclassical constructions and modes of understanding that had contributed so centrally to unifying it and lending it an enhanced prestige within the range of social sciences. For example, the objective of economics has gradually come to be conflated with the mechanistic project launched by Walras and his contemporaries. Economics is frequently defined as the study of rational man, of *homo oeconomicus*, or, more generally, of the principles that govern the efficient allocation of given means in relation to given ends.[24] Indeed, it has become very difficult to define the microeconomic project without reference to vocabulary native to Neoclassical theory (e.g., maximization, equilibrium, efficiency, etc.).[25] Similarly, the views of the nature of man and of thought inherent to Neoclassical theory have acquired formal status within economics. Just as the mechanics of self-interest gives new meaning to the terms 'rational' and 'rationality', so economists subscribe to the rational ideal.

The rational ideal

During the nineteenth century the prestige physics enjoyed among the sciences had a major effect upon the development of theoretical structures in many disciplines. However, in no case was the authority of theoretical practices in physics more apparent than in the emergence of Neoclassical economics. In taking classical mechanics, together with the Newtonian calculus, as their exemplar, Walras and his contemporaries were attempting to demonstrate that disciplines studying man were capable of generating theories with the characteristics that had made physical theories so impressive in the realms of prediction and control. In line with physical examples, economic theories of this period dealt primarily with quantities, not qualities, hence with cardinal, nor ordinal, measures. Economic analysis was directed towards the elucidation of the laws governing valuation and exchange, and to this end arithmetic formalisms were erected and elaborated until every detail of the underlying mechanics had been pursued. In this latter process 'completeness', in the sense of the integration of all spheres of economic life into a closed axiomatic system, was a compelling, if never fulfilled, goal of much theoretical work. 'Consistency' across theoretical categories also became an important objective in the development of economic theory as economists attempted to ensure that the Neoclassical reconstruction did not encounter challenges as a result of contradictions latent in its structure (witness the debates concerning cardinal and ordinal utility, and, more recently, revealed preference).[26]

Moreover, the affiliation with mechanics and, hence, with physics proved propitious. Economists have employed models and analytical devices derived from disciplines other than physics. Marshall, for example, drew upon biological analogies for many of his economic explanations. However, as the twentieth century progressed the prestige of biology waned, particularly after the First World War, and the biological analogies introduced into economics were not pursued. Physics, on the other hand, came to dominate the sciences in the twentieth century, especially in the wake of the weapons research and development that accompanied two World Wars and the Soviet–American confrontation of recent decades. The high status of the Neoclassical reconstruction was, therefore, assured, and the mechanics of self-interest has remained at the core of economic analysis, even in the wake of the 'Keynesian revolution'. As a result, economists acquired prestige as the exponents of numeracy and, by implication, exact knowledge within the social sciences. This, combined with the special understanding of human relations that a study of Neoclassical economics provided, formed the basis of a new professionalism.[27] A central feature of this professionalism was the belief on the part of many economists that the Neoclassical reconstruction has a variety of potential applications, that a 'technology' of business, or perhaps politics, is possible on the basis of Neoclassical insights.[28] This conviction led to the progressive institutionalization within many settings of what may be designated as the 'rational ideal'.

Rationality is the epistemological expression of the necessity to bridge the gulf between ends and means, between man and nature, that is characteristic of the Neoclassical reconstruction. As indicated earlier, Neoclassical theory is not concerned with the nature of ends and means, and for this reason ends–means complementarity has taken a second place to ends–means separation or juxtaposition in the development of economic thought. None the less, the Neoclassical reconstruction, like all economic theories, reconciles ends and means, and rationality constitutes the individual orientation whereby this is accomplished. It invokes a parallelism between the nature of the commodities that are manipulated in the market and the nature of the physical and mental attributes available to man with which he appropriates these commodities for his own uses. Under strict rationality the problems associated with the acquisition of human knowledge, both psychological and social, are reduced to the assumption that matter fits the needs of man. The question of how human beings formulate their wants is not dealt with in this context because Neoclassical theory denies the independence of ends.[29] The same is true of questions regarding how men identify means suitable to their ends. Thus, for example, the processes involved in developing appropriate materials and technologies for specific types of production are non-problematic. On a broader front, consideration of whether ends and means might be integrated or ordered in ways different from that implied by the maximization rule is not possible within this format. Yet it is this very simplicity that constitutes the foundation for the rational doctrine's considerable social authority. Rationality permits the analyst who embraces it to set aside the many particular problems associated with the way in which man sustains himself in his environment, and, therefore, to concentrate upon the fundamental laws governing human conduct in the marketplace.

Rationality also derives authority from its monolithic character. Parsons has observed that positivistic theories, of which the Neoclassical reconstruction is one, typically do not employ subjective categories in portraying action, but rely, instead, upon appeals to objective processes in interpreting individual behaviour.[30] It is exactly this abandonment of subjective categories, along lines described in the previous paragraph, that lends rationality its monolithic character and, hence, part of its social authority. Rational man acts not as a result of a selective awareness of his means, ends and conditions but in accord with a 'public standard'. In order for this standard to be realized, the individual's thought processes must be of a specific type. Therefore, rationality allows little or no scope for epistemological variation. In contrast, for example, to the arithmetic doctrine underpinning the arithmetic ideal of the physical sciences, which has historically been differentiated, particularly at the epistemological level, into a variety of stances ranging from positivism through Neo-Kantianism to realism, rationality is one and indivisible. This characteristic lends great authority to the doctrine, for its adherents seldom have to explain away contradictions internal to the doctrine's structure. Moreover, the doctrine's appeal has not been diluted by disputes between groups committed to different interpretations of mind and, therefore, of matter.[31]

The social authority of the rational doctrine is further sustained by the way in which it appeals to certain widely held understandings both of the nature and the desirability of specific types of social action. There are many circumstances in which accumulated social lore is such that it is possible to identify the 'right' selection of means for a certain end.[32] The doctrine of rationality lends generality to this particular, but widely perceived, phenomenon by portraying *all* market transactions as 'right' in this sense. There are, therefore, relatively few difficulties for the layman in assimilating the general thrust of the doctrine (although perhaps not its technical details), and its authority is thereby increased. In addition, the identification between market transactions and 'right' action inherent to rationality constitutes the basis of an ethical imperative that lends further support to the rational doctrine. The Neoclassical reconstruction is both descriptive and prescriptive. Laymen are urged to employ the insights provided by the model as a guide to the market and to a type of conduct that is enterprising yet moderate, hence to be emulated. 'Commonsense' in many walks of life is derived from the Neoclassical worldview. Thus, in business and politics we are urged to admire and support the rational contender. An important point to note in this connection is that individuals or groups that do not accede to this type of commonsense are often said to act 'irrationally' or 'non-rationally', and, by implication, to undermine the welfare of the collectivity. This type of labelling can serve to isolate and neutralize adherents to opposing worldviews, thereby reinforcing the social authority of rationality.

The strength of the rational ideal both within economics and beyond the boundaries of the discipline also derives from the connection between rationality and scalarity. There are two aspects to this. In the first place, as noted earlier, the juxtaposition of ends and means characteristic of rationality encourages questions (Which is the greater?, etc.) that invite arithmetically expressed answers. The social authority of rationality stems in large part from the simplicity and determinate character of these questions and answers. Second, rationality facilitates the extension of scalarity to new subject areas. Neoclassical theory posits that man is rational in making choices in the marketplace. Furthermore, the theory represents rational conduct in arithmetic terms. If, then, other types of human action can be construed as having an economic dimension (that is, as involving choice) there would appear, according to this perspective, to be few barriers to the application of arithmetic or scalar argument in many spheres of social investigation. The theoretical vehicle most frequently used in the extension of scalar argument to new subject areas is the pair of juxtaposed 'opposites' mentioned earlier.

This project is, of course, not without its limits. For reasons of taste or credibility economists may refrain from applying scalar arguments too explicitly in areas in which religious belief, patriotism or human mortality are central, although in this context it is also important to note that the valuation of human life has recently emerged as a speciality within applied microeconomics. In addition, there have been conflicts, at times heated, between economists and other social scientists as a result of the extension of economic modes of reasoning into spheres in which other than economic doctrines are dominant. Nevertheless, in general, the authority of the rational doctrine has been strengthened by the attempts to construe a variety of social questions in arithmetic terms. Not only has the range of microeconomics been expanded, but the mode of reasoning that has been instrumental in extending scalarity to new subject areas also has properties that reinforce rationality by comparison with other disciplinary doctrines. For example, for each problem or 'application' social sciences other than economics usually offer *many*, often non-arithmetic explanations. In contrast, economics employs pairs of juxtaposed opposites that are a manifestation of *one* arithmetically informed explanation with, apparently, many applications. This difference permits economists to be more efficient than other social scientists in handling the problems of new subject areas, and thus, more adept at expanding the horizons of their discipline.

Finally, there are two important features of the economics discipline that both reflect and reinforce the social authority of rationality. The first of these is the lack of 'experimental' or 'testing' philosophy within microeconomics. In a discipline dominated by a doctrine that asserts that the way in which man is conceived is consistent with the way in which he comprehends and that these are, in turn, consistent with a well-defined public standard, there is little incentive to test the theoretical postulates supporting the doctrine. To do so is to attempt to abstract oneself from the theoretically defined totality, and generally economists have felt little need to take this direction. Microeconomic theory suffers from a lack of rigorously empirical support. For example:

A cornerstone of microeconomics, both theoretical and applied, is the belief that the marginal equivalences of the neoclassical model are achieved, to a tolerable degree, in whatever economic situation is being analysed. To date, that belief – for all its importance – is largely untested hypothesis.[33]

There also seems to be little prospect that this situation will be altered. Interest in methodological questions among economists has, if anything, waned in recent decades. In Boland's words, most members of the profession 'endorse some form of Conventionalism and struggle against Empiricism'.[34] Moreover, it is not remarkable that they should do so. The lack of a testing philosophy within microeconomics serves to strengthen the authority of rationality. In the case of the physical sciences, experimental work has often been accompanied by epistemological controversy (as, for example, in the revitalization of Kantian doctrine associated with Helmholtz's physiological experimentation).[35] The doctrine of rationality has not been fragmented, and therefore made vulnerable, in this sense. Hypothesis testing in economics is a product of the twentieth century, and in the main is confined to the largely inductive field of macroeconomics.

The other feature of microeconomics that both reflects and reinforces the authority of rationality is the importance of what Stigler has called 'casual knowledge' both in the development and in the current practices of microeconomics.[36] The adequacy of Neoclassical economics depends not upon the accuracy of the representation of market actors and market relations that it encompasses, but upon the *coherence* of its deductive description of the market and the *insights* it seems to provide concerning how men conduct affairs in order to ensure their own welfare. As Stigler has noted in discussing the development of utility theory, in the past these insights acquired their support from the casual observations of intelligent men (often economists) concerning how men earn and spend their incomes.[37] Moreover, in the absence of a testing philosophy within microeconomics, casual knowledge continues to play a central role in supporting Neoclassical theory. When questions regarding the validity of Neoclassical tenets are raised, the profession often resorts to appeals to the informed judgement of the initiated. A typical instance would be Blaug's observation about demand curves:

From casual observation we feel sure that most demand curves are negatively inclined.[38]

At other times the layman's sense of proportion is invoked. Thus, economists often attempt to validate the convexity of indifference curves by noting that to assume they are otherwise implies monomania, an orientation they feel most laymen and students will find unrealistic or abnormal. Like the lack of a testing philosophy in microeconomics, this type of casual knowledge is both a product of the monolithic character of rationality and a guarantee of the continued authority of the doctrine. In particular, it is a function of the Neoclassical reconstruction's capacity to assimilate its apparent objects of study. Thus, it is 'loose and relatively timeless'. It is 'better calculated to detect new error than to enlarge old truth'.[39] Yet, for exactly these reasons, it also serves to reinforce the stability and authority of the rational doctrine.

Social corollaries of the rational ideal

In the decades since the emergence of the Neoclassical reconstruction the rational ideal has played a leading role both in the development of economics and in the emergence of several other fields of study. The dominant worldview in business administration is rationalistic, and the rational ideal (if in a modified form) has its advocates in modern public administration.[40] Moreover, as emerging academic disciplines assimilated the ideal, business and government, which had previously been callings that demanded apprenticeship not training, increasingly came to accept the legitimacy of the rationalistic standard.

In each case the progressive institutionalization of the rational ideal had the effect of altering patterns of social authority, organization and work practices. One manifestation of this is the contrast between teaching practices in economics and those in other social sciences and the humanities. More than any other social science, economics, like the physical sciences, organizes its materials into well-defined units. Since Marshall's time, therefore, the main teaching vehicle has been the text, now often accompanied by manuals or work books that advocate specific study plans. While other social sciences give emphasis in teaching to wide reading and synthetic argument, economics encourages a specific focus and analytical discourse. Neoclassical economics is a closed, arithmetic and, more recently, axiomatic construction.[41] Within the Neoclassical framework criteria of excellence centre upon the successful manipulation of arithmetic formalisms and the plausible reduction of social phenomena so that arithmetic analysis may be employed. Thus, teaching in economics is focused on a variety of educational problems designed to illustrate the properties of the formalisms. Recognition is awarded for spare, yet complete and theoretically informed, answers to these problems and, in examinations, for the ability to recognize new problems as variations on an underlying logic and solve them accordingly. This orientation toward instruction may be viewed as a social corollary of the rational ideal in that it embodies the assumption that teaching is most effective when the study process is organized in accord with the nature of the theoretical commitments that are being transmitted.

A commitment to the rational ideal is also evident in the organization of the economics discipline. Two forms of specialization prevail. One centres on subject area, whether agricultural economics, industrial organization, public finance, pricing, labour economics, or public policy, to cite a few examples. The other derives from the operational distinctions between descriptive, applied and analytical economics. Neither, however, reflects a vision of the structure of economic knowledge or a developmental strategy that the economics discipline might pursue to substantiate its claims to special expertise in each of its areas of endeavour. Instead, specialization has led to a compartmentalization rather than a division or differentiation of labour within the economics profession.

This may be illustrated by noting that specialization by subject in economics is not associated with the development of theories about the relations between specialities. Economic subject areas are frequently affiliated with, and in many instances defined by, a certain type of microeconomic or macroeconomic treatment. Thus, the income–employment–price question is largely a product of Keynesian, and later monetarist, macroeconomic preoccupations. A large part of the public policy field relies on microeconomic theory, of both the positive and welfare varieties. Yet, as McClelland has observed:

> A curiosity of economics is its failure to relate in any precise manner its theories about individual behavior to almost all of its theories concerning aggregate behavior. General equilibrium theory is the one exception.[42]

Economists have recognized this disjuncture for decades, but such is the strength of the rational ideal, with its emphasis on the discrete and self-contained, that the existence of a gap between microeconomic and macroeconomic theory has remained largely unproblematic.[43] In a similar vein, within the microeconomic sphere theoretical differentiation between subject areas and theoretical novelty within a new subject area are rare. Instead, Neoclassical tenets are exported from subject area to subject area,[44] and, therefore, theoretical premises in fields as apparently diverse as labour economics and pricing are likely to be identical. This type of homogeneity across categories is particularly evident in the field of public policy. For example, in dealing with transport, health, defence, the environment and housing, the welfare economist will be likely to employ the same theoretical format.

This tendency to compartmentalize is also apparent in the contrast between the analytical–applied–descriptive classification of economics with the theoretical–experimental–analytical and pure–applied–technological classifications characteristic of the physical and biological sciences. The analytical economist resembles the theoretical scientist in that each is involved in manipulating, expanding and evaluating the theoretical formalisms that constitute the foundation of their respective disciplines. However, professional equivalents to the experimentalist and analyst of the physical and biological sciences are rare within economics, particularly within microeconomics. The rational ideal has served to weaken the distinction between theory and knowledge in economics, and hence, the enterprise of substantiating theoretical claims through experiment or hypothesis testing tends to be neglected within the discipline. As a result, applied and descriptive economics, unlike applied science and technology, are not necessarily related to processes of testing the value and adequacy of hypotheses. Most applied and descriptive economists are best described as 'theorists' with problem-centred inclinations.[45] Applied and descriptive economists at the microeconomic level tend to employ theory as a guide to sampling and analysing their cognitive environment. What appears to be a differentiation of tasks similar to those of the physical and biological sciences in which each set of tasks both sustains the legitimacy and enlarges the scope of other sets is, instead, a compartmentalization of tasks along pragmatic lines allowing the efficient projection of theory into a number of applied areas. The importance that the rational ideal attaches to formal argument means that analytical economics is more prestigious than applied economics, which is, in turn, more prestigious than descriptive economics. Yet the consistency of rationality ensures that to some degree all economists are 'theorists'.

There are a number of further social phenomena associated with the dominance of the rational doctrine within economics that are particularly significant given the content of subsequent chapters of this book. Many economists in Britain, especially those who choose to work in government, business or other non-university spheres do not proceed beyond the first degree or the Master of Economics. In general, economists entering non-academic settings after this level of training regard themselves as interpreters of the store of theoretical knowledge contained in their discipline, even if they are in an applied or descriptive speciality. This has meant that the profession tends to be quite egalitarian in these environments.[46] Each professional regards himself, and is regarded, as an analyst bringing the weight of his expertise to bear upon each problem at hand. Distinctions between professionals tend to centre upon differences in age, experience and skill rather than upon differences in activities undertaken.[47]

This theory-inspired egalitarianism does not, however, extend to relations between economists and other professionals. The economic worldview centres upon rationality, and the theoretical edifice of microeconomics is, therefore, self-contained. As a result, economists are sensitive to the challenges to this structure that are latent in the intellectual goals of other professions. For example, the behavioural orientation of a variety of scientifically trained professionals who have come to work in policy areas in which economists have a stake are sometimes seen to threaten the rationalistic edifice. Empirical investigations by scientific personnel on occasion highlight areas of economic activity in which social actors apparently do not conform to economic prescriptions about rational action. A challenge of this type is often met by attempts on the part of economists to place the intellectual foundations of the particular profession in doubt. However, this task is not always simple, and conflicts can become exacerbated if the behaviourally oriented profession is sufficiently well established as to have developed a coherent worldview that it can deploy in disputes with economists, as is the case with operations research specialists who characteristically contrast their multi-valued logic with the single-valued logic of economics.[48]

Economists also encounter challenges, implicit or explicit, to their cognitive commitments from the opposite end of the professional spectrum. The emphasis upon rationality and arithmetic argument in economics can lead economists to become impatient with the codes of conduct that apply in such non-numerate, learned professions as law and medicine. The point at issue is usually the affirmation of ethically founded professional rights within the learned professions versus the economist's desire to apply rational, universal and non-structured criteria to action both within the marketplace and without.

Finally, competition and conflict of a more limited nature may centre upon competing claims to a subject area from neighbouring professions with rationalistic commitments. Economic problems and, for example, engineering problems often overlap. At times, they are almost indistinguishable, especially in the case of fixed investment projects. The question then arises: which profession should be given which role in dealing with such problems? In situations of this kind, economists generally argue that their worldview is more universal, more attuned to the full panoply of human aspirations than the more particularistic and operational rationalities of disciplines like engineering.

In conflicts with other professions of the type outlined above, the position of the economist is often enhanced by those features of rationality that first engendered disagreement. The rational ideal encourages economists to subsume problems of knowledge and technique in the interests of an apparently more general level of understanding, and, therefore, conflicts with instrumental professions such as engineering and the various behaviourally oriented sciences can be designated as arising from incidental rather than substantial counter-claims. Indeed, the generality, the simplicity, and the ethical appeal of the economic theoretical edifice are usually sufficient to gloss over the challenges economists encounter as a result of competing classifications arising from competing theories. Furthermore, for most purposes the juxtaposed opposites economists employ as a vehicle to extend economic arguments to a variety of spheres lead to very open analytical categories. In setting up economic systems of analysis in the first instance, economists usually borrow theoretical and empirical propositions from other disciplines in order to lend structure and plausibility to these open categories. Thus, if at a later time conflicts erupt as a result of other professions wishing to assert their authority by dictating changes in the structure of the analytical system, economists can cite their original pragmatism in establishing the system, and appeal to the desirability of stability and coherence in intellectual and organizational matters in order to subdue debate.

If challenges to rationality emerge from the opposite end of the professional spectrum, the difficulties for economists tend to be more profound. The learned professions, particularly medicine and law, are founded upon ethical codes of longer historical duration and greater social authority than the ethical imperative associated with economics. These codes appeal to humanity and justice, while economics appeals to tempered self-interest, and modern Western institutions, including governments, usually cannot openly violate the ethical precepts of the learned professions in favour of economic considerations without grave political and social consequences. Thus, open conflicts between economists and members of the learned professions are relatively rare, and economists usually attempt to focus their analysis upon subject matters in which there is likely to be a complementarity of professional interest. Despite these limitations, however, economists are playing a more developed role than previously in areas such as health policy and regulatory policy where the learned professions have historically held sway. The learned professions typically base their claims to authority upon the unique and novel features of every professional–client relationship. Hence, these professions are frequently loath or unable to offer aggregate prescriptions concerning the evolution of their subject areas and responsibilities. Economists have recently occupied this territory by taking on an increased role in the study of resource allocation in the medical and legal fields, while studiously avoiding any obvious infringements of professional discretion at the level of professional–client contact. In this case, rationality, which eschews analytical distinctions between the individual and the universal, has facilitated the aggregate analysis of what are normally considered configurational subject areas, analysis that is often seemingly beyond the capabilities of the professions governing these configurational fields, bound as they are by 'richer' cognitive commitments than those that apply in economics. None the less, this is a delicate balance of influence for economists to establish, and they encounter more difficulties in the field of social policy than they do in other fields.

In disagreements or disputes with other professionals the authority of economists in non-academic institutional settings is also strengthened by the frequent identification of rationality with efficiency in administration. As noted in the above discussion of specialization within economics, the rational ideal encourages a specific type of disposition of labour, one that is pragmatic with regard to subject matter and relatively indifferent to relations between objects that are more complex than the additive. When this type of disposition of labour is extended into non-academic settings, administrators often find that it has certain advantages in comparison with other ways of deploying labour. In many instances this has resulted in the fusion of rational and administrative goals (as, for example, in the case of programme budgeting).

The typical rationality-based administrative system is organized such that each participant in the administrative process is responsible for one or, at times, a series of fixed delimited tasks, each of which usually results in the generation of an end-number. Each task operationally defines a distinct system component, and the system as a whole is comprised of many such components. Participants may employ a variety of disciplinary perspectives in fulfilling their tasks, and they may draw upon expertise from many levels of organizational activity. Yet, ultimately, the objective is to generate *one* number per component that represents that component's relative importance within the total system. The end–numbers for the many components are then fed into a calculating mechanism designed and updated by the exponents of rationality within the institutional setting, in many cases, economists. The mechanism orders the components of the administrative system according to ends and means, or some other dichotomy, and then adds the numbers in each category so that aggregate end-numbers are produced. These are then compared to see which is greatest, smallest, and so forth.

This type of administrative apparatus brings certain advantages that have reinforced the position of economists and other exponents of rationality within administrative hierarchies. For example, it facilitates the aggregation of knowledge from a variety of disciplines covering a variety of subject areas. When confronted, as is frequently the case, with the task of making sense of diverse activities involving many kinds of expertise, the administrator may well be induced to adopt a rational administrative format. In addition, administrative systems of this type are able to encompass a large number of analytical categories (the number of components in the system may be expanded infinitely). If they are employed, therefore, the appearance of administrative plurality is maintained, and organizational diversification (along, for example, national–regional–local lines) is possible.[49]

Of much greater importance, however, is the role rational administrative systems play in minimizing administrative instability. Some of this centres on the numbers that the system yields. In particular, difficulties and uncertainties associated with generating component end-numbers are secondary to the numbers themselves. Therefore, conflicts between administrative participants with different disciplinary or professional affiliations over the processes whereby the end-numbers are generated do not tend to proceed very far because the rational doctrine ensures that precedence is given to numbers over debate about the structure of variables. The focus on numbers within the administrative process also discourages speculation across component categories and questioning of the calculation mechanism. Finally, in this context, recognition for satisfactory work is premised upon generating end-numbers that are not out of line given the previous experience of the exponents of rationality who operate the calculating mechanism. There is, therefore, a tendency for each participant in the administrative process to become increasingly concerned, not with the inherent validity of his own estimates, but with the relation between the numbers he produces and some long-run average. For all of these reasons, rationality-based administrative systems, once established, are relatively rarely destablized as a result of interprofessional conflict.

The stability of this type of administrative apparatus is also enhanced because of its monolithic character. As rational administrative systems become institutionalized the conventional and often disruptive divisions of administrative culture (for example, between policy formulation, implementation, evaluation, etc.) usually begin to blur due to the overwhelming consistency of rationality.[50] An ends–means apparatus may be introduced inititially as an evaluative instrument designed to ensure that, for instance, investment patterns conform to certain normative standards derived from welfare theory. Later the evaluation system may evolve into a device to assign priority to particular projects at each stage of their implementation. Finally, the same system may be reinterpreted as a broad guide to appropriate patterns of investment in the formulation of general policy. This progression may occur quite naturally without any reconsideration of the original assumptions used in setting up the system because rationality is founded upon the assumption that man's capacities conform with the characteristics of his environment and, therefore, there is no need to draw distinctions between, for example, policy formulation and implementation. In such circumstances 'recycling through the phases of the problem'[51] by comparing and contrasting formulation, implementation and evaluation strategies is likely to be at a minimum.

In summary, then, the rational ideal has the potential to restructure the administrative environment in major ways, especially given that rationality-based administrative systems lend themselves to the manipulation of large amounts of data, particularly when they are coupled with computer technologies.[52] Of course, just as the economics profession is but one of a number of professional groups seeking influence within Whitehall, so the doctrine of rationality is but one of a series of doctrines structuring administrative practice. Therefore, in all instances, its application has been conditioned by competing claims. Nevertheless, the rational ideal has had a significant impact on the operations of British central government. We may now turn to a consideration of the specific type of economic analysis that is the subject of this book. The next chapter explores the nature of the cost–benefit methodology in preparation for investigating how it has been applied in a number of government settings.

2

Measuring social benefits and costs

Theory and application

When cast in a microeconomic framework, economic questions typically resolve themselves into problems of counterpoint. One of the most overt examples of this tendency is cost–benefit analysis, an evaluative methodology legitimized by welfare theory. As the name implies, cost–benefit analysis involves the use of a pair of juxtaposed opposites to order the various categories of a subject area so that the magnitude of each half of the pair can be assessed and policy recommendations thereby derived. Thus, cost–benefit analysis is one of a number of analytical instruments founded upon what one might call the ends–means grammar of the mechanics of self-interest. As such, it can be, and has been, employed to extend economic reasoning to many different fields of study. The way in which this has occurred in a number of public policy areas and the obstacles that have been encountered in the process are the subject of subsequent chapters. However, before turning to specific instances of the application of cost–benefit analysis within central government, it is appropriate to review some of the principal features of the cost–benefit methodology in theory and practice. The following pages briefly outline both the conceptual foundations of the methodology and the way in which it is typically implemented.

Cost–benefit analysis derives from a multipolar conception of market relations, although the connections between the methodology and the multipolar model have not always been explicit. Many discussions of modern cost–benefit analysis begin by noting that the methodology first came to prominence as an administrative tool in the US water resources development field during the 1930s, and it has been argued that the American engineers who developed and employed the methodology in this context owed nothing to economic theory.[1] However, cost–benefit calculations have a much longer history and are much more closely integrated with the development of the economics discipline than this would suggest. In particular, Jeremy Bentham, the foremost eighteenth century advocate of the principle of utility, urged the merits of a pleisure–pain (benefit–cost) calculus in deciding which undertakings yield the 'Greatest Happiness of the Greatest Number'. Subsequently, utilitarian doctrines were refined by French engineer–economists as they groped towards the theory of marginal utility. Among the most prominent of these was Jules Dupuit who, during the course of analysing the optimum provision of public goods in the 1840s, developed the concept of 'consumer's surplus' upon which modern CBA is founded.[2] In recent decades most economists and other types of CBA practitioners have come to argue that the methodology is best sustained theoretically by referring to Pareto's work regarding the conditions that define a position of 'maximum ophelimity' (in present terms, maximum efficiency) for an economy. This facet of Paretian theory is a direct extension of Walrasian general equilibrium analysis.[3] Hence, CBA cannot be divorced from Benthamite utilitarianism and Neoclassical theory, both of which have been central to the development of the multipolar model and the discipline of economics.

Pareto's major contribution to what is now called welfare theory consisted in developing criteria for determining whether or not a particular change in economic circumstances enhances the efficiency of an economy (in Pareto's terms, increases the ophelimity for the collectivity). The central tenets of his presentation are: (1) that a position of maximum efficiency for an economy is one in which no individual can be made better off (i.e. increase his 'ophelimity' or, in present terms, his utility) without someone becoming worse off; and (2) that this condition is fulfilled when equilibrium is achieved in a perfectly competitive economy.[4] The object of Pareto's work in this area was to specify which types of changes in non-equilibrium positions for an economy lead unambiguously to efficiency improvements or increases in what is today called economic, or Paretian, welfare. Put in modern terms, his analysis leads to the conclusion that if a change in economic circumstances results in an increase in utility for at least one individual, and a decrease in utility for none, then there can be no doubt that it is productive of an efficiency, and hence a welfare, improvement.

As it happens, however, instances in which change can plausibly be said to be of this kind are rare. The much more common case is that a change in economic circumstances apparently leads to increases in utility for some and decreases for others. Under these circumstances, Pareto contended, it is impossible to say on economic grounds whether or not a welfare improvement has been achieved because, as noted in the last chapter, Neoclassical theory does not provide for knowledge of the preferences of others among market subjects and by extension, interpersonal comparisons of utility on the part of the analyst.[5] There is another major difficulty involved in attempting to apply Paretian criteria in the assessment of the impact of changed economic circumstances upon collective welfare. Paretian logic is suitable for comparisons between optimum and non-optimum positions, but it cannot be used in the comparison of sub-optimum positions, although it is these comparisons that are frequently the subject of policy debate. In the latter case, the economist should resort to the General Theory of Second Best, first developed by Lipsey and Lancaster in the 1950s, but, in practice, this is rarely done.[6]

As indicated above, Paretian theory is rigorous, particularly in so far as it shuns interpersonal comparisons of utility. Yet it is also limited in that it is applicable to only a relatively restricted range of problems. There have, therefore, been a variety of efforts during this century to extend or modify the theory so as to broaden its range of application, although without exception these have involved the sacrifice of theoretical rigour. The most concerted attempts to extend the applicability of Paretian theory centre upon the case of changes in economic circumstances that involve gain to some at the expense of loss to others. With the objective of concretizing the welfare implications of such changes, a number of theorists engaged in recasting the Paretian criteria until they had acquired the qualitatively new form known as the Kaldor–Hicks–Scitovsky variation on Barone's compensation principle. Under this normative regime a change yields a Pareto improvement if and only if, first, the gainers could have compensated the losers and still be better off, and, second, the losers could not have compensated the gainers for their forgone welfare increase without becoming worse off than in the original situation.[7]

Several points should be made concerning this formulation of a welfare improvement. To begin with, neither Barone, who originated the compensation principle, nor the other economic theorists who later built upon his work insisted that compensation actually be paid, perhaps on the assumption that instances in which voluntary compensation could be achieved were too limited in number. Secondly, Scitovsky's contribution to the compensation principle, set out in the second condition above, is an attempt to separate efficiency from equity in the evaluation of the welfare implications of economic change by insisting that the welfare effects of simply redistributing income within the collectivity be taken into account in assessing whether or not some change leads to a Pareto improvement. In both instances there is an implicit assumption that an analyst is able to compare individual utilities, even in situations involving different income distributions. Thus, the Kaldor–Hicks–Scitovsky variation on the compensation principle is a marked departure from the strictly Paretian tradition. Its proponents argue, however, that it is a viable extension of Paretian theory and, therefore, an effective means of gauging improvements in efficiency or Paretian welfare.[8]

Economists have devised a variety of means to assess the individual's 'capacity to compensate' which is so central to the Kaldor–Hicks–Scitovsky regime. However, one method is cited more frequently than any other in this context. It centres upon the consideration of the effect on a consumer's (or producer's) level of utility of a fall in the price of a particular product resulting from an alteration in market conditions (for example, a new investment project). Under these circumstances the consumer is said to have a 'surplus' in utility arising from the difference between the price he would be willing to pay rather than forgo the product and the price he actually has to pay. As noted earlier, Dupuit first developed the consumer's surplus concept, but we owe its detailed elaboration to Marshall.[9] A variety of measures have been advanced for consumer's surplus,[10] but for present purposes it is perhaps best, and most simply, represented by the Marshallian one consisting of the area under an uncompensated demand curve and between the original price of the product in question and the new lower price resulting from altered market conditions (see Figure 2.1). This measure of the individual's 'capacity to compensate' is fundamental to cost–benefit analysis, for it is one, and often the most important, means of specifying the benefit accruing to the individual from changed economic conditions.

However, Marshallian consumer's surplus presents a variety of difficulties when economists attempt to employ it as an applied measure. As is evident from Figure 2.1, the Marshallian measure of consumer's surplus is defined by a fall in the price of a particular product. Yet an individual's real income increases along a Marshallian demand curve as price falls. This has the effect of decreasing the individual's utility with the result that the Marshallian measure for consumer's surplus remains ambiguous unless it is restricted to small changes in the quantity consumed of an unimportant product and, at the same time, the fall in price is small.[11] In other words, Marshallian consumer's surplus is a particular or partial equilibrium concept, and like all such concepts is only meant to apply to what Shackle calls 'a minute portion of the economy'.[12] It, thus, has a very circumscribed range of appropriate uses, although it is not uncommon for it to be applied in situations involving substantial changes in either the quantity consumed or the price of important products, or both.

The partial equilibrium nature of the consumer's surplus concept is particularly evident when the aggregation problem is addressed. Marshallian consumer's surplus, complete with the restrictions outlined above, is a credible Neoclassical construction in the case of one individual and one product. This situation is, however, seldom very interesting from a policy perspective. Yet when questions regarding aggregate economic welfare,

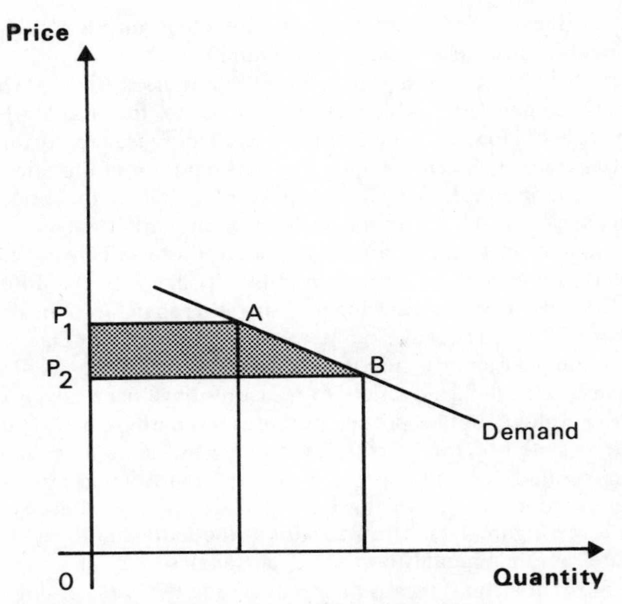

Figure 2.1 Marshallian consumer's surplus (as hatched)

or indeed the individual's total capacity to compensate, are raised, the limits of the consumer's surplus concept become apparent. For example, 'the individual's utility function for a particular commodity varies with the amounts of other commodities consumed',[13] and, therefore, it is inappropriate to add together an individual's consumer's surpluses for a variety of products.[14] More importantly, there are serious difficulties involved in aggregating the consumer's surpluses of different individuals arising from a fall in the price of one product. In accord with the teaching of Bentham, it is often assumed that individual utilities, and hence individual economic welfare, can be added in this context to yield measures of aggregate welfare. Yet this presupposes equal incomes for all the individuals concerned, the only case in which interpersonal comparisons of utility are said to present no difficulty. In practice, of course, the economist seldom encounters situations in which he can plausibly assume that the distribution of income is perfectly equal. Despite this, cost–benefit analysis assumes that measures of individual economic welfare can be added.[15]

There is a final, but none the less very important, point concerning consumer's surplus which should be mentioned before turning to other subjects. This is that the knowledge of individual demand curves required to arrive at an accurate Marshallian measure of consumer's surplus is 'rarely, if ever, available'.[16] For this reason, in cost–benefit analysis, as in other microeconomic methodologies, little emphasis is placed upon absolute magnitudes in the estimation of individual or aggregate benefit. Rather, welfare economists conventionally work with various types of approximations for consumer's surplus, often based upon prevailing market prices. The nature of some of these types of approximations will become evident in subsequent chapters.

The efforts welfare theorists have made to preserve the general conceptual framework and vocabulary of the Paretian tradition in the face of the difficulties involved in stretching Paretian categories to take in applied problems is an important illustration of the authority of the rational doctrine within economics. At the same time, one of the most notable aspects of the progression from Paretian theory to consumer's surplus and cost–benefit analysis is the surrender of the theoretical integrity of the Neoclassical mechanics of self-interest. This type of conceptual development is manifestly contradictory, and, indeed, has proved to be the source of much of welfare theory's vulnerability. Yet at another level it has its own logic.

The most important feature of the progression from Paretian theory to cost–benefit analysis is the attempt to broaden the applicability of Pareto's insights by abandoning the emphasis on the whole market characteristic of his work and focusing, instead, on changes in individual levels of welfare, witness the contrast between the Paretian criteria for defining a welfare improvement and the compensation principle. In large part, this project aimed at attaining measures for individual welfare improvements on the assumption that utilities are additive and can, therefore, be simply aggregated to yield measures of welfare for the collectivity. In this sense, applied welfare theory came to be largely synonymous with 'welfare theory applied'.

As noted earlier, this enterprise rapidly encountered difficulties, many of which centred on interpersonal comparisons of utility and the partial equilibrium nature of the concepts involved, thereby indicating that commitments to the deeper structure of Neoclassical economics were at stake. This did not, however, result in a retreat from the applied field. There is little in the history of the multipolar model to induce great concern for the structural integrity of the Neoclassical mechanics as long as its reputation remains unchallenged. Within the multipolar framework, market subjects are individuals, and a market is a collection of individuals. When an economy is viewed in this light, there is little to inhibit the analyst from assuming that aggregate measures are simply the sum of individual measures. Indeed, there is a strong incentive to do so, for the scalar character of economic reasoning is thereby enhanced. True, by positing that the apparently chaotic actions of market subjects are integrated as a result of the maximization rule, Neoclassical theory asserts that the market as a whole is more than the sum of its parts. Yet, as noted in Chapter 1, even the Neoclassical system encourages one-to-one dichotomies, and, by extension, individual measures and scalar argument. In the case of applied welfare economics this is evident in the emphasis on gains and losses (hence, benefits and costs) that is latent even in pure Paretian theory.

Alternatives and choice

The emphasis to this point in the present chapter has been on the Neoclassical, and specifically Paretian, theoretical underpinnings of cost–benefit analysis. As we have seen, cost–benefit methodology takes the Paretian efficiency standard to be the source of its legitimacy, and the Kaldor–Hicks–Scitovsky variation on the compensation principle constitutes an extrapolation of the Paretian criteria for defining a welfare improvement. At the same time, the analyses of the compensation principle and consumer's surplus presented above strongly indicate that cost–benefit analysis can be characterized as a recessive version of Paretian theory. If this is the case, we may ask: are there other aspects to the Paretian cost–benefit divergence, and where does this divergence lead?

Consider, first, the circumstances in which one is able to apply Paretian welfare criteria. If the conditions of the economy are assumed to be such that equilibrium is fully determinate, then, given any non-equilibrium position, change can only be of one type, that which leads to equilibrium. If, however, certain of the conditions necessary for a determinate equilibrium are assumed to be relaxed, then there are an infinite number of positions of maximum efficiency (now often referred to as Paretian optima), and, given any non-equilibrium position, a variety of changes are possible. It is in this latter situation that Pareto's welfare criteria are relevant. In particular, they can be used to distinguish which of a series of different changes lead unambiguously to improvements in welfare for the collectivity. Thus, Pareto's realization that equilibrium need not be determinate means that his welfare theory is concerned with alternatives.[17] Not surprisingly, therefore, cost–benefit analysis is also about alternatives, although, as will become evident shortly, in a sense quite different from the Paretian.

The progression from alternatives in the Paretian sense to alternatives in the cost–benefit sense begins with the sacrifice of the aggregate measures of Paretian theory in favour of the individual measures of cost–benefit analysis. Alternatives in the Paretian sense refer to the different effects of various changes upon the welfare for the collectivity taken as a whole. In this presentation, choice resides with market participants, and alternatives are assessed with reference to the aggregate result of the preferences of all those engaged in exchange. But with the introduction of the compensation principle the Paretian focus upon the collectivity as totality was abandoned, and replaced by a preoccupation with the different effects of various changes upon individuals. Moreover, in the cost–benefit context the individual is no longer the self-contained rational actor, the agent of choice, of pure Neoclassical theory. Rather, by virtue of the fact that CBA countenances interpersonal comparisons, the individual is a gainer or a loser with reference to the particular type of change under consideration at any one time. This does not mean, however, that the vocabulary and conceptual apparatus of rationality have no place within the cost–benefit framework. They have simply been shifted for use at another level of abstraction. To be precise, cost–benefit analysis establishes a parallelism between the choices undertaken by the Neoclassical rational actor and the type of decision-making directed towards the collectivity that cost–benefit analysis is intended to assist. Just as under Neoclassical theory the rational actor confronts choices between different bundles of goods, so in the CBA context the collectivity confronts choices between different alterations in economic circumstances. Just as the rational actor makes his choices with regard to the ends and the means at his disposal, so the collectivity is guided in its decisions by a consideration of the gains and losses, benefits and costs, associated with a particular type of change. In effect, for all intents and purposes cost–benefit analysis identifies the collectivity with the rational actor of Neoclassical theory, and operates with a conception of choice that reflects this. Thus, in CBA, the term alternative refers, not to the aggregate result of myriad individual choices, but to one of several options facing the collectivity seen as agent of choice.[18]

Once the identification described above is noted, many of the principal features of cost–benefit analysis become comprehensible. Perhaps the simplest way to illustrate this is, first, to re-examine the concept of rational action and then, on that basis, review the structure of the cost–benefit methodology.

The rational actor operates within a framework in which proximate potential ends are numerous, and proximate potential means are scarce. His task is to grope towards a situation in which the means at his disposal are allocated so as to maximize his well-being or satisfaction. Given this *ultimate* end, the rational actor focuses upon the relative merits of proximate ends and the relative uses of proximate means, for the choices that he makes in these two areas 'make(s) a difference' to the attainment of the demonstrably optimal. Rational action, therefore, consists in making the right choices given any particular set of economic circumstances, choices that will enhance the actor's well-being and, at the same time, ensure that equilibrium is a possibility.[19]

Cost–benefit analysis, too, is about choice with the difference that the necessity to distinguish between the relative merits of proximate ends and the relative uses of proximate means resides with the collectivity rather than the rational actor. Thus, CBA is typically said to be concerned with the alternatives that society has available to it, both in terms of the ends that it might pursue and the various uses to which means might be put.[20] The object of the methodology, which also appeals to the rational action analogy, is to determine which choice of ends and means is right given the ultimate end of maximizing benefits relative to costs for the collectivity across all fronts. This is accomplished in two phases. First, ends and means are juxtaposed to determine whether or not the benefits of a course of action exceed the costs, and in certain cases cost–benefit analysts have limited their attention to this issue exclusively. In the second phase different combinations of ends and means are juxtaposed to determine which yields the highest level of benefits relative to costs. The most sophisticated cost–benefit analyses treat arrays of ends and means, and use some decision rule (several have been proposed during the development of cost–benefit methodology) to identify those combinations of ends and means that are apparently most advantageous.[21]

The flaw in this methodological logic is, of course, that in Neoclassical theory choice resides with the market subject, not with the collectivity. Indeed, there is a curious sense in which the cost–benefit methodology embodies a recognition of this flaw. In depriving individuals even of those minimal cognitive capacities with which Neoclassical theory endows them (the gainers and losers of post-Paretian theory are not involved in choice, but are simply reacting to projected change) and in locating choice at the level of the collectivity, economists confronted the necessity for an active agent capable of actual choice. Clearly, the collectivity of CBA, composed as it is of passive individuals, is not such an active agent, although, as we have seen, choices are made in its name. Instead, the cost–benefit analyst has assumed this role. It is the economist who posits who the gainers and losers from change are and in what ways they suffer or are rewarded. Many within the economics profession argue that CBA is founded upon an objective efficiency standard and that most cost–benefit analysts derive their conception of social ends and available means from standard sources. (Politicians, government administrators and the business community are frequently cited in this context.)[22] Yet it is important to note that in conducting cost–benefit studies economists define not only their research questions, but also the parameters that are employed to answer them.[23]

Another of the consequences of the transformation of the meaning of choice that has accompanied the progression from Paretian theory to cost–benefit analysis has been the abandonment of the marginalist framework of discourse. Choice in CBA resides with the collectivity seen as individual. But, of course, the collectivity is not an individual, and it is for this reason that the analogy between the rational actor and the collectivity of cost–benefit analysis eventually breaks down. The rational actor operates as one among many, and the rightness of his choices depends upon the choices of others. In contrast, the collectivity of CBA is simply one, and the rightness of the choices it exercises depends upon some decision rule that bears no relation to the actions of others. In these circumstances the marginal conditions of Neoclassical theory cease to be relevant. The result has been that the vocabulary and conceptual apparatus of marginal theory have acquired a questionable status within cost–benefit analysis. The way in which the opportunity cost concept is used to concretize losses within a cost–benefit context constitutes perhaps the best illustration of this phenomenon, despite the fact that most CBA theorists are determinedly marginalist in discussing opportunity cost.[24]

Costing and CBA

All laymen have confronted choices between different commodities having similar uses. In common parlance, rationality demands that the individual should consider the general suitability of the various commodities for his purposes (often this will amount to an evaluation of their relative technical efficiencies), and weigh the results of this assessment against the *cost* of each before making his choice. Economists in this century (Wicksteed, Davenport, Knight, Robbins, von Mises, Hayek, Thirlby, Coase) have elaborated this understanding of rational choice by asserting that the true cost of each commodity under discussion is its value in the best alternative use to which it could be put – otherwise designated as its opportunity cost.[25] The crucial point to note in this connection is that, while the selection process described above is often said to be rational, it is only distantly related to the strict rationality of the Walrasian system. Indeed, the above-mentioned economists indicated that they may have recognized this in that they each, at one time or another, distinguished between cost as an obstacle subjectively perceived by an individual at the point of choice and cost objectively measured in the Neoclassical marginalist sense as the market value of the alternative product, although the term opportunity cost is conventionally used in both ways. Thus, the exact meaning of opportunity cost is ambiguous in economics.

In the cost–benefit context the concept is employed as a measure of the loss suffered by certain members of the collectivity as a result of change, a use that suggests that CBA theorists and practitioners, perhaps unwittingly, take a subjectivist view of cost. Yet this usage, too, is curious. For example, there is no psychological reason why the obstacle an individual confronts in choosing should be identical to the loss he suffers once a choice is made. In practice, however, economists elide what Buchanan has called 'choice-influencing cost' and 'choice-influenced cost'. Moreover, while it may appear odd on first inspection, this behaviour is consistent with the analysis of choice in CBA presented earlier, for, as Buchanan has observed in a somewhat different context, opportunities lost:

> . . . more accurately reflect the value of potential alternatives as judged by others rather than by the chooser himself.[26]

If, then, cost in cost–benefit analysis is not synonymous with cost in the strictly Neoclassical sense, how is it be viewed? The cost issue was clarified a few years ago by Hicks, who stated that the concept of cost, as presented in the welfare economics we have inherited from Pareto and Pigou, is descended from the attempts of Classical economists, most notably Smith and Ricardo, to impose 'a common measure' upon heterogeneous commodities, often by invoking a labour theory of value.[27] In this latter project the concern was not, as in the Walrasian era, to explain how markets operate, but to find a means of aggregating values so that the wealth of a household, a firm or, indeed, a nation could be determined. The business analogy was very important in this context. Firms may produce a variety of different products, but these are reduced to a common measure through the medium of money. The Classics rapidly discovered, of course, that the measuring rod of money presents many difficulties (for example, the reconciliation of money values over time), but they persisted with attempts to elaborate this type of valuation procedure (in the guise of both private and social accounting) and to elucidate how money valuation is possible (Ricardo's labour theory of value). Costing in modern welfare economics is, according to Hicks, another, and perhaps less sophisticated, version of this Classical enterprise. With the emergence of marginalism and the concomitant abandonment of the labour theory of value, economists ceased to view costs as founded upon homogeneous labour. The economics profession continues, however, to postulate, either implicitly or explicitly, that resources have a certain homogeneity, and, therefore, costs in today's terms are resource costs. What has been lost in this progression is some sense in which cost has a deeper meaning than money valuation of resources would imply. Modern economists have, therefore, resorted more and more to simple money measures and, hence, business standards in the costing process.

In CBA, as in other parts of welfare economics, the aggregation problem is at the centre of analysis. The total cost of change is determined by aggregating individual costs (losses). This total is, in turn, juxtaposed against aggregated benefit, conventionally determined by adding the consumer's surpluses accruing to the gainers from change. Thus, CBA compares and contrasts aggregated Neoclassical measures (consumer's surpluses) with aggregated non-Neoclassical, if not Classical, measures (costs). Given Hicks's remarks about the costing process in welfare economics (hereafter referred to as the cost approach), CBA is perhaps best described as a methodology consisting of a Neoclassical superstructure, various parts of which have degenerated in the first phase through the sacrifice of Paretian rigour, and in the second phase through the adoption of pre-Neoclassical modes of reasoning. The question that immediately arises is: What advantages has this latter type of degeneration brought?

As was the case with the progression from Paretian welfare criteria to the compensation principle and consumer's surplus, the answer appears to be greater applicability. If, for instance, the economist were to confine himself to valuation in marginal utility terms, he would be obliged to limit the direct applicability of his analyses:

> to that part of the Social Product which is sold to final consumers, who alone can be supposed to be making their purchases by comparison between prices and marginal utilities.[28]

In contrast, the cost approach, which assumes all resources are homogeneous, allows economists to broaden their brief to include the consideration of losses and gains (benefits are often valued in other than consumer's surplus terms in CBA) that are not normally a part of market transactions. We have already seen how, by equating opportunity cost with the cost of opportunities lost, economists have divorced cost from individual choice. Given this, it is simply an extrapolation to apply the cost approach to areas in which the rational actor cannot be said to be central, such as the investment sector and the public sector. In the public sector case studies presented in later chapters of this book costs range from the opportunity cost of a particular government investment (e.g. training) for the individual to the opportunity cost incurred by the state in administering that investment.

By the same token, one of the distinguishing features of cost–benefit analysis is the attention that its practitioners devote to externalities, or those spillover effects from change that affect individuals 'directly, and not indirectly through prices'.[29] The classic instance of this type of effect is, of course, the soiling of laundry arising from factory smoke, but externalities are not necessarily nuisances. The enjoyment that a community derives from the construction of a beautiful building is also an externality. In both cases the market can be invoked only indirectly in attempts to place values upon these effects, for, by definition, externalities lie beyond the range of market transactions.[30] The valuation problem for externalities is conventionally solved in the cost–benefit context by asking what minimum sum the individual would be willing to accept in order to accommodate himself to some negative externality, or what maximum sum the individual would be willing to pay rather than forgo some positive externality (Mishan's compensating variations).[31] In this instance the cost approach has allowed valuations that would not have been possible, indeed, conceivable, within a strictly marginalist framework.

With the incorporation of costing into the post-Paretian framework, therefore, the almost universal applicability of cost–benefit analysis was assured. The methodology is suited to the valuation of welfare in both the private and public sectors. In addition, it allows economists great flexibility in choosing topics within these sectors because the cost approach facilitates the consideration of externalities. Indeed, CBA practitioners are relatively rarely concerned with their ability to *define* the gains and losses arising from particular types of change. Instead, their problem has been to develop criteria for limiting their attention to a *manageable* number of costs and benefits among the *many* that might be considered (externalities, for example, are, to use Mishan's term, 'unlimited').[32] Fortunately for the economists involved in CBA, the cost approach does have certain constraints associated with it. The most prominent of these is that it ceases to have much meaning if the gain or loss under discussion cannot be assigned a plausible measure. Thus, at any particular point in the history of CBA there have been certain intangibles (visual amenity is one) that economists concede are not measurable in any definitive way, and are, therefore, beyond the range of the methodology's brief. It is important to note, however, that what is intangible is highly relative over time.[33] Creativity in the cost–benefit field is frequently associated with devising measures for externalities that were once considered intangible. The valuation of health and human life in recent decades are cases in point.

Welfare accounting

The issue of measurability is at the heart of cost–benefit analysis and, some would argue, of welfare economics. At the beginning of this century Pigou, following the example of Marshall, asserted that economic welfare should be defined with reference to the 'measuring rod of money'.[34] Pigou valued welfare in marginalist terms (for example, in his presentation of welfare economics optimum output for an industry can be achieved by equating marginal social net product with marginal private net product) and, therefore, much of what is today accepted as welfare measurement would not have had a place in his scheme. However, his emphasis upon the necessity to find a common measure, indeed, a money measure for economic welfare is both distinctly Classical and distinctly modern. Since Pigou's time economists have been preoccupied with developing both direct and indirect means of concretizing welfare in money terms and aggregating the resulting money measures – in short, with welfare accounting. Moreover, with the incorporation of the cost approach into the Paretian welfare framework,[35] this task became easier, if less sophisticated. Many of the principal features of CBA which have still to be reviewed in this chapter are essentially accounting devices used to reconcile different types of welfare accruing at different points in time.

The first of these is the shadow price. When no market exists for some gain or loss, CBA practitioners often resort to indirect evidence regarding the values individuals place upon these effects. Thus, for example, the values individuals place upon travelling time are frequently imputed from the choices travellers make between modes of transport with different fare structures and journey times. Shadow pricing is also employed when the cost–benefit analyst is convinced that certain goods or bads are, for his purposes, unsatisfactorily priced in the market. In most cases this type of shadow pricing is associated with anticipated changes in supply or demand conditions. If, for instance, international political circumstances are such that it is reasonable to anticipate sharp increases in the price of oil in the near future, the economist may choose to adjust prevailing market prices to reflect this during the course of a CBA evaluation. In general, shadow prices for specific gains and losses are derived either by examining markets in which similar items are traded, by investigating trade-offs of an administrative nature, by adjusting existing market prices or, more rarely, by resorting to the prices developed in connection with exercises in linear programming.[36]

Other accounting devices that are indispensable to the conduct of CBA are related to the reconciliation of costs and benefits accruing at different points in time. Many cost–benefit studies, for example, contain provisions for dealing with changes in relative price levels over time (through reducing all prices to some base year). In addition, analysts are conventionally required to incorporate considerations of consumer and social time preference into their studies through the use of a discount rate. The argument is that individuals, and, by extrapolation, the collectivity, place a higher value on present than on future income. This requires that benefits received a year from now be discounted by some percentage before being compared or aggregated with those received today (the same applies to costs).

There is, however, disagreement among economists as to what annual percentage should be used, particularly in the case of public sector studies. The literature devoted to this issue is vast.[37] Suffice it to say, economists have debated which, if any, of the plethora of interest rates found in the private sector is applicable in the CBA context. They have asked if there is any justification for assuming that a market-determined interest rate would be appropriate for decisions involving the collectivity. And if not, what is the *social* rate of discount, and what are the implications for efficiency of applying different rates of discount in the private and public sectors? There is also the question of whether the discount rate for public projects should be put on a social time preference or a social opportunity cost basis, or both. Yet, in practice, the foundation for the discount rate employed in public sector analyses in Britain during the 1970s is clear. The project of developing a social rate of discount has never commanded much enthusiasm in official circles. Hence, the government's 'test discount rate' has been set at the average rate of return on private sector investment. During the period when the analyses discussed in the following case studies were conducted this rate was deemed to be 10 per cent.[38]

Once costs and benefits have been assessed and a discount rate determined (either by choice or fiat) the analyst is almost in a position to aggregate his results. Before doing so, however, he may apply a number of testing criteria to his work in order to demonstrate that the assumptions he has employed are plausible and that his welfare accounting has been sound. For example, great attention is usually given in discussions of cost–benefit methodology to the dangers of double-counting, and the economist may well scrutinize his work to ensure that he has not, for instance, mistaken a transfer payment for a true benefit or cost.[39] Similarly, he may review his analysis to ensure that he has not assigned an excessive value to the cost of bringing unemployed factors into use. The opportunity cost concept implies, for example, that the cost of employing an unemployed man is not his wage in a former job, but the value of his leisure.[40] In the same vein, the economist may apply sensitivity analysis to the more uncertain estimates in his study. This procedure consists in providing alternative values for these estimates with a view to determining what effect this has upon the final outcome of the analysis. It is a means of determining which of the more uncertain estimates are crucial for the study and the limits of variation consistent with a positive result for the analysis as a whole.

It is at this point that the analyst must undertake the task of aggregating benefits and costs in preparation for determining which, if any, of the alternatives he has chosen to examine are economically viable and, among these, which is the most advantageous. As the earlier mention of discounting suggests, cost–benefit analysts seldom employ the crude investment criteria characteristic of many financial analyses (for example, cut-off period, pay-off period or average rate of return). Rather, they generally use the net present discounted value criterion in assessing the merits of change. This consists in reducing benefit and cost streams to present value, and then comparing their magnitudes. A specific type of change is considered economically viable if the present value of the benefit stream (B) exceeds the present value of the cost stream (K). There remains, however, the question of which of an economically viable set of alternatives is the most advantageous. Several decision rules of varying sophistication can be employed in this context. Some analysts select the option with the highest net present value (B–K). Others select the option with the highest benefit to cost ratio (B/K or (B–K)/K) in the belief that the choice of options the economist recommends should take into account the resource constraints in operation in any given situation.[41]

One issue that frequently emerges at this stage in an analysis is the consideration of the distributional effects of change. Economists are ill-equipped to comment on this question for reasons connected with a number of the fundamental tenets of the Walrasian mechanics. The maximization rule of the Walrasian system is founded upon a specific psychology, which posits that an individual's preference for an additional unit of some commodity, as measured by the incremental flow of some other commodity which he is willing to sacrifice in order to obtain the additional unit, diminishes as the absolute amount of the first commodity in his possession increases. It follows from this that an individual's preferences vary with the means at his disposal to achieve satisfaction, or, in other words, his income. Thus, the nature of the maximization rule is such that what are conventionally denoted as efficiency and equity cannot be separated within the Walrasian framework. Moreover, the connection between individual preferences and income clearly places approaches to the estimation of welfare improvements based upon interpersonal comparisons and individual measures in question. Yet, as indicated earlier, cost–benefit analysis is premised upon exactly such interpersonal comparisons and individual measures. The result has been that applied welfare economics, and especially CBA, has been characterized by unfocused debates both about the meaning of equity and efficiency in competitive economics and about whether society should be using improved efficiency (Paretian welfare) or improved equity (or both) as a standard to assess altered economic circumstances.

As Stafford has noted, the efficiency-based Kaldor–Hicks–Scitovsky variation on the compensation principle is silent about the equity status of any particular initial income distribution and about the redistributional effects of changes within the economy.[42] This does not mean, however, that the equity–efficiency question has not prompted debate. Indeed, the weaknesses of post-Paretian theory in this respect have obliged economists to address the issue, if only to protect their claims to have applied expertise in the welfare field. A number of groups of economists have articulated various positions corresponding to the different cognitive dimensions of the equity–efficiency question. The orthodox stance, advanced most forcefully in Britain by Mishan, is that applied welfare economics must remain true to its Paretian origins and claim an efficiency standard as the foundation for its prescriptions.[43] Economists at the other end of the spectrum of opinion on this issue have argued that, while the techniques of applied welfare economics are useful, the post-Paretian theory that sustains them is too inconsistent to allow the profession to adopt any one interpretation of applied variables.[44] These economists have suggested that moral and ethical judgements are inevitable in applied microeconomics and have advocated cooperation with other disciplines in the estimation of the effects of changed economic circumstances upon equity, efficiency and other components of a liberally interpreted welfare.

The range of opinion that exists within applied welfare economics concerning the equity–efficiency issue is symptomatic of a variety of attempts within the profession to strengthen or reformulate the foundations of this branch of the discipline in the face of theoretical contradictions (often with strong ethical overtones). Purists insist upon grounding cost–benefit analysis firmly in Neoclassical doctrine, even when there is a risk that the assumptions underlying the methodology will be considered implausible. Pragmatists, by contrast, wish to make applied welfare economics more generally acceptable by relaxing Neoclassical strictures and broadening the interpretation given to applied variables. The purists have commanded the greatest following, thereby indicating that those who are strict in upholding the rational ideal continue to be accorded the greatest prestige even when circumstances are as difficult as they have been in the welfare field. It should not be taken from this, however, that the purists have succeeded in a clear competition for authority within welfare economics, for the contributions of the purists and the pragmatists to the equity–efficiency debate have been complementary, if not consistent. Purists may emphasize the efficiency standard, but they do so in the knowledge that applied welfare economics has evolved through the abandonment of pure efficiency. Pragmatists may advocate liberal interpretations of welfare and urge cooperation with other disciplines, but the status of CBA is too enmeshed with the multipolar model for analysis to proceed, at least in the first instance, on any other than economic terms (e.g. rational terms, liberally interpreted). In practice, this means that, while certain analysts have developed elaborate balance sheets indicating the incidence of change upon a variety of social groups,[45] there is no obligation to address the equity issue. The efficiency standard is sufficiently authoritative, for example, that none of the analysts involved in the work examined in the following case studies dealt with the equity–efficiency question.

Such, then, is the calculating mechanism at the heart of cost–benefit analysis. Before concluding, we should briefly consider the purpose conventionally ascribed to this type of welfare accounting.

Boulding has asserted that all of welfare economics, including cost–benefit analysis, is about riches and it appears that few economists would question this.[46] Opinion has not been uniform, however, regarding the specification of what welfare theory has to say about riches and the nature of the validity of welfare postulates. Many, if not most, welfare economists, including CBA practitioners, adhere to the view that welfare postulates derive from the scientific analysis of allocative efficiency embodied in Neoclassical theory and, therefore, applied welfare economics may be regarded, not as ethically neutral, but as ethically unproblematic. Seen in this light, cost–benefit calculations provide an objective means of determining the effect of change upon efficiency or economic welfare. Other economists have been less certain about the exact nature of welfare, and, hence, have argued that welfare theory and applied welfare economics encompasses a specific set of value judgements concerning the nature of human happiness that can either be accepted or rejected. Viewed in this manner, cost–benefit calculations are value-laden in ways that must be clearly specified if the economics profession is to avoid ridicule.[47]

The important point to note in connection with the two positions outlined above is that, while they appear diametrically opposed, the implications of each for the clarification of the purpose of CBA merge. Economists who are convinced that welfare economics is scientific, and, hence, ethically unproblematic feel little requirement to ask whether cost–benefit calculations assist the achievement of desirable ends because the ethics of CBA is subsumed in the analysis. Those who stress that welfare theory is founded upon value judgements also feel little incentive in that direction because value judgements cannot be questioned. They simply are. Thus, in both cases, the purpose of CBA remains uninvestigated. In these circumstances, it is the accounting method, the calculating mechanism, whereby results are obtained that looms large for its own sake.

Conclusions

The preceding pages have not contained an exhaustive survey of cost–benefit methodology. Rather, they have explored the theoretical and methodological underpinnings of some of CBA's principal features with a view to elucidating both the nature and the consistency of the logic at the centre of cost–benefit analysis. What is clear from this review is that the Neoclassical ends–means grammar is a crucial, and almost infinitely malleable, instrument for the extension of economic reasoning to new and wider spheres of application. The uses to which the ends–means dichotomy is put in cost–benefit analysis allow the economist to isolate sets of discretely distinct ends and means, to compare specific ends with specific means (which is greater, etc.) and to compare different combinations of ends and means (which is the most advantageous, etc.). Whether or not these ways of portraying the ends–means counterpoint are legitimate in Neoclassical terms is less important than the increase in the range of questions economists feel able to answer which follows from the above format. Similarly, the loose interpretation that the term opportunity cost has received is overlooked in view of the advantages that the Classically-based cost approach to valuation brings to CBA (the extension of economic analysis to the public sector, etc.; the valuation of externalities). Moreover, in both cases, the particular interpretation that the ends–means counterpoint received in the CBA context facilitated the extension of scalarity. Cost–benefit analysts are concerned with both the magnitudes of ends and means and ends–means ratios. The cost approach, furthermore, permits the valuation of effects, which, until the twentieth century, were considered beyond the range of economics or, indeed, intangible. In all cases, the emphasis is on the scalar, on the measurable.

The evidence suggests, then, that Neoclassical theory, while, in strict terms, of limited applicability, embodies a vehicle (the ends–means dichotomy) that has been very effective in bringing rational argument to new areas. Yet, at the same time, this vehicle is at the centre of the unravelling of Paretian welfare economics. Generally speaking, the economics profession has succeeded in emphasizing the advantages of the ends–means format as it is employed in CBA and in de-emphasizing the contradictions to which its use has led. But there are certain circumstances in which these contradictions come to the surface of economic debate. One of these is the continuing discussion of what constitutes a legitimate discount rate for use of CBA (especially CBA applied to the public sector). Another is the discussion of the scientificity and ethical character of welfare economics, including CBA. In the first case, questions regarding what is public, what is private, what concerns the individual, and what concerns the collectivity come to the fore, but remain largely unresolved. In the second case, certain economists, perhaps recognizing that methodologies like CBA are in many respects far removed from Paretian theory, have questioned the majority view to the effect that applied welfare economics is rooted in scientific analysis, and, hence, is ethically unproblematic.

It is important to note, however, that debates like these have not led to profound challenges to the logic of CBA. For example, the questions posed in the debate over the discount rate have not immobilized analysis because, as conventionally presented, they are essentially about numbers, and it has been possible to generate consensus in this area through appeals to commonsense and the examples set in the private sector (witness the government's test discount rate). In the case of the debate over the scientificity and ethical character of applied welfare economics it would appear that the only certain way to challenge the scientificity of welfare theory is to subject its postulates to testing. However, in this respect, the minority of economists who question the scientific character of welfare theory are relegated to inaction, for they, more than the majority, argue that welfare theory is ethically informed, and in these circumstances 'no questions of testable implications can arise'.[48] Hence, not only have welfare economists not been concerned with testing the postulates of Neoclassical theory before transferring them to a welfare framework, but they have also not devoted much attention towards ensuring that the assumptions underlying the constructions of welfare theory are plausible within an applied context (witness the ambiguity of the Marshallian measure of consumer's surplus in any but certain highly restricted circumstances and the assumption of universal equality of income underpinning the additivity of utilities). The lack of a testing philosophy within microeconomics and the integration of analysis and ethics within the Neoclassical framework (something that is particularly marked in welfare theory) have served to minimize the likelihood that rational economic doctrines will be successfully challenged. Clearly, welfare theory and cost–benefit analysis embody significant defences against theoretical disintegration, as well as being highly effective vehicles for the amplification of Neoclassical theory. In subsequent chapters we shall examine how economists have fared in attempting to apply this theoretical apparatus within government.

3

Economics and the administrative process

The most prominent examples of the use of cost–benefit analysis and related methodologies in the last ten to fifteen years have been concerned with public expenditure. Some, like the economic evaluations of the Channel Tunnel proposal and the plans for a Third London Airport, have had a very high public profile. Others, like the many CBA assessments of road and rail investment projects undertaken by economists in the Ministry of Transport and its successors, while no less important to the allocation of public moneys over the long term, have received much less public attention. Whatever the case, however, a full understanding of the way in which CBA has been applied in any particular instance of public sector expenditure appraisal presupposes some knowledge of the history of the methodology's uses in government and, just as importantly, an acquaintance with the reputation its exponents have had within Whitehall.[1]

In most cases, public sector cost–benefit analyses have been undertaken by professional economists employed within the Civil Service. Thus, the manner in which CBA studies have been conducted, the degree of influence such studies have had within government and the importance of CBA relative to other ways of evaluating policy have been closely related to the position economists occupy within the Whitehall structure. Several aspects of this position should be taken into account in any review of the use of CBA in government: first, the nature of the division of labour between economists and administrators and between economists and other types of civil service professionals; second, the status of government economists *vis-à-vis* other members of the Civil Service; third, the strengths and weaknesses of the economic worldview in relation to the many different demands that the administrative process places upon the economist; and finally, the degree to which economists are able to substantiate their claims to special knowledge and professional expertise within the administrative environment. This chapter explores each of these subjects as part of an analysis of the way in which the economics profession acquired a place in Whitehall. To provide a context for this analysis, the chapter begins with a discussion of the position CBA has occupied within the range of evaluative techniques used in central government and of the types of policy concerns to which these techniques, and especially CBA, are directed.

Taking a long and a wide view

Cost–benefit analysis is but one of a range of quantitative approaches to the problems of resource allocation that have been used in central government. Comparative cost evaluation, cost-effectiveness analysis, output (or programme) budgeting, economic forecasting (both for public expenditure and for the economy as a whole) and macro expenditure coordination procedures such as the Public Expenditure Survey Committee (PESC) and Programme Analysis and Review (PAR) constitute other examples of methodologies that officials have routinely deployed in the interests of efficiency and effectiveness in spending.[2]

The evaluative procedures that have been employed in Whitehall can be ordered vertically according to the degree to which they are applicable to large-scale, as opposed to small-scale, expenditure decisions. There would, of course, be much overlapping in such an ordering, but if a hierarchy of quantitative techniques were developed on this basis, CBA would occupy a relatively low-level position. Traditionally, CBA has *not* been employed to evaluate the appropriateness of large-scale, aggregated expenditure directed at a multitude of objectives.[3] Instead, CBA has generally been employed to evaluate specific projects, in other words those in which objectives are well defined and limited and in which the profile of projected expenditure is clear. Most projects with these characteristics lie within the administrative jurisdictions of the spending Departments and, therefore, CBA has been very much a departmental methodology.

Specific projects fall into at least two categories. Some are investment projects, either in existence or contemplated. Others, including regulatory procedures, pricing schemes, and legal regimes, have minimal spending implications for government, but may have substantial economic effects upon a variety of groups in the private sector.[4] While information about the number and nature of CBA studies in the Departments of central government was collected only intermittently during the 1970s, that which does exist suggests that CBA was applied most frequently to the first category of projects.[5] Furthermore, many of the investment projects to which CBA was applied either were or were envisaged to be schemes involving repeated expenditure (e.g. annual expenditure on vocational training, or long-term-care packages for the elderly). Frequently, CBA studies of investment projects involving recurrent expenditure have been undertaken in the hope that the initial analyses would suggest ways of developing a regular system of year-on-year expenditure review. Thus, CBA studies conducted in central government seem to have been geared to immediate administrative requirements in at least two senses: with few exceptions, they have been concerned with projects having *direct* departmental investment implications; in addition, many of them have been focused upon schemes involving repeated expenditure or, in other words, those most in need of monitoring over the long term.

Taken together, government cost–benefit analyses have had another prominent feature. They have been very heterogeneous in terms of subject matter. CBA has been used in an enormous variety of policy areas (e.g. defence, transport, employment, education, health, social services, agriculture, aid provision for developing countries, industrial development, civil service management). Moreover, the methodology has rarely been modified upon transfer from one policy area to another. For example, in terms of logic, there is little to distinguish a cost–benefit appraisal of a military investment from a cost–benefit appraisal of an investment in education, despite the much greater ambiguity that the investment concept has in the latter case. Where the distinctions, if any, have tended to lie is in the degree to which CBA is deemed to be successful or credible in these two policy areas. In the 1960s Prest and Turvey observed that CBA 'is more useful in the public utility area than in the social services area of government',[6] and this judgement has been substantiated in the British case to the degree that transport projects have predominated in most compilations of public sector CBA studies. Indeed, CBA first acquired a reputation as an aid to policy-making through the 1963 Victoria Underground Line study by Foster and Beesley. More recently, however, certain qualifications have had to be added to the Prest and Turvey assessment. In the late 1970s cost–benefit studies relating to manpower, education, health and other social services became much more common than they had been in the 1960s. As later chapters indicate, there have been major difficulties involved in applying CBA to social expenditures. Nevertheless, cost–benefit analysts have had some success in recent years in persuading senior officials that they are able to transcend the divide between the public utility and social services areas of government. Thus, more, rather than fewer, policy areas have come within the range of the CBA practitioner.

The fact that CBA has been applied in a great variety of policy areas, some of which are far removed from the water resource field in which it was pioneered, indicates that the methodology has come to be widely perceived as a *flexible* analytical tool. Moreover, its flexibility is not confined to questions of subject matter. For example, the methodology encompasses accounting devices (notably discounting) that allow the analyst to take what Prest and Turvey have called a long view of expenditure.[7] If the appropriate annual indices are available, analysis can begin in any year, end in any year, and extend over any reasonable period of time. Thus, the cost–benefit analyst confronts no particular difficulties in undertaking prospective or retrospective evaluations.

In this last sense CBA has been very much in step with many developments in the general field of public sector expenditure control. Beginning with the Plowden Committee Report of 1961, and throughout the negotiations surrounding the emergence of PESC and PAR, those interested in expenditure control have stressed the rolling nature of public spending and the necessity for coming to terms with the short-term future in resource allocation.[8] Part of this emphasis has been embodied in the Treasury's long-standing insistence that discounting be incorporated into all expenditure reports from the Departments and the nationalized industries.[9] The commitment to discounting was crystallized in the 1967 White Paper, *Nationalised Industries: A Review of Economic and Financial Objectives*,[10] which left little doubt that discounting methods were to become central to expenditure control in the nationalized sector and, by extension, to departmental work focused on the nationalized industries. The review established a test discount rate for the public sector, and this was set at the average rate of return on investment in the private sector (then considered to be approximately 8 per cent). Henceforth, the nationalized industries were required to employ a test discount rate as a target in planning all investments regardless of their specific nature.[11] By extrapolation, the government expected that all departmental reviews of the investment activities of the nationalized industries, and, indeed, departmental evaluations of public expenditure generally, would incorporate discounting methods, including the test discount rate. Cost–benefit analysis and discounting have always been integrally linked, and, therefore, it was an obvious instrument to be used in the government's bid to ensure that all participants in public sector expenditure review acknowledged the difference between yesterday and today, today and tomorrow.[12]

The 1967 White Paper also indicated that the Treasury wished to take advantage of another aspect of CBA's flexibility as an analytical tool. The document made mention of the social costs and benefits that may result from certain types of investment by the nationalized industries, and noted that Departments supervising the activities of the nationalized industries should be prepared, on occasion, to undertake cost–benefit studies of particular types of investment if their wider implications seemed to warrant review. Thus, the government came to associate cost–benefit analysis not only with a long view of investment, but also with a *wide* view. Moreover, this wide view was said to reside in the Departments, not in the industries. By introducing a discussion of social costs and benefits into the 1967 White Paper the government was reasserting the right of the Treasury and the Departments to ensure that the public interest was protected in the course of planning state-financed investment in the nationalized industries. Moreover, Ministers and officials were confident that cost–benefit analysis offered a means of making the public interest more explicit than had been possible in the past. Thus, cost–benefit methodology was juxtaposed against commercial criteria and traditional financial methods of appraisal, as a symbol of the government's wish both that the more socially unacceptable aspects of business practice should be mediated in the consideration of public sector investment, and that the Treasury and Departments be seen to be developing their own rigorous standards of public efficiency.[13]

One of the more obvious, although probably intentional, weaknesses of the 1967 White Paper was that it did not provide Departments with any specific guidance as to how social costs and benefits were to be identified or interpreted.[14] Clearly, the government, acting in large part on the basis of the Treasury's view of public expenditure, wished to standardize investment review procedures across the public sector, but this did not mean that it was prepared to prejudge the concerns of individual Departments in specific cases. Rather, as long as officials employed the evaluative formats outlined in the 1967 review, the government appeared willing to accept whatever interpretations of the public interest emerged as a result of departmental history, experience and institutional patterns, and the state of play between the Departments and their respective nationalized industries. In consequence, the White Paper's guidelines regarding investment review procedures were seldom applied uniformly or consistently. Indeed, so much have the particular circumstances of each Department influenced the way in which expenditure has been evaluated that in many cases the application of evaluative methods such as CBA to their nationalized industries has taken second place to other developments.

In 1973, the Select Committee on Nationalised Industries issued a report, *Capital Investment Procedures*, that illustrates these last points.[15] The Treasury's presentations to the Committee reaffirmed the importance of the investment review procedures (including CBA) advocated in the 1967 White Paper,[16] but presentations from other sources indicated that departmental investment appraisal was displaying some contradictory features. A number of these were revealed in an exchange between members of the Committee and officials from the Department of the Environment (DOE).[17] From this exchange, and the DOE's memorandum, Committee members learned that, in accord with the thrust of the White Paper on nationalized industry investment, cost–benefit approaches to the evaluation of British Rail investment had taken hold within the Department, in large part because the introduction of corporate planning into British Rail had proved less satisfactory than originally planned in removing official doubts about certain investments. It also emerged, however, that the Department had applied CBA much more extensively to the evaluation of roads (a strictly departmental concern) than to the evaluation of railways. The DOE officials justified this imbalance by stating that because British Rail is a revenue earner commercial criteria give the analyst a more critical hold on performance. In the words of one official:

> . . . one can do a financial analysis and then one knows one is relying on facts of the market and getting an answer which may not be a final answer, but which through the market process reflects the needs of the community in so far as one can establish them.[18]

Roads, alternatively, were given CBA treatment 'because there is simply no other way of doing it'.[19] One Committee member queried this distinction. He argued that the social dimension to railway investment should not be ignored, regardless of British Rail's position as a revenue earner, and pointed out that the application of different methods of evaluation to road and rail prevented any meaningful comparative policy with regard to these two modes of transport. The arguments of this Committee member were raised again, and to some degree amplified in *The Role of British Rail in Public Transport*, the First Report from the Select Committee on Nationalised Industries for the 1976–7 session, but the imbalance in the evaluative treatment of road and rail persisted.[20]

The DOE example illustrates several aspects of the way in which CBA and similar, non-financial methodologies have been applied in central government. In general, when there has been a plausible case for employing commercial criteria in the evaluation of an investment, CBA and like methodologies have been applied sparingly. Indeed, departmental officials have usually been loath to substitute CBA for financial analysis in these circumstances because they have felt that the latter yields more direct results and, therefore, greater control over the investment in question (particularly investments undertaken by the nationalized industries). Alternatively, CBA (and similar techniques) have been applied fairly extensively in a variety of policy areas that have traditionally been difficult to evaluate using conventional financial analysis. It is the 'wide view' of investment embodied in CBA that has made this possible. At the same time, however, the exact meaning of 'a wide view' has remained ambiguous beyond the context of specific cases. For this reason, there have been few attempts to arrive at any kind of comparative assessment of evaluations undertaken in different policy areas (even when the methods used are similar).

CBA is considered to be a flexible analytical tool because of the long view and the wide view of investment that it encompasses, but there are also other features of the method that are perceived to be advantageous depending upon the application. For example, the logic of CBA allows the worth of a project to be assessed in absolute or relative terms. If the project under evaluation is historically unique, the cost–benefit analyst confronts few difficulties in developing a cardinal measure of its net worth. Alternatively, if his audience is somewhat sceptical about absolute evaluations, in instances in which a number of projects of a similar kind are to be reviewed, the analyst can argue that at least CBA yields valid ordinal measures of the relative merits of each project with respect to others of the same type. In addition, CBA is said to sharpen judgements concerning the phasing of investment. Discounting certainly highlights the pattern of investment over time for any particular project, and, therefore, encourages the analyst to consider the relative merits of lumpiness versus accretion in investment phasing (what is less frequently mentioned is that CBA biases the search for a solution to investment problems towards accretion). Finally, cost–benefit analysis is well suited to the reconciliation of quantitative results obtained from a diversity of analytical methods (and disciplinary or professional perspectives).

The preceding pages have reviewed some aspects of the way in which CBA has been applied in central government and, in particular, a number of the reasons why the methodology has been so readily accepted into administrative culture. However, the specific features of the manner in which departmental officials have applied CBA only become fully comprehensible when one locates the methodology within the larger system of public expenditure control of which it is a part and identifies the institutional structures and relations of authority that are associated with this system.

Assessing inputs and outputs in the public sector

If one examines the methodological structures of the quantitative approaches to the problems of public sector resource allocation mentioned earlier in this chapter, it is apparent that all of these methods are addressed to the task of specifying an efficiency relationship between the inputs and outputs of some system (whether it be a departmental programme or an investment project). The particular inputs and outputs will differ from case to case, as will the relationship that is posited to exist between them, but the fundamental logic of evaluation remains the same.

Given this, each method either incorporates, or assumes, some means of specifying the nature and magnitude of the imputs into the system under consideration. Much academic and non-academic debate is concerned with determining which inputs should be included in the definition of various government systems (witness, for example, the perennial public discussions about which types of outlays should be included in the computation of total public expenditure levels). Indeed, there is often a sense in which the preoccupation with inputs precludes consideration of other elements in the system. In so far as they provide valuable indications concerning the way in which the system in question is conceived, the degree of attention given to inputs is justified. However, there are also other, less convincing reasons for the preoccupation with inputs. In particular, they receive a disproportionate amount of attention because, superficially at least, most of the inputs we currently choose to label as such lend themselves to money valuation. Thus, inputs are usually identified with costs, for in many minds a project is fully defined when each component that can be assigned a cost-price in the market, or by administrative fiat, is itemized.[21] Moreover, since money values are subject to a wide variety of arithmetic manipulations, the treatment of inputs is very much simplified. Outputs, however, are quite a different matter.

Outputs are far more complex than inputs, even from a superficial standpoint. To begin with, particularly in the last two decades, analysts have come to recognize that outputs can take the form of either costs or benefits. Furthermore, output costs are different in kind from input costs. If, for example, the system under consideration is seen to yield some form of pollution, analysts encounter great difficulties in costing this effect because there is no long-run historical process of market or administrative adjustment fixing a price in these circumstances. Consequently, pollution effects are never costed directly. Rather, they are approximated by cost measures developed at some remove from the polluting process (for example, as when noise pollution from an airport is measured with reference to the cost of demolishing homes in zones of intolerable noise, relocating the occupants of these homes and providing sound insulation for those dwellings that are less affected).[22] The same applies to other output costs, such as congestion, that resemble the pollution phenomenon, but are not normally grouped with it. The problems surrounding the costing of negative outputs indicate that market-oriented models do not provide an adequate framework for understanding these effects. In the case of pollution, Georgescu-Roegen has observed that 'there is no such thing as the cost of undoing the irreparable harm, of reversing the irrevocable depletion'. As a consequence, he has urged us to think again about how we conceptualize 'process' either in the economic sphere or in other contexts.[23] Moreover, this recommendation acquires added weight when we turn to a consideration of output benefits.

Output benefits associated with government expenditures tend to be even less concrete than output costs. Despite the difficulties mentioned above in costing negative outputs, their effects are usually tangible (for example, we generally identify pollution effects through some concrete form of deterioration in our surroundings) and some (e.g. road accidents) have a great immediacy owing to their sporadic, individual and often dramatic or horrific nature. Alternatively, effects that are considered beneficial are more abstract. This is perhaps best illustrated by a recent dilemma that has confronted policy-makers in the health care field. Consider the case of a vaccination programme designed to reduce the incidence of a common, serious disease which, as an unintended effect, leads to a small number of cases of serious disability or even death. In these circumstances it is very difficult for politicians or the medical profession to argue convincingly for the benefits of the vaccination programme (or, indeed, vaccination programmes in general) because the costs of the programme have an immediacy and a concreteness that a benefit such as 'greater freedom from disease for the population as a whole' cannot evoke. Benefits like that just cited are part of Georgescu-Roegen's 'still mysterious *immaterial flux* of the enjoyment of life',[24] and therefore, to one degree or another evade measurement. Surrogate measures are always being advanced, however, because ultimately benefits, and their generation, are at the heart of the governing process.

Given the above observations about the differences between inputs and outputs, it should not be surprising that the history of the development of evaluative procedures with regard to public expenditures in Whitehall has been marked by a distinct imbalance between the speed of development and the administrative plausibility of evaluation procedures directed at inputs and those directed at outputs. Heclo and Wildavsky have commented upon this imbalance explicitly.[25] Lord Diamond has referred to it implictly.[26] In the 1970s the most obvious contrast was that between PESC and PAR.

The PESC system involved a yearly review of the expenditures to be undertaken by Departments on particular programmes. Thus it focused on the input dimension of public expenditure. The PAR apparatus, alternatively, was designed to assess the effectiveness of particular departmental programmes in achieving specified objectives given a range of alternative programme options, or the output dimension of public expenditure. While neither approach to public expenditure review was wholly successful, the PESC system proved more flexible. The general identification of inputs with costs permitted the elaboration of monitoring and control mechanisms using models derived from private sector financial information systems. Thus, in the wake of the 1975–6 inflationary spiral and rapidly accelerating levels of public expenditure, the PESC system came to be supplemented by short-term monitoring of expenditure in all fields, cash limits and new breakdowns of expenditure according to volume and price changes.[27] This extension of PESC during the 1970s is in direct contrast to the sporadic development and then the demise of the PAR apparatus. From the outset PAR had an uneven record and reputation. The outputs of government activity are simply not of the same concreteness, either in physical or monetary terms, as the outputs of private sector production. They, therefore, eluded the maximizing or satisficing standards so characteristic of the private sector, with the result that no overall monitoring of efficiency could be said to be taking place. Eventually, officials gave up the attempt.

These differences between input evaluation and output evaluation have also been reflected in the institutional divisions and relations of authority that characterize the expenditure review system. It is the general identification of inputs with costs and the concomitant parallels between input evaluation and evaluation procedures characteristic of the private sector that have provided the basis for the Treasury's position at the centre of the public expenditure review system. The homogeneity that inputs, valued as they are in money terms, are considered to have has allowed the Treasury a large amount of leverage with respect to expenditure decisions on the basis of relatively simple scrutiny procedures.[28] In contrast, the heterogeneity of outputs and their more indeterminate character necessitate that reviews focused upon 'what government systems produce' be undertaken by those who have most familiarity with the systems, that is by departmental officials. Thus, it is the Departments that conduct the expenditure review procedures directed towards outputs, although they do so at the behest of the Cabinet and the Treasury. However, this function has not lent the Departments the same degree of authority that input monitoring has lent to the Treasury. The principal reason for this is that the heterogeneity of outputs has been at the root of the competition for funds between Departments. Objectivity in output monitoring has, therefore, required some mechanism for ensuring that each Department does not exaggerate the benefits of its programme *vis-à-vis* those of others. In the PAR procedure objectivity was sought by subjecting the results of PAR studies undertaken in a particular Department to the scrutiny of Ministers and officials from other Departments and the Treasury. However, since no Department wished to lose funding as the result of criticisms from its peers, this process led to all of the difficulties and compensation mechanisms of a collective exercise in 'saving face'.[29] Consequently, PAR exercises did not gain a reputation for rigour and in-depth scrutiny. Indeed, within the Departments they were often dismissed as rather pointless attempts to usurp the prerogative of Ministers and senior civil servants to assess the merits of particular policies through internal committee decisions and comprehensive (if not always systematic and quantitative) examinations of the results of policies.

Cost–benefit analysis has acquired much of its methodological significance in government because it constitutes a bridge spanning the input evaluation and output evaluation modes. The methodology incorporates ways of assessing inputs (most often conceived as government costs) that closely parallel those characteristic of conventional financial analysis, and, therefore, draws upon the prestige private sector practices have enjoyed in the public sector.[30] At the same time, CBA embodies a view of outputs (both costs and benefits) that is much more comprehensive than that generally found in private circles. Indeed, its methodological distinctiveness rests upon the identification and evaluation of as many of the effects, both direct and indirect, of a particular system upon 'society at large' as the analyst, together with his official audience, deem to be important. This type of analysis is possible because CBA is characterized by a very 'open' logical structure – in fact, one that demands that the analyst fill in the cost and benefit categories on the basis of his particular perceptions of the system or project to be evaluated. There has been no sacrifice of the arithmetic character of economic analysis, and, except in unusual circumstances, CBA practitioners endeavour to provide a plausible arithmetic measure for each of the system's outputs so that they can be reconciled with the inputs, and the system's efficiency thereby specified. The arithmetic character of CBA means that private sector analogies are important in the evaluation of outputs as well as inputs, but in the case of the former there is also much room for what Peacock has called 'the qualities of the "guesstimator"'.[31] Moreover, it is these qualities that lend CBA its special character. In particular, the methodology derives its meaning from the attempt to find measures for costs and benefits arising from public spending that are, by private sector standards, intangible and, therefore, require creative approaches to measurement if they are to be assessed. Thus, unlike output budgeting, corporate planning, management by objectives and accountable management, all practices that, although in use in government, were developed in the private sector, cost–benefit appraisal has been closely associated with the public sector and the administration of public expenditure.

Cost–benefit analysis resembles the PAR approach to expenditure in that its primary focus is upon outputs, and, therefore, like PAR studies, cost–benefit analyses have usually been undertaken within Departments by departmental staff. However, unlike the PAR analyses of the 1970s, cost–benefit exercises have usually embodied a reasonably stringent requirement to present results in a quantitative form. This has meant that cost–benefit studies are usually focused upon areas of concern that are relatively tangible, such as the smaller, single-objective, investment projects cited earlier. Moreover, this focus has had certain advantages over time. Unlike PAR studies, which were often at least a potential threat to the reputation of Ministers and senior officials and, therefore, to the funding levels of the Departments, CBA studies have usually been somewhat removed even from the periphery of ministerial discussions, and, hence, have not jeopardized major aspects of the Departments' operations. Indeed, in most cases, CBA studies have been considered to be in-house reviews.

This does not mean, however, that cost–benefit analysis has been divorced from central expenditure control procedures. In the background to most CBA reviews one finds that Treasury officials have put informal pressure upon departmental officials to institute a study of the outputs in a particular policy area. The Treasury's interest has been to supplement input monitoring with the evaluation of outcomes.[32] One way of accomplishing this without alienating the Departments has been to suggest that the latter establish internal review procedures, the details of which are specified by departmental officials, while the general standards for review are agreed between the Treasury and the Departments.

The open structure of CBA is well suited to this type of division of responsibility. The Departments have decided which types of costs and benefits are to be evaluated, but the Treasury also has had leverage because it sets the discount rate, and has usually specified what is an unacceptable final result (i.e., a negative cost–benefit ratio).[33] Arrangements of this kind allow Treasury officials to be somewhat more systematic in the review of certain kinds of expenditure without a corresponding increase in the Treasury's workload. Moreover, through them, the Treasury has obliged the Departments to make some sense of the many types of outputs arising from policy regimes with spending implications.

Thus, the relations that have existed between the Treasury and the Departments in regard to cost–benefit analysis reflect two complementary, but distinct, orientations. First, there has been the Treasury's emphasis upon objectivity and control in the review of expenditure, which has been to one degree or another reflected in all cost–benefit evaluations. In addition, there has been the Departments' concern that the variegated nature of outputs not be suppressed during the course of evaluation, for it is in the interpretation of the often complex outcomes of policy that departmental expertise traditionally lies. The case studies contained in the following chapters illustrate that each application of cost–benefit analysis reflects the tension that exists between these two orientations. This tension is also apparent in a more general sense in the insitutional structures, and accompanying organizational arrangements, most closely associated with the use of CBA and other economic modes of analysis in public expenditure review.

The Government Economic Service

CBA's position within the public expenditure review system has derived in part from the fact that cost–benefit studies have been seen to complement departmental operations. Just as importantly, however, CBA has been a major symbol of the expertise of a recognized professional group within government Departments, namely departmental economists, members of the Government Economic Service (GES).

By the 1970s the GES had emerged as the career service for all professional economists in Whitehall.[34] Its headquarters was in the Treasury, although most of its membership was located in the Departments and other organizations of central government. Thus, through GES channels, and routine contacts between the Treasury and the Departments, Treasury officials were well placed to monitor the progress of cost–benefit and other forms of economic evaluation. The head of the GES, whose official title was Head of the Government Economic Service and Chief Economic Adviser to the Treasury, held a position in the Treasury equivalent to that of a Second Permanent Secretary, and was responsible for that sector of the Treasury providing short- and medium-term economic forecasts and specialist advice concerning macroeconomic policies. In addition he had a staff located in the Treasury which undertook the management of the GES including recruitment, assignment, training, promotion up to the Senior Economic Adviser level, the development of guidelines for promotion, and secondments to outside or foreign organizations.

Beyond the Treasury the GES was divided along departmental lines, with varying numbers of economists in each Department (see Table 3.1). Most Departments with substantial numbers of economists had some type of separate establishment for them. Some (Energy; Health and Social Security; Agriculture, Fisheries and Food; Overseas Development and the Foreign and Commonwealth Office) had internal groups or divisions of economists headed by an official either of Deputy or Under Secretary rank and sometimes designated as a Chief Economic Adviser. Others sought economic expertise from a group or division of economists (headed by a Chief Economic Adviser) within a common services organization used by a number of Departments (Industry and Trade relied upon common economic services, as did Environment and Transport). In addition, there were the Departments with substantial numbers of

Table 3.1 Economists distributed by Department, August 1977

Department	*Number*
Agriculture, Fisheries and Food	32
Cabinet Office	6
Civil Service Department	7
Customs and Excise	2
Defence	2
Education and Science	7
Employment	23
Energy	20
Environment	80
Fair Trading	8
Foreign and Commonwealth Office	12
Health and Social Security	19
Home Office	4
Industry	54
Inland Revenue	2
Manpower Services Commission	10
Overseas Development	45
Scottish Office	23
Trade[1]	3
Transport[1]	2
Treasury	74
Welsh Office	1
Other organizations (for example, the Monopolies and Mergers Commission)	11
Total	447

[1]The figures for Trade and Transport should be grouped with those for Industry and Environment respectively for an accurate representation of the number of economists engaged in the Industry–Trade and Environment–Transport policy areas.

Source: Interview, civil servant, HM Treasury, 18 October 1977.

economists in which these professionals were either integrated into the research and planning division (Employment) or distributed in units throughout the Department's structure (Scottish Office). The remaining Departments and organizations generally had complements of economists too small to warrant distinct establishments.

The composition and organization of the GES in the 1970s were products of highly uneven historical development. When the Wilson Government created the GES in 1964 not all government economists were incorporated into it. For example, the economists in the then Ministry of Agriculture were not regarded as full professionals by those creating the Service, and, in any case, wished to manage their affairs independently. Thus, it was several years before the GES became truly government-wide. Moreover, the growth in the number of economists in different Departments after the creation of the GES depended very much more upon ministerial preference than upon central planning. For example, despite the many instances in which economic analysis has been applied to military spending in the United States and elsewhere during the 1960s and 1970s, economists were very scarce in the Ministry of Defence in 1977. In contrast, the Ministry of Overseas Development and the Department of the Environment had sizeable complements of economists in that year, in large part reflecting the progress of Mrs Barbara Castle through various ministerial posts in the 1960s. Finally, it should be noted that a substantial number of economists within a Department did not guarantee a considerable and uninterrupted economic input to policy. Paraphrasing one civil servant, the nature of the work in which they were engaged, rather than the numbers of economists in the Department, determined the type and degree of influence they had.

Within the GES, the Treasury, with its large number of economists in a variety of fields, was clearly dominant. As the body responsible for economic management, both of government and the economy at large, it had charge of the coordination of the GES. It followed, moreover, that economists outside the Treasury were heavily influenced by the intellectual climate and administrative style prevailing within the Treasury.[35] An economist's prospects for promotion (regardless of his location within the Civil Service) depended upon the type of impression he made with Treasury officials (both economists and, to a lesser degree, administrators). Furthermore, most of the more desirable GES positions were located within the Treasury and Treasury officials had virtually exclusive influence over the choice of GES personnel assigned to these positions. Finally, the Treasury derived a great degree of influence over GES economists from the fact that, although its total staff complement was small, it had more economists in relation to administrators and other personnel than any organization in Whitehall. This meant that once an economist became established in the Treasury it offered the broadest spectrum of promotion possibilities in government.[36]

The dominance of the Treasury within the GES meant both that Treasury officials were continuously involved in monitoring the work of all GES members and that the latter looked to the Treasury for indications concerning which developments in the economics discipline were judged to be applicable to government, the type of work that would be approved in the future and the areas of specialization likely to offer promotion prospects. This, however, did not constitute a rigid system for the control of economic intelligence. The nature of the work undertaken by government economists and the type of influence they had were also very dependent upon the composition, structure and social climate of the Department to which they belonged. The most important point to note in this connection is that, with a few exceptions (some of which are discussed later in this book), government economists were *advisers* to their respective Departments. Unlike their administrative colleagues, they had no responsibility either for the formulation and implementation of policy or for the consequences following upon policy decisions.[37] Rather, their task was to improve the processes of policy formulation and implementation by counselling administrators as to the *economic* merits of following one course of action over another. Therefore, the nature of the work performed by government economists was greatly influenced by the degree to which administrators believed economic advice to be useful in particular policy areas. Certain GES members were 'bedded into' programmes for which administrators felt long-term economic advice was required. Other government economists were 'floaters' moving from problem to problem, policy area to policy area depending upon where administrators felt their skills were needed.[38] In both cases there was a constant dialogue between economists and administrators as to the skills of the former and how those skills could be best deployed. GES members relied upon their association with the Treasury to ensure that their views were not overwhelmed in this dialogue. They were also sustained in their discussions with administrators by a general belief within government (one that was especially marked within Departments having large numbers of economists) that economics has an important contribution to make to many policy problems. Despite these advantages, however, there were many times when economists failed to persuade administrators that their methods had some role to play in the interpretation of administrative problems.

The degree to which administrators proved amenable to economic advice was determined by many considerations. Some of the departmentally-specific and problem-specific considerations that influenced administrators in this regard are dealt with in the case studies. There are, however, certain broader determinants of the degree to which administrators proved open to economic advice that should be mentioned here. For example, on occasion, the predilections of a particular Minister meant that economic analysis was given more weight during his term of office (and sometimes after) than might ordinarily have been the case. Thus, when Dr David Owen was Minister on the health side of the Department of Health and Social Security economic evaluation received greater attention from administrators in that part of the Department because Owen believed in the merits of in-depth economic appraisal of health care problems.[39] In addition, key personalities within the Civil Service hierarchy have had a substantial effect upon administrative practice. When Sir William Armstrong was at the Treasury, and then head of the Civil Service Department, economic analysis and management techniques were assigned considerable weight across the Departments.[40] Furthermore, the appointment of personalities like Sir William

Armstrong was, at least in some measure, a function of changes in the general political climate of opinion regarding the machinery of government and the nature of effective administration. For example, the interest of the 1964–70 Wilson Governments in improved management within the public sector, perhaps best exemplified by the Fulton Committee's investigations of Civil Service operations,[41] induced more concern for the subtleties of quantitative analysis in administrative circles and spawned certain institutional innovations like the introduction of sizeable numbers of economists into a variety of Departments.[42] The 1970–74 Heath Government was also preoccupied with improved management, as indicated by the introduction of PAR and the creation of the Central Policy Review Staff. In consequence, more technical, more systematic approaches to policy formulation, implementation and evaluation were favoured in this period as well, although the Fulton Committee's suggestions for a radical reorientation of the Civil Service along more managerial lines were not carried out.

However, while considerations of this kind were important in ensuring a hearing for economists within the Civil Service and in breaking down barriers to certain institutional innovations involving economists, the status of economic advice within the bureaucracy also depended upon the degree to which the economics profession was able to adapt its training and experience to the demands of the Civil Service. This was particularly true given the dominance within Whitehall of an administrative ethic favouring judgement over analysis and breadth of outlook over in-depth scrutiny.[43] What we know of the challenges economists confronted in moving from the universities and other institutions into the Civil Service is by no means systematic. We must rely upon the often anecdotal descriptions of the work of government economists given by those few professionals who have a detailed familiarity with the Civil Service and have written about it. Nevertheless, from this testimony one can discern certain broad strategies that economists have employed in accommodating themselves to the administrative environment – strategies that make the ready acceptance of cost–benefit analysis in certain policy areas comprehensible.

Economists adapt to the Civil Service: the early years

For economic expertise to have credibility within the Departments of central government, government economists had to be able to persuade their administrative colleagues of the efficacy of economic methods in at least some phases of the process(es) whereby policy is assessed. In the past this task has not been easy. For example, government economists have not been able to rely upon their associations with the community of academic economists to confirm the advantages of their disciplinary orientation within government circles.[44] In the late 1960s Hutchison observed that in the 1946–66 period policy advice stemming from the British community of university economists was fragmented, contradictory, very much subject to the vagaries of political and intellectual fashion and often ill-informed.[45] He also noted that academic economists, rather than fully acknowledging the role of guesstimation, or speculation, in the economic policy advice that they proferred, tended to stop any obvious gaps in their knowledge with a 'dubious temporary filling', which may have deflected criticism but, in the long term, did little to enhance the credibility of the profession.[46] Moreover, when economic advice from the academic economists did have an impact upon policy formulation and implementation, all too often the results damaged, rather than bolstered, the latter's reputation. After examining a number of policy areas in which economic advice from the academic community of economists was applied, Hutchison concluded that there had been a 'predictability gap' between the theoretically-based prescriptions of university economists and the outcomes of the actions these prescriptions inspired.[47]

Given the dubious early record of academic economists in various government policy areas, Hutchison was of the opinion that the judicious application of economics to policy would be accomplished, if at all, by those economists who emerged 'for the first time in Britain in business and government, in significant numbers, in the middle of the nineteen sixties'.[48] He observed, moreover, that the prospects in this regard were not entirely bleak. If nothing else, economists both inside and outside government had succeeded in extending economic analysis, of both the macroeconomic and microeconomic varieties, to encompass most of the new policy areas in which the state had become engaged since the Second World War.[49] In addition, the mathematical modelling techniques which became much more prevalent in all parts of the economics discipline after the War had been taken as exemplars in the public policy field. What was considered adequate in the way of policy evaluation within government had become more quantitative than in the past. This, in turn, had prompted a greater interest in the 'criteria or "methods" aspired to, attempted, claimed or considered "professionally adequate" by economists'[50] within the Civil Service and the public sector generally. The pertinent question was, therefore, had government economists succeeded in integrating themselves into the Civil Service environment and, if so, how had this been accomplished.

In 1955 A.K. Cairncross published an article entitled 'On being an economic adviser'.[51] In it he recounted his experiences as a civil servant at the Board of Trade during the early 1950s. This was the period when single, illustrious economic advisers to government (for example, Sir

Henry Clay) were gradually being replaced by economists who had permanent staffs and were 'bedded into' specific government organizations. Cairncross focused his attention almost entirely upon the issue of how a man with some experience of economics as an academic discipline, who is hired by the Civil Service to advise others on that basis, could best integrate himself into the apparent chaos of a sprawling administrative organization. He recommended that a government economist should accommodate himself very quickly to the administrative complexion of his working environment. Cairncross noted, for example, that initiative is valued in the Civil Service, but only when it is directed at the salient, that is to say urgent, administrative problems at hand. Therefore, economic advice is only given attention when it arrives tersely argued on the right person's desk at the right moment. Timing, speed in the preparation of briefs, and a knowledge of how the administrative system operates were, in Cairncross's view, essential qualifications for an economic adviser. In addition, an adviser had to be able to perform many tasks that were not directly connected with the provision of economic advice, such as speech-writing, committee work and the reception of foreign delegations interested in British economic policy. More importantly, he had to be able to assess work in progress in his own organization and elsewhere in government in order to identify those areas in which work needed to be done. Finally, an adviser was expected to help administrators with their 'figures' and to take on the more quantitative, often statistical, aspects of policy advice. Cairncross warned, however, that this last task often involved simply confirming that an administrator had, indeed, sorted out a particular problem in the appropriate way.

This early description of the work of a government economist was amplified some years later by E. Devons.[52] Writing in 1959, Devons stressed that economists in the public sector were best advised to avoid the complexities involved in elaborate academically-inspired theories and to concentrate, instead, upon the simple, elementary propositions showing the functional relationships between, on the one hand, supply, price and demand and, on the other, income, expenditure, production and employment. He noted, furthermore, that these propositions only give indications as to the likely economic tendencies that would follow upon different policy regimes – something all economic advisers would do well to remember. He warned that if economists were to attempt to proceed beyond the identification of tendencies to try to predict specific outcomes at specific times, they would debase their standing both with their government colleagues and with the public at large. Fundamentally, Devons believed that the standing of economists in the public sector could be best enhanced by the succinct presentation of the commonsense of economics in all policy spheres. He saw the public sector economist as a guide to the simple logic of economic life, as a determined scrutinizer of the economic assumptions upon which policies were to be erected.

In 1961 P.D. Henderson published a paper in which he analysed the contribution that trained economists were making to public policy formulation both by examining the numbers and positions of economists in central government and by reviewing a number of policy-making episodes in which adequate economic advice, he argued, had been lacking.[53] He found that the level and quality of economic advice available to central Departments were unacceptably low, and recommended that steps be taken to change the situation. However, for present purposes, the most significant part of Henderson's paper is that in which he criticized the lack of economic advice in the numerous specific areas of policy formulation that are the responsibility of the Departments – that is, those areas that were later to be the object of evaluative methods like CBA. Henderson recommended that economic analysis be coupled with administrative debate in these areas. Moreover, in doing so, he carefully balanced claims for the professionalism of economists (using analogies with other established government groups like accountants and engineers) with recommendations for the development of the economist class which would make it closely resemble the administrative class (for example, the routine movement of economists from Department to Department every few years to prevent the undermining of independence of mind).

Clearly, Henderson was attempting to reinforce the claims of economists to a larger place in Whitehall by emphasizing that they, like administrators, could be sensitive to the specifics of departmental problems, and at the same time contribute a new and valuable dimension to policy review through their special expertise. Moreover, the role of the economist would be enhanced if, like the administrator, he were able to acquire a breadth of economic experience in government. The similarities between the role of the economist and that of the administrator and the potential overlap and complementarity between these roles were stressed in Henderson's call 'to increase both the number of economists who are civil servants and the number of civil servants who are economists'.[54]

To summarize, then, Cairncross had asserted that the economist could not afford to ignore certain fundamental features of the civil service environment if he was going to be effective within it, while Devons had argued that the economist must focus his attention upon those types of expertise that are likely to be best received in the public sector and resist all temptation to 'over-sell' his specialized knowledge. Taken together, these presentations stressed the merits of simplicity, clarity and timing in the delivery of economic advice. In part, this constituted a response to the need to make advice both comprehensible and useful to administrators, but, more importantly, it reflected a realization that economic advisers had constantly to confront the danger of debasing their credibility by failing, as economists, to integrate the diverse facets of government policy concerns into well defined 'wholes' with some foundation in non-commonsense reasoning. The central imperative was to use the intellectual resources of the discipline of economics to develop conceptual frameworks that could both accommodate the variety of issues with which government had become involved and preserve the cognitive cohesion that was necessary to reinforce the group position of economists within government.

One tactic that could contribute to the achievement of this last mentioned goal was, as Henderson had recommended, to align the use of economic expertise more closely with ongoing administrative debate in settings such as *ad hoc* interdepartmental committees in which the full range of government policy questions were regularly discussed.[55] Not only did this offer the prospect of broadening the range of questions that government economists would have some opportunity to analyse (especially at the microeconomic level), but it also promised to counter any tendencies for administrators and other members of the bureaucracy to identify economists with separate and overly technocratic approaches to policy. In connection with the last point, it should be noted that commentators like Henderson wished, above all, that government economists should avoid the fate of government accountants who were, more often than not, regarded as mere technicians by their civil service colleagues.

The question Henderson left unanswered was: what types of economic methodologies would be most acceptable in the civil service environment given the coupling of economic and administrative expertise that he envisaged. Although many of the examples he cited to illustrate the value of economic reasoning in the public sector involved the application of welfare economics to policy, Henderson remained vague about the form in which economic advice should be cast. Three years later, however, economists had identified a number of methodologies that they felt had great potential in the public sector, and were advocating their merits with great confidence. Even in 1960, an issue of the *Bulletin of the Oxford University Institute of Statistics* was filled with articles about economic and investment criteria, and, in the same year, Coburn, Beesley and Reynolds published the now classic cost–benefit assessment of the London to Birmingham motorway.[56] Then in 1961 the publication of the Plowden Committee Report, which dealt at length with ways of improving the efficiency of public expenditure, encouraged some economists with an interest in Whitehall operations to propose new applications of economic methodologies within the public sector.

M.S. Feldstein, for example, published two articles in this connection.[57] Feldstein was convinced that the economist had a role to play as an 'economiser of the nation's resources'.[58] Moreover, he had advice to offer concerning how they could best fulfil this role. In his view, the then most obvious sources of methodological guidance for the government economist were the application of cost–benefit analysis to water resource programmes by US engineers and, later, economists, and the use, both in Britain and America, of operations research techniques supplemented by economic reasoning in the generation of budgetary profiles for military spending.[59] Like many others, Feldstein was intrigued by the 'common expression' that the budgeting function could lend to a variety of problems. He believed, furthermore, that applied welfare economics (and particularly CBA) could be used to supplement and improve upon then standard budgeting practices. If, he argued, the expenditure planning process were undertaken by economists, it could be more than an exercise in budget minimization and/or project maximization. The reason for this was that, armed with applied welfare theory, economists would be equipped to identify policy options and evaluate them by determining benefits *in relation to* costs.

Feldstein's formulation of the economist's potential role in policy-making did not prejudice the latter's position within Whitehall because it apparently conformed to the budgeting function and because it was not sufficiently 'concrete' to carry damaging social or historical associations for specific applications. At the same time it promised to allow economists to treat a wide variety of policy areas and, therefore, broaden their influence within Whitehall. It was on this basis that Feldstein recommended the application of cost–benefit analysis to the National Health Service – a field far removed from those in which the methodology had normally been employed before 1964.[60] In this case, as in others, the economist would be able to use the open categories of CBA to accommodate a *variety* of cost and benefit effects, plus *limited* degrees of diversity, uncertainty and inconsistency, thereby generating a specific and historically-based assessment. Simultaneously, he would be able to control the configuration of the proliferation of the variables studied so that they fell within the bounds consistent with comparative economic analysis.

The tenor of Feldstein's work indicates that by 1963–4 at least some economists were much more confident than five years previously concerning their ability to make a viable contribution to the evaluation of public policy. Furthermore, this confidence was confirmed and given added impetus by developments such as Foster and Beesley's precedent-setting, cost–benefit evaluation of the Victoria Underground Line, the results of which were published between 1963 and 1965.[61] However, the application of welfare-derived methodologies within government might well have remained fairly idiosyncratic for some time, even within the transport policy area, had it not been for the emphasis given to concepts such as effectiveness and efficiency within the public sector following the 1964 Labour victory. Harold Wilson had acquired notoriety, and in large part his office, because of his incisive and forcefully argued attacks upon the Conservatives' capacity to manage the economy. After the 1964 election, therefore, many observers anticipated that the new government would adopt approaches to economic problems significantly different from those employed by the Conservatives. Moreover, many expected that these different approaches would involve the extensive use of economic expertise. In the event, Labour did introduce new approaches to policy, a large number of which were premised upon extensive consultations with economists, although the results that followed were not precisely what either Labour politicians or the economics profession had wished.

The impact of the Labour Government

Prior to 1964 the number of economic advisers in Whitehall was fairly low.[62] From the turn of the century until 1939 there were usually a few distinguished economists serving within the Civil Service at any one time, but, while these men were often very influential within particular policy areas, it was only with the advent of the Second World War that the economics profession could be said to have established an institutional base within Whitehall. During the War a sizeable number of economists entered government Departments, and, although many left to return to the universities at the War's end, a nucleus of economic advisers endured in the form of the Economic Section of the Cabinet Office. In 1953 the Economic Section was transferred from the Cabinet Office to the Treasury, and during the 1945–64 period the number of professional economists slowly expanded to reach a total of twenty-five at the time of the Labour election victory. Despite these changes, however, many of the economists who entered the Civil Service before 1964, even those senior men with access to ministerial and, at times, Prime Ministerial deliberations, found that their status was not such as to allow them to make what they considered to be meaningful contributions in the policy sphere. The situation changed in several ways when Labour came to power.

To begin with, the potential importance of economic expertise within the Civil Service was acknowledged in the creation of the Government Economic Service. Furthermore, the Labour emphasis upon good management in government allowed the development of teams of policy-oriented economists in a variety of non-central Departments (most notably Transport and Overseas Development). These teams were led by senior, experienced men with ready access to Ministers (indeed, the teams were often regarded as ministerial 'private armies'). More importantly, they were of a sufficient size that they could perform the type of in-depth, long-term work that ensured their members a greater influence upon policy than pre-1964 economists and guaranteed that the teams survived after their initial sponsoring Minister moved on to other Departments or other activities. Finally, Wilson appointed 'a handful of politically-committed advisers'[63] in the economic area. Although their influence has often been exaggerated, these men did have a direct impact upon certain key aspects of the Labour Government's economic policy, especially in the macroeconomic sphere. The most prominent among them were Professor Nicholas Kaldor and Dr Thomas Balogh.

The departmentally-based teams of economists that emerged under Labour were important in that they gave many economists with no experience of government a taste of the opportunities that public sector economics presented. Moreover, they gave many younger men a chance to accustom themselves to government service at an early stage in their careers. The teams also provided a setting in which the methodologies that Feldstein had described could be tested, and where found satisfactory, implemented. Economists like C.D. Foster, who joined the Ministry of Transport, were primarily interested in the microeconomic issues associated with government investment and the delivery of government services, and many of them had experience in operating the new evaluative methodologies such as CBA. In the next several years these men had an impact upon the organization of their Departments, upon recruitment, upon work patterns and, more generally, upon the norms that were to govern future decisions about public sector services. The number of economists involved in these changes was not large (in 1969, for example, there were still under 200 economists in the GES).[64] Furthermore, many of these economists had short tenures in government. Most of the important original contributors had left the Civil Service by 1970. Nevertheless, the framework for economic advisory work that they introduced endured, and was taken up by others. So great was their impact, in fact, that the majority of their successors were career civil servants as opposed to short-term staff. Moreover, the new recruits occupied positions in a much broader range of Departments than their predecessors had done. Finally, it should be noted that the efforts of the departmentally-based teams of the Wilson years prepared the way for a sizeable expansion in the number of government economists outside the Treasury during the 1970s. (The number of departmental economists more than doubled between 1970 and 1977.)

These departmentally-based developments were obscured to quite an extent, however, because of seemingly much more radical changes that were taking place during this period in the area of macroeconomic, if non-

Keynesian, policy. Labour Ministers and certain senior officials had come to believe that in the war against inflation and low levels of industrial productivity fiscal and monetary weapons had to be supplemented by more selective, more specific economic policies which could be employed to remedy structural deficiencies in the economy. In the words of Sir Eric Roll, 'we were in danger of suffering from "macroeconomicosis"' (of the Keynesian variety).[65] The remedy was to be the development of a sectoral economic strategy. This strategy had various facets, the most obvious of which was the attempt at indicative planning launched by the newly created Department of Economic Affairs (DEA). Other aspects of the strategy included the development and implementation of the Selective Employment Tax, the Corporation Tax, the Capital Gains Tax, and the Prices and Incomes Act. The failure of the majority of these policies is well-documented.[66] What is of interest for present purposes is that many of these failures came to be identified in the public mind with the influence of economic advice upon the policy-making process.

By 1967–8 the status of the economic advice that the government was receiving at the macroeconomic level was so low that Graham Hallett, a Cambridge lecturer in economics, was prompted by public criticism of 'adviser-inspired' programmes like the Selective Employment Tax to write an *apologia* for the influence of economists upon the Labour Government.[67] He concluded that there were two senses in which policy formulation within the Wilson Government had been adversely affected by the type of economic advice that Ministers and civil servants had received. First, the Wilson Government had placed too much reliance upon the counsel of economists like Kaldor and Balogh who were not embedded in the civil service hierarchy, and this meant that a variety of traditional, administrative filtering mechanisms (for example, the civil service committee system and consultations with special interest groups) were bypassed during the development of a number of important economic policies with the result that administrators encountered many practical difficulties in attempting to implement them. In addition, much of the advice that Ministers received in the 1964–7 period came from senior economists of a 'scholastic' or 'polemical' type. According to Hallett, the former had little awareness of the limits of academic theory in an applied context, and the latter too often attempted to portray their politically inspired recommendations as objective analysis.

As a remedy for this situation, Hallett, like Devons before him, recommended that government economists should focus their attention upon elucidating the 'basic relationships' of economics.[68] He also urged them to have more respect for 'factual knowledge and professional experience'.[69] Indeed, the conclusion to be drawn from his observations appeared to be that senior advisers in the Wilson Government had failed to heed the recommendations of men like Cairncross and Devons regarding the proper conduct of a government economist, and by the late 1960s were reaping the consequences in the form of a public backlash which threatened the credibility of all economists in the Civil Service. Other economists, commenting on similar issues, went further than this. M.M. Postan, for example, believed that, given the inadequacies of Keynesian economics and the highly questionable nature of the sectoral policies which certain economic advisers within the Wilson Government had advocated, economists would be well advised to proceed very cautiously in the macroeconomic sphere and concentrate their attention, instead, upon microeconomic issues.

The incipient swing among economists towards the micro-economic problems of government ought to be a sign of their being after all a collection of sensible men.[70]

Also in the same period the role and status of economists in government service became a sub-issue of the debates associated with the investigations of the Fulton Committee into civil service operations. For example, Roger Opie of New College, Oxford, who had experience as an economic adviser in both the Treasury and the DEA, responded to the Fulton Committee's interest in pursuing the merits of more managerial approaches to policy-making by noting that the government had not taken full advantage of the capacities of the professional economist during the expansion of the GES.[71] He argued that too few economists had been introduced into too few Departments and that the potential for economists to act as special 'expert' advisers to Ministers in order to highlight the inadequacies of departmental orthodoxy had been neglected. Not surprisingly, Opie's arguments were interpreted as special pleading within Whitehall, and senior government economists could not afford to associate themselves with Opie's criticisms, especially as they formed part of a larger discussion concerning whether or not civil servants were wielding excessive influence over Ministers. Nevertheless, the discussions that followed upon Opie's analysis, both inside and outside the Civil Service, served to highlight a number of the strengths and weaknesses of the position of economists in Whitehall during the 1960s.

To begin with, most of those concerned with the issue agreed that policy formulation and implementation in central government was suffering as a result of a lack of adequate economic analysis in many policy areas. Most also agreed that the need for economic analysis was particularly acute in policy areas such as social services and defence. Furthermore, in attempting to answer outside criticism, government economists were obliged to concede that the role of the economic adviser was still not very well established within Whitehall. Many GES members were convinced, however, that this situation could not be corrected by attempting to transform the government economist into an expert ministerial adviser, as Opie had suggested. This, they argued, was an unworkable option both because it threatened the claims of administrators, other professionals and politicians for a hearing from Ministers and because it breached the hierarchical chain of command characteristic of the Civil Service. But what were the alternatives? Some within government were attracted by the open and quantitatively-oriented approach to economic inquiry and discussion characteristic of the American federal government, but even those, like Sir Eric Roll, who greatly admired the American system of consultation between economists, administrators and politicians acknowledged that it could only be imitated to a limited extent within the British context because of obvious differences between the political systems and research establishments of America and Britain.[72] In these circumstances, it seemed prudent to seek indications as to the most appropriate ways for the role of the economic adviser to evolve in British experience and, then, to supplement the latter, where suitable, with models from abroad.

In the late 1960s, as in the 1950s, the major imperative for government economists was to maintain their credibility in the policy field by effectively integrating themselves into the civil service hierarchy. Through trial and error they had discovered that effective integration implies cooperation with all types of civil servants and a certain subordination *vis-à-vis* administrators. In connection with this last point, economists found they were well advised to ensure that the economic advice that administrators received was directed towards the administrative requirements of the moment, easy to assimilate, and credible. This meant, in general, devoting less attention to advanced theory and more to the basic propositions of economics, less to macroeconomics and more to microeconomics, less to the problems at the leading edge of academic research in economics and more to the applied problems regularly confronting the administrator, particularly those associated with the budgeting function. In this last regard, economists gradually found that they could be of most service in finding ways to expedite the flow of administrative work in existing programmes (through the establishment of information systems and the like), in using economic logic to organize certain policy areas at the conceptual level for purposes of evaluating existing or projected administrative action and in outlining possible productive extensions to current administrative systems.

It was in this context that a number of economic methodologies, many of which were developed principally in the United States, assumed importance within British Government. In November 1967, a Management Accounting Unit (MAU) was established within the Treasury. The Unit was closely associated with the Management Services (General) Division, and its brief was to assist 'in the wider application in

Government (and where opportunity offers in the public sector generally) of economic techniques which seem likely to lead to a more economical or effective use of resources'.[73] As part of this objective, it was 'to promote the wide application of systematic costing, especially comparative costing'. Thus, Feldstein's belief that economic analysis could contribute to the process of planning public expenditure had been given institutional expression by the latter half of the 1960s.

One of the methodologies that the MAU advocated with most vigour was cost–benefit analysis. Both CBA and the investment appraisal techniques which are integral to it (e.g. discounting) were discussed at some length in one of the Unit's first products, a *Glossary of Management Techniques* published in 1967.[74] As was made clear at an early stage, the MAU did not have the resources to undertake major cost–benefit studies of its own, but it hoped to persuade a variety of Departments of the merits of calculating social costs and benefits in the assessment of public expenditure, particularly given the contents of the previously mentioned 1967 White Paper on nationalized industries.

The vehicles that the Treasury, including the MAU, used most frequently to publicize CBA and other quantitative methodologies were the Treasury's Centre for Administrative Studies (CAS) and its series of Occasional Papers. In June 1967 some two dozen CBA practitioners were invited to a conference dealing with the merits of using the methodology in the public sector, and some two years later a non-technical review of some of the topics discussed at the conference was published by H.G. Walsh and A. Williams as a CAS Occasional Paper, 'Current issues in cost benefit analysis'.[75] In presenting the results of the conference to a wider audience, Walsh and Williams stressed the *administrative* importance of CBA, stating that its primary value lay in 'marshalling data systematically' and in 'rendering it [the data] as commensurable as possible'.[76] The compromise between administrative ends and economic means that had been achieved by the end of the decade is indicated by the fact that the group of cost–benefit practitioners that the Treasury had assembled was willing to suspend debate about many of the theoretical aspects of CBA in view of the technique's usefulness. In the words of Walsh and Williams:

> Some of the thorniest theoretical issues (e.g. that surrounding the appropriate conceptual foundations for the discount rate) may have relatively little immediate import for the practice of cost–benefit analysis, whilst other apparently theoretically insoluble problems (like the proper way to handle the redistributory impact of the projects between different groups in the community) can (and perhaps should) be left explicitly to the judgement of the *policy makers*. Thus devices which appear to be 'arbitrary' methods of solution to the economist *qua* theoretician may be perfectly acceptable in a wider context.[77]

At the same time, those in the CBA field recognized that even a pragmatically ordered CBA would be unacceptable if it appeared to be interfering excessively with conventional policy-making patterns. The conclusion to Walsh and Williams's review is replete with caveats to the effect that cost–benefit analysis does not involve the suspension of judgement, but rather its amplification through the development of a systematic and synoptic view of the problem at hand.

Conclusions

By 1970 Whitehall economists had surveyed the administrative environment with a view to determining the opportunities and limitations that this environment presents to members of the economics profession. They rapidly discovered that survival in central government demanded the development of strategies for the integration of their expertise into existing programmes – some of which have already been discussed. The concepts of 'government economic adviser' and 'economic advice' weathered the Wilson years intact, not because of the high political profiles assumed by men like Kaldor and Balogh, but because during the 1960s economists made conspicuous gains in imposing their worldview upon areas such as the enumeration of criteria for public investment, pricing policy in the nationalized industries and regional and transport policy. These successes, together with the established role of the economics profession in fields of macroeconomics like demand management and international and domestic finance, indicated that civil service economists could have a substantial impact in government by offering cogent, consistent and administratively relevant advice of a kind that cannot be gained by episodic soundings of the community of outside economists.[78] By employing economic logic to regularize and systematize some parts of the administrative process, government economists demonstrated the usefulness of their methods within the bureaucracy, and made themselves an important part of the smooth operation of certain policy areas, thereby establishing their autonomy with respect both to their non-government colleagues and other professional groups within government. This was achieved largely by progressive efforts at blurring the demarcations between economist and administrator, economic advice and administration. In this process, however, enough differentiation of approach was preserved that the group position of economists in Whitehall was not jeopardized and economists' claims to have special knowledge in dealing with policy problems could be substantiated.

One of the instruments that greatly facilitated the transition described above was cost–benefit analysis. As noted earlier, all microeconomic methodologies are focused upon the identification and manipulation of discretely distinct ends and means, but CBA also has the distinction of assigning approximately equal importance to each half of the ends–means dichotomy. The cost–benefit approach to economic evaluation addresses both sides of the budgetary question – costing and the benefits to the community that flow from public expenditure. Therefore, in comparison with conventional budgeting practices, CBA was sufficiently innovative in the 1960s and early 1970s to enhance the reputation of economists as custodians of the nation's resources and evaluators of the expenditure process. Furthermore, CBA's pragmatism with regard to the subject matter it treats, especially on the benefit side of the cost–benefit juxtaposition, allowed economists a common expression for the many public sector variables with which they were confronted. At the same time, while it drew upon the prestige afforded by the concreteness of private sector costing procedures, CBA was not simply another type of financial analysis, and, hence, could be claimed as a special preserve of the government economist. Thus, in 1970 Alan Williams could apply CBA to areas as diverse as the London underground network, nuclear versus coal-fired power stations and trunk road improvements, and observe:

> My three exhibits were presented in order to demonstrate situations (1) where cost–benefit analysis would tell you to do something which private sector financial appraisal would not tell you to do, (2) where cost–benefit analysis would tell you not to do something which private sector financial appraisal would tell you you ought to do, and (3) where cost–benefit analysis takes on board such a wide range of considerations that we are led to confront questions of valuation which, in their private capacities, people do not need to confront, and in some cases would prefer to ignore.[79]

Such comparisons with conventional types of appraisal meant that the CBA methodology came to be perceived to have a variety of administrative uses. The Plowden and Fulton Committees had both emphasized that expenditure review and evaluation procedures were not sufficiently rigorous, even in so far as the Treasury had control over spending. In the wake of such criticism, CBA appeared to provide a means of supplementing existing practices directed at expenditure control. Upon Cabinet and Treasury urging, the Departments employed it as a way of assessing the social impact of investments undertaken by the nationalized industries in their jurisdiction. More importantly for present purposes, during the late 1960s, through the Management Accounting Unit and other devices, the Treasury promulgated the use of CBA in the evaluation of departmental programmes. From the Treasury's standpoint, the methodology offered a way of informally monitoring, not only departmental spending patterns, but also the economic benefits, if any, that followed from particular types of departmental expenditure. Moreover, the open structure of CBA meant that this could be accomplished without unduly alienating the Departments because the undertaking could be presented as a cooperative one. Admittedly, this scheme could be no more than partial because it relied upon exhortation from the Treasury, and some Departments were more enthusiastic than others. However, in so far as it succeeded, small evaluative empires with links to the Treasury were established in Departments, and, within these, government economists increasingly took responsibility for the procedures, evaluative and otherwise, that they operated.

CBA's very open structure served to ease this integration of economists into departmental administrative structures. For example, CBA was often instrumental in coordinating different types of expertise in the review of a single programme, thereby facilitating the development of consensus in policy areas involving contributions from a variety of professionals. In addition, the methodology's expansiveness with respect to the number of analytical categories that it embraces meant that it could be used to serve a variety of administrative ends. CBA could be employed to plan prospective expenditure or to review previous expenditure, to rationalize the presentation of programmes with many facets, to organize the contributions of many interest groups to a particular programme. However, while CBA could encompass as many categories as was necessary for the evaluative task at hand, it was not premised upon the universal application of rationality within the administrative environment, and, therefore, seldom threatened the policy-making prerogatives of senior officials. Unlike output, or programme, budgeting, which requires the imposition of total efficiency in order for any one part of the system to operate,[80] CBA could be applied experimentally in a piecemeal fashion until it had demonstrated its merits. A corollary of this is that the methodology did not endanger long-established administrative divisions, such as that which has traditionally been maintained between road and rail. Indeed, the arithmetic character of CBA facilitated the differential treatment of issues that administrators deemed to be separate.

Cost–benefit analysis also proved useful to economists and administrators alike because it could be employed to introduce the basic propositions of conventional economics to an audience (namely administrators, other professionals and the public) that could not be assumed to have any special expertise, or, indeed, interest, in the area. The rationality embodied in CBA was not very removed from the 'common-sense maxims' that govern much day-to-day economic life, and was, therefore, readily interpretable to non-economists. Moreover, the methodology encompasses a remarkably effective 'distillation process'. During the course of any one analysis massive amounts of data may be sifted, sorted, made commensurate and manipulated, but the end-product is usually a set of relatively simple comparative tables, or perhaps even one number, from which policy implications can be drawn, even by the non-initiated. Thus, CBA could serve as an educative tool, as well as a strictly administrative one, introducing those principles of applied economics that 'seem often mere banalities, almost an anti-climax after the formidable controversies amid which they evolved'.[81] It was in this sense that cost–benefit analysis was attuned to the simplicity and the clarity that economists, often by trial and error, had found are so highly prized in the administrative environment.

CBA further enhanced the position of economists in the Civil Service because its open-ended nature seemingly gave vent to the philosophical and speculative predilections of economists. This identification served a dual purpose. On the one hand, it aligned the worldview of the economist more fully with that of the administrator. On the other, it prevented civil service colleagues from associating economic analysis with mere technocracy, or the output of a low-status civil service profession such as accountancy. CBA might, on occasion, degenerate into the kind of overly numerate activity that Cairncross, Devons and others feared,[82] but initially, at least, it was the means by which economists were able to make whole the many disparate facets of particular policy areas.

Finally, CBA has assisted the integration of economists into government administration by focusing attention upon manageable problems within the public policy field. In particular, the methodology acts as a symbol that the discipline of economics is highly relevant to the public sector even when, as is so often the case, government economists operating in the macroeconomic sphere fail to command the confidence of their peers and superiors. For example, in 1977 Alan Peacock, formerly Chief Economic Adviser (CEA), Departments of Industry, Trade and Prices and Consumer Protection, offered a description of the work of a CEA which clearly indicated that very little had changed since the 1964–70 Wilson Governments in the field of macroeconomic advice, except perhaps that economists in this area retained a lower profile than their predecessors.[83] As Peacock observed, in order to maintain the confidence of outside professional critics and Parliamentary review bodies such as the Expenditure Committee, the Government Economic Service had to be seen to be delivering consistent economic advice based upon a common analytical and statistical framework. However, in many macroeconomic policy areas (Peacock was particularly concerned with those pertaining to industry and industrial development), the many economic interests involved, the heterogeneous nature of the subject area and Cabinet rivalries had resulted in the fractionalization of economic advice. Moreover, even discounting political and bureaucratic pressures, economists of right and left had been forced to admit that macroeconomic theory is sparse in many areas and often inadequate and that empirical work may be non-existent. The difficulties associated with giving advice to competing members of Cabinet, of integrating information from a wide variety of sources and persuasions, and of developing a politically tenable theoretical structure upon which to base policy had often served to weaken the credibility of the economics profession in Whitehall. In these circumstances, economists frequently retreated, either out of government (as in Peacock's case), or into lower level, less politically salient, and generally more micro, fields of government work. In the latter arena, cost–benefit analysis apparently constituted a highly flexible means of applying Neoclassical logic to a variety of policy problems, and many economists have been gratified by the relative intellectual security it has afforded.

4

Investing in roads

Economics and roads

Physical planning, and especially planning connected with transport facilities and services, has been a traditional area of interest for applied economists both within government and in other institutional settings like the universities. Moreover, in the 1970s certain aspects of the economist's role in transport planning came to the attention of a large expert and lay audience as a result of the Roskill Commission's work on the location for the Third London Airport and the economic analysis undertaken in connection with the Channel Tunnel proposal.[1] In general, this exposure did not enhance the reputation of the economics profession, but it should also be noted that the economic evaluations conducted in association with the Third London Airport and the Channel Tunnel were not particularly representative of the type of work in which most transport economists have engaged. The economists working for the Roskill Commission and those who examined the Channel Tunnel proposal were obliged to estimate the economic impact of large, historically singular projects with the potential to affect many sectors of the British economy. In contrast, the vast majority of transport economists have confined their attention to relatively small projects of a type that were likely to be repeated and were unlikely to have substantial effects on the economy as a whole. Indeed, the controversies surrounding the economic assessment of plans for the Third London Airport and the Channel Tunnel proposal should not be allowed to obscure the activities of the economics profession in certain more mundane, less publicized, but in the long term equally important areas of transport. In particular, over the last fifteen years, within a variety of governmental and non-governmental settings, the profession has succeeded in institutionalizing the routine application of micro-economic analysis, especially of the cost–benefit variety, in the assessment of inter-urban roads, urban public transport and urban road projects.

There have been several dimensions to these developments. To begin with, there is evidence that indicates that in the 1970s economists acquired substantial authority within university-based transport research – authority that lent credibility to recommendations on their part for the adoption of economic methods in non-university organizations concerned with transport problems. In contrast to the situation in the United States where consultants and research institutions (e.g. the Rand Corporation and the Brookings Institution) played a substantial part in the analysis of transport issues, most non-governmental transport research in Britain was undertaken by the universities. A study by Heggie of the distribution of university transport research projects for 1967–8 and 1972–4 suggests that in the period from the late 1960s to the early 1970s the disciplinary orientation of university-based transport research shifted away from engineering, science and technology and towards planning and economics.[2]

This is not to say that planners and economists became numerically predominant within university transport research. Heggie's data for 1972–3 and 1973–4 show economists and related specialists to have been in a minority within transport research.[3] At the same time, however, they tended to be more academically senior than their colleagues with training in science, engineering and technology and were apparently more intellectually self-sufficient than the scientists, engineers and technologists. While the latter were given to launching multi-disciplinary efforts in the transport field, planners and especially economists did not find it necessary to 'mobilise multi-disciplinary research projects'.[4] Furthermore, although planners and economists constitute only 20 per cent of Heggie's 1972–3 and 1973–4 samples of university-based transport researchers, upwards of 45 per cent of the projects in which these workers were engaged fall within the planning–economics category because significant numbers of engineers, scientists and technologists had adopted theoretical approaches and methodologies from economics and related specialities during the course of their research. Thus, economic logic apparently commanded wide respect within university-based transport research, and economists and planners seem to have had a more secure position within the speciality than numbers indicate. The work of academic economists and affiliated professionals on transport has constituted a solid foundation for the extension of economic methods into other institutional spheres, including government.

A number of extra-academic circumstances also hastened the routine application of microeconomic analysis to transport, especially within central government. During the 1950s, the Ministry of Transport (MOT) was the scene of an important set of administrative and organizational innovations whereby professional engineers and administrators there succeeded in suspending their professional differences in the interest of a unified approach to transport problems.[5] Thus, by the early 1960s engineers and administrators within MOT were working in teams down to the sub-divisional level.[6] The most obvious product of this new alliance was a series of reforms in administrative practice based upon a combination of professional and non-professional expertise that had the effect both of rationalizing work programmes within the Ministry and of extending the planning horizon for such programmes from a few months to several years. For example, in 1960 the roads programme was still only projected from one year to the next, but the application of critical path analysis to the programme later in the decade served to define investment priorities, and thereby facilitated longer-term planning.[7] Initiatives like this were designed to regularize programme development through the use of rational methods of forward planning. Ultimately, the objective was to curtail the large fluctuations to which transport investment has historically been subject by persuading the Treasury that the Ministry's projections were founded upon stringent analysis of transport requirements and priorities.[8] In this connection, it rapidly became apparent that it might be advantageous to couple engineering knowledge and expertise with economic expertise, particularly in the area of resource allocation. The economics profession was an obvious source for the skills required to reduce the many features of transport investment programmes to the monetary measures favoured by the Treasury and to specify and evaluate the full range of direct costs and benefits associated with transport projects. It was against this background that transport economists became participants in the efforts to modernize administrative practice within MOT that punctuated the 1960s.

Early in the decade several academic economists began to explore the applicability of cost–benefit methods to government-sponsored transport projects. The best known of these attempts are the evaluation of the London to Birmingham motorway by Beesley, Coburn and Reynolds and Foster and Beesley's work on the Victoria Underground Line.[9] These early efforts suggested that the economics profession did, indeed, possess the means to assess the economic merits of inter-urban road or public transport projects either individually or as components of a total programme. In the years that followed, the methods employed by Foster, Beesley and others were adopted and perfected both by the expanding number of economists in the Ministry and by engineers who had perceived that methods for planning resource allocation derived from economics might constitute acceptable means of organizing often disparate pieces of technical analysis. Moreover, after 1965 the use of economic appraisal methods accelerated as a result of two other concurrent sets of circumstances.

In the first place, during the second half of the decade British officials began to learn the details of the Planning Programming Budgeting System

(PPBS) that the United States Department of Defense had developed in order to achieve a greater degree of control over military spending. While officials in many British civil Departments and Ministries regarded PPBS with scepticism, the system did combine economic appraisal with systems analysis, and therefore, had an obvious appeal for Ministries such as Transport, which, like the Ministry of Defence, had traditionally been preoccupied with physical planning under resource constraints. In the case of MOT, PPBS served to focus attention upon the potential administrative implications of the models of urban transport that were beginning to appear at that time as US transport engineers followed in the steps of the military systems analysts. These models, frequently based upon large-scale computer use, permitted the simultaneous evaluation and aggregation of the numerous components of very large investment programmes. In their wake strategic programme appraisal founded upon the coupling of economic methodology with relatively sophisticated mathematical modelling techniques and the use of computer technology seemed both possible and desirable.[10]

The second set of circumstances that accelerated the routine application of economic analysis to transport was a product of choices made in the national political arena. Britain had emerged from the 1950s with a transport system that differed markedly from the railway-dominated systems of Europe. Motorization had proceeded much further in Britain than, for example, in France or Italy. On the other hand, the railways had not received the kind of massive post-war capital investment that had served to establish the continental railways as undisputed universal carriers. In addition, the degree of state intervention in the transport sector was far lower in Britain than in many European countries. The unified and nationalized transport system that Labour attempted to establish through the Transport Act of 1947 had been substantially dismantled by subsequent Conservative Governments in the interests of efficiency through competition, especially in road haulage. Thus, in 1964 Labour inherited responsibility for a transport system dominated by roads, and governed by market precepts even within the nationalized sector. Partly on the basis of past experience, the Wilson Government did not attempt a radical restructuring of the transport sector. Rather, under the guidance of Mrs Castle, the then Minister of Transport, Labour adopted a pragmatic approach that was designed 'to combine the advantages afforded by the automatic processes of the market mechanism with those of direct control'.[11] There followed a series of Green and White papers culminating in the 1968 Transport Act. The provisions of the 1968 Act, including the establishment of Passenger Transport Authorities to control and coordinate urban public transport, the creation of the National Freight Corporation and the National Bus Company, the reorganization of road haulage licencing, restructuring the accounts and activities of the railways, and the use of subsidies to support 'socially necessary' transport services, are generally well known. What is perhaps less well appreciated is that the development of the Act and its subsequent implementation were founded upon a much higher degree of discrimination between, for example, profitable and unprofitable services and market and administrative measures than had previously informed policy. Unlike the Conservatives, Labour did not subscribe to the belief that many, if not most, transport problems can be resolved through competition between the transport industries without resort to some type of coordination of the market as a whole. At the same time, Labour did not consider that nationalization and other forms of direct control were viable political options in all situations. Thus, the Labour policy depended upon distinguishing between those areas of transport in which society is generally well served by market precepts and those that require regulation or more direct forms of control. Moreover, from a political perspective it was felt that it would be advantageous if these distinctions could be sustained through the use of universal criteria, given the many entrenched interests characteristic of the transport sector.

In this regard the Minister herself favoured the extensive use of economic expertise in the development of policy, and for this reason was responsible for substantially enlarging the number of economists in the Ministry. She intended that these professionals should act as impartial guides to the most efficient choices that could be made in the transport field, although she was not averse to tempering economic analysis with judgements concerning the social necessity of sustaining certain services, as in the case of the railways. This approach seemed to permit selective amendments to the system supported by a logic that commanded respect in many quarters. (In this context, one measure of the success of the approach is that it survived four years of Conservative Government, from 1970 to 1974, virtually intact.) From the standpoint of the economics profession, Mrs Castle's policy offered an unprecedented opportunity to exercise skills in the analysis of a wide variety of questions, as is evident, for example, in D.L. Munby's review of the 1968 Act.[12] Latterly, as well, the accumulation of economic manpower within the MOT, which the Minister had encouraged, permitted a number of administrative innovations founded upon economic logic and economic expertise.

Economists within the transport field thus benefited both from the emphasis that US transport analysts and certain MOT engineers gave to economic methods and from the type of discriminatory measures involved in Labour's transport policy. Economists were also integrated very rapidly into the operations of the Ministry of Transport, in large part because many of the traditional barriers to the effective use of professional expertise in the MOT had been bridged by the Ministry's engineers in the previous decade. The present chapter is concerned with one of the more notable products of this influx of economic expertise into the Ministry of Transport, the COBA (cost–benefit) system of economic evaluation used in appraisal of certain types of inter-urban roads. Later sections of this chapter explore the COBA system in detail. First, however, it is appropriate to examine the economist's role in the assessment of roads generally, so as to clarify the context in which COBA developed.

Trunk roads and economic expertise

In the mid-1950s only three of the Ministry of Transport's sixteen Under-Secretaries dealt with roads or road transport. By 1969 the number of Under-Secretaries within the Ministry specializing in road-related matters had increased to ten.[13] This growth in the administrative apparatus connected with roads was a function of commitments on behalf of both major parties to expand and improve Britain's inter-urban road network through the building of motorways and the upgrading of other major trunk roads. For practical purposes, the 'Motorway Era', from which we are now emerging, began with Harold Watkinson's Parliamentary Statement of 1957 announcing the commencement of five major inter-urban road projects costing approximately £240 million over four years. These road projects contributed to the one thousand mile motorway programme of 1963, and this, in turn, was amplifed under Labour with the result that in the 1960s and early 1970s motorway construction accelerated, culminating in a 1971 peak of 232 miles opened in one year.[14] Before leaving office in 1970 the Wilson Government published the White Paper, *Roads for the Future*, which advocated 'a comprehensive national system of trunk roads' and outlined a programme of road building designed to provide 2200 miles of motorway and extended carriageway as well as 1800 miles of improved trunk roads by 1985–90 at a cost of some £3400 million.[15]

During the 1960s, road planning and road building required the extensive mobilization of professional and administrative expertise, the more so as planning horizons lengthened, building standards acquired more precision and administrative procedures involving order taking, land acquisitions and financial control were elaborated in response to the challenges encountered in managing an expanded road programme. Administrators, engineers and other experts including economists, lawyers and scientists cooperated in developing, implementing and refining operating procedures designed to ensure that a wide variety of types of expertise were integrated into the planning and construction of any particular trunk road.[16]

For the economists' part, this process offered a number of opportunities. To begin with, since the late 1950s politicians in both major parties have frequently resorted to citing economic objectives in justifying the expansion of the inter-urban road network. Consequently, economists have had a role in discussions concerning which types of roads would best fulfil economic aspirations ranging from increased industrial development and improved international competitiveness (generally cited by Conservatives) to more equitable regional economic expansion and more efficient inter-regional distribution (generally cited by Labour). In addition, economists have been concerned with the allocative efficiency of choices between roads of a single type, and have developed methods to assess user costs and benefits associated with road investment in order to facilitate choices between road schemes. Using these evaluative methods, economists have played a part in formulating the procedures for the assignment of priority among projects in the road programme. In this latter capacity they have contributed to the micro-management of road building, including the ranking and phasing of projects or parts of projects.

Transport economists had varying degrees of success in the foregoing areas. For example, they were not successful in fully defining the relationship between trunk road provision (particularly in the form of large projects or collections of projects) and economic expansion or redistribution (often referred to as indirect economic benefits). Writing in 1971, A. Peaker noted:

> The direct effects of transport improvements in the economy are observable and may be estimated, but the indirect, dynamic effects we can neither estimate nor describe with any confidence as yet.[17]

Traditionally, the complexion of the strategic road network and the construction of specific large links in that network (such as motorways) have been justified by an appeal to economic objectives, although often it was not especially apparent which combination of economic objectives a specific link was designed to serve. Yet while economists engaged in the overall debate about the merits of road building, they were not able to clarify the economic impact of one type of network over another, and, as Judge and Button remarked, it was difficult to discern any 'explicit process' within government for evaluating the appropriateness of the whole road system or large sections of it either from an economic or a non-economic standpoint.[18] The profession also encountered difficulties in establishing the credibility of its assessments of the indirect economic impact of *single*, large road projects such as motorways. A number of economists (Gwilliam, Peaker, Judge and Dodgson) investigated the possibility that 'traditional cost–benefit analysis might be an inadequate indicator of the true social worth of . . . primary road projects'.[19] In general, these writers concluded that, although on theoretical grounds there might be circumstances in which the indirect benefits of primary roads would be significant, such circumstances are unlikely to be encountered very frequently in practice. This interpretation of the effects of primary roads was tested to a limited degree during the 1970s in Dodgson's work on the M62, Cleary and Thomas's work on the Severn Bridge and associated motorways and Peaker's examination of a road in outer Metropolitan London.[20] These studies tended to reinforce the contention that the indirect effects of primary roads are minimal. Nevertheless, neither the theoretical nor the empirical work that appeared in connection with this multi-faceted problem proved to be definitive. As a result, Ministers and officials dealing with road transport did not feel obliged to question the link between trunk road provision and economic objectives. In the late 1970s the Department of Transport acknowledged that economic studies provided little evidence to support a connection between the building of primary roads and indirect economic benefits, but also cited alternative studies (derived from other than economic perspectives) that, the Department argued, sustained the contention that the location of trunk roads has a substantial influence upon industrial location and therefore regional growth.[21]

In contrast, the profession has been highly successful both in developing normative economic methods for the evaluation of the direct (or user) benefits connected with road building and in instituting these methods as part of the routine assessment of the road programme. Direct benefits include, along with other things, time savings associated with the opening of a new or improved road and reductions in the number of accidents associated with less congested roads or roads built to a better standard. Much of the literature on road assessment has been preoccupied with perfecting what Mills has called the 'conceptual aspects' of direct benefit appraisal (e.g. operational measures for consumer's surplus, time savings and accident loss).[22] However, the evaluation of the direct benefits and costs of any particular road project using these measures is only plausible if the project under consideration can be isolated from the more general highway pattern of which it is a part. This places distinct limits upon the size of the project that it is feasible to evaluate,for projects that are large are presumed to influence traffic flow patterns well beyond their own boundaries. Furthermore, the size of a project that can be feasibly evaluated using cost–benefit methods is constrained as a result of considerations connected with traffic prediction and ease of calculation. Thus, the great majority of road projects that are evaluated using economic methods are sufficiently small that they may be plausibly regarded as fixed trip matrices. This means that the number of trips between any origin and destination within the project network may be regarded as constant before and after the proposed network improvement. In short, it is assumed that the improvement neither generates trips nor redistributes them, but only serves to reassign traffic between routes.

One consequence of the pattern of disciplinary endeavour described above is that the status of economic expertise within the field of road transport has not been especially dependent upon the magnitude of the road programme or upon its relative importance within transport policy as a whole. Many of the methods of economic evaluation that acquired prominence in the Department of Transport's road operations were developed in the mid- and late 1960s when building was at its height. However, the reappraisal of the road programme in the 1970s, which began with Peter Walker's 1971 review of inter-urban road needs, did not greatly diminish the stature of these methods.[23] In reassessing the inter-urban network against a background of economic stringency and increasing public disillusion with massive road projects, both the Conservatives and Labour stressed the value of small-scale road projects designed to relieve specific local pressures, for example intolerable congestion in historic towns.[24] This emphasis led to the progressive abandonment of commitments to comprehensive improvement of entire routes. As a result, small improvement schemes and bypasses assumed a larger and larger place within the road programme as a whole.[25] These were exactly the kind of small-scale projects to which economic expertise is apparently most applicable. Thus, as expenditure upon new road construction by central and local government authorities fell from £1000 million in 1971–2 to £630 million in 1977–8,[26] and as officials were obliged to economize by turning their attention to smaller scale projects, economic appraisal became more and more central to the allocation of road investment.

However, this occurred during a period when the need for roads was being challenged on environmental and other grounds. Quantitative, including economic, forms of road appraisal received extensive public criticism in the late 1970s, although most of this was directed towards the government's methods of traffic forecasting rather than the cost–benefit and other economic formats that had been employed in the evaluation of roads. In the wake of highly vocal protests from road objectors questioning the fundamental assumptions of the road programme and major disruptions at road inquiries, the government became increasingly concerned that its methods of road evaluation should be seen to have validity. It, therefore, launched an independent inquiry into these methods, the results of which were published in the *Report of the Advisory Committee on Trunk Road Assessment*.[27] During the course of its deliberations the Advisory Committee, chaired by Sir George Leitch, dealt with the economic evaluation system called COBA and its consequences for the detailed management of the inter-urban road programme. It is the COBA system of inter-urban road appraisal that will be the focus of the remainder of this chapter. The Leitch Committee's evaluation of the COBA system of economic appraisal, as well as its conclusions and recommendations, will be taken up later. Before this, however, the manner in which the COBA system came into being and the structure it assumed during the 1970s warrant some consideration.

COBA and its predecessors

The COBA system of trunk road evaluation derives from many years of effort, at times sporadic, by government transport engineers, scientists and economists, sometimes working separately, sometimes in concert. The economic evaluation of inter-urban roads is usually said to originate with a paper by Paisley and Charlesworth published in 1959.[28] This introduced the merits of cost–benefit analysis in the assessment of road projects to the engineering profession. In addition, it prompted a number of investigations within the Road Research Laboratory, which were published in the early 1960s as the Road Research Laboratory's Technical Papers 46 and 48. The first of these papers consisted of a prototype post-construction assessment of the M1, and the second developed the method employed in the first into a general appraisal format for inter-urban roads.[29] In 1963 the Ministry of Transport gave formal recognition to the work that had been proceeding in the field of trunk road evaluation by introducing methods of appraisal that closely resembled those advocated by the Road Research Laboratory. These, in turn, were elaborated and standardized to form Technical Memorandum T.5/67, which was later metricated and decimalized and reissued as Technical Memorandum H.1/71.[30]

The first method of economic appraisal that was widely applied after 1963 was called TAL (Travel and Accident Loss). Under this regime timed runs over the road network under consideration and historic accident rates were employed to yield measures of economic losses arising from congestion and accidents compared with free flow conditions in the network. TAL was superseded in 1967 by T.5/67, which introduced the now classic, then novel, classification of the most important quantifiable benefits, or returns, accruing from road projects, that is, time savings, savings in accidents, and savings in the costs of vehicle operations. However, by contrast with later methods, both T.5/67 and its successor H.1/71 were restricted to the evaluation of benefits in the year of opening of a specific road project. These relatively simple manual methods were employed to calculate what was known as a 1st Year Economic Rate of

Return (ERR) in which the benefits estimated for the first year of opening were expressed as a percentage of the capital costs of the project. Under normal conditions, officials expected that the ERR should exceed 15 per cent before a road became eligible for entry into the road programme. This approach to appraisal became standard in the years before the 1972 introduction of COBA, and all but the smallest schemes were assigned an ERR.[31]

The COBA system descends from these early methods, but it is a much more elaborate form of appraisal. It dates from the period when the influx of economists into the Ministry of Transport under Mrs Castle allowed a number of administrative and technical reforms in the evaluation and management of transport. By 1967 economists had become sufficiently numerous in the Ministry and the problems associated with the economic evaluation of highways sufficiently specialized that the Minister and senior administrators approved the creation of the Highways Economics Unit (HEU). At the time, the Treasury was urging the Highways Directorate to develop more sophisticated management tools for the road programme, and, in part, the HEU was established in order to fulfil some of the Treasury's requirements in that direction. Prior to 1967 the economic evaluation of roads had been one of the responsibilities of the Ministry's Economic Directorate. This responsibility was transferred to the HEU in 1967 when it was established as a separate unit. However, liaison between the two bodies remained close, and C.D. Foster, then head of the Directorate, reviewed the progress of work in the HEU, including the work on COBA.[32]

At the time when the HEU was first created, C.D. Foster wanted engineers to advise on some aspects of a Transport Costs Model then in the first stages of development. One of the engineers who joined the HEU in that capacity, R.D. Law, was later to be the inventor of COBA. Early in the history of the HEU a review of the Unit's objectives was undertaken, and as part of that review, officials decided that one of its tasks should be the development of a cost–benefit method that highway engineers could employ in assessing highway schemes. A central part of this project was to be the introduction of up-to-date discounting techniques, and given the amount of arithmetic involved in discounting, officials decided that the economic evaluation of highways projects should be computerized. As one of the few in the HEU with computer experience, Law undertook to write a program for highway evaluation that incorporated thirty-year discounting. He took as his model a simple length of road, and posited 'do-something' and 'do-nothing' scenarios, allowing for reassignment of traffic between the two. With this basic concept, Law then proceeded to add on procedures for cost and benefit assessment based upon such engineering expertise as was extant at the time.

With the aid of a number of young economists and in consultation with senior economists in the HEU, Law produced an initial program in a period of six months. However, several years were to elapse before the program became operational. The delays in implementing COBA stemmed primarily from two considerations. In the first place, the results of test runs using the new program displayed very much lower benefits than would have been the case under T.5/67. Indeed, the T.5/67 benefit range could only be approximated with the introduction into COBA of benefits arising from the reduction of junction delays. However, even with reduction of junction delays, there were frequent cases of road schemes with lower rates of return under COBA than under the previous method. Initially, project engineers had been reluctant to have economists examine their schemes in depth during the COBA test runs, in large part because they were concerned that the new form of analysis might reveal that certain schemes were not as viable as formerly supposed.[33] The results of the test runs confirmed their suspicions, and, therefore, prompted resistance to the new method. In the end, it required much discussion and argument to reinforce the case for the practicability of the COBA method among project engineers.

Delays also arose in connection with the mechanics of launching the system. The initial HEU program had to be refined before becoming operational. This latter task was eventually given to a group of outside computer consultants who made the program modular and introduced 'beyond-capacity' features that allowed the system to handle, along with other things, traffic-saturated junctions. Delays in obtaining authorization and departmental staff changes meant, however, that the program did not become operational until 1971.[34]

In November 1972 a Road Circular containing COBA instructions was issued to all road project designers, partly as the result of the concerted efforts of the man then in charge of the project, an Under-Secretary seconded from the Treasury. In the same year the Department of the Environment published a booklet explaining the COBA system entitled *Getting the Best Roads for our Money: The COBA Method of Appraisal.*[35] In addition, G.A.C. Searle of the Highways Economics and Modelling Analysis Division of the Department of the Environment informed the Department's professional audience of the COBA project through an article published in *Traffic Engineering and Control*.[36]

Implementation of COBA was scheduled for April 1973 for major Road Construction Unit (RCU) schemes. During 1973 road projects costing over £1 million were brought under COBA, and the next year projects costing under £1 million were brought under the system. The original operative version of COBA was designated as COBA 5 M3, but there have been major revisions to the system since 1972. The revision that was initiated by the oil crisis of 1973 and the concomitant oil price rises yielded COBA 6 M1 in the spring of 1975. In this revision the methodology of the original system remained intact, but a number of changes were made in traffic parameters in the light of the new world oil pricing regime.[37]

During 1975–6 Economics, Highways and Freight (EcHF), the division in charge of the COBA program, was given formal responsibility for vetting the economic aspects of all road schemes during the preparation of the 'firm programme report'. This report was a detailed examination of the overall justification of a road scheme, and was employed by the Finance Division in assessing the merits of each project. It was prepared at the same time as the draft statutory Orders defining the line of the proposed road (the line Order) and alterations required to roads adjoining the proposed project (the side road Orders), but prior to the public local inquiries into line and side road Orders. Thus, the officials in charge of the COBA program ensured that COBA analyses were performed satisfactorily by engineers in the field before any scheme was forwarded to the Finance Division. If a scheme had a positive Net Present Value it was recommended to the Finance Division for approval. In the event of a negative Net Present Value, the project was referred to the Treasury for consideration.[38]

The arrangements described in the previous paragraph constituted a departure from normal practice in other Whitehall Departments. COBA, as an economic appraisal method, was developed under the supervision of members of the Government Economic Service. Generally, government economists act as advisers in the formulation and implementation of government policy. Therefore, the formal responsibility for vetting the economic aspects of road schemes that economists within EcHF acquired is an indication both that COBA developed into an integral part of the management of the roads programme and that the transport economists were successful in convincing senior administrators within the Department that cost–benefit analysis can provide a plausible means of appraising individual projects and of assigning priorities between projects. In actuality, COBA evolved from a means to assess the economic worth of a single road scheme into a management system controlled from departmental Headquarters and extending into every Road Construction Unit and Regional Controller's Office (Roads and Transportation) in England. This network served to assemble and analyze massive amounts of data needed for road planning. Engineers in the regions collected data concerning their projects and prepared their economic evaluations in accordance with the instructions contained in the COBA procedure manual.[39] They then ran their respective programs on the computer, and forwarded the results to Headquarters, where EcHF staff vetted the data and assumptions underpinning the regional presentations using their previous experience as a guide to what does and does not constitute an adequate COBA evaluation. If EcHF staff were not satisfied with a specific presentation, they had a responsibility to voice their objections and withhold their recommendation. In general, however, they attempted to maintain a sound basis of cooperation with the regional groups using COBA, and joint work on presentations to the Finance Division was, therefore, favoured whenever possible.[40] Some of the detailed aspects of this management system will be addressed at a later point, but first the various aspects of the COBA methodology deserve elaboration.

The COBA methodology

The COBA methodology of the late 1970s consisted of two main facets: a normative economic framework that served to make a number of costs and benefits associated with road building commensurate, and a series of modelling procedures based upon engineering expertise. In contrast to previous evaluative methodologies, it also incorporated thirty-year discounting, a feature that officials felt was of particular relevance to the highway programme because of variations in benefit growth over time between schemes and the implications of these for the relative phasing of interdependent schemes. COBA also introduced a number of engineering innovations into the assessment of roads, especially with regard to the treatment of junctions.

A COBA evaluation began with the program user positing two types of road networks. One category consisted of the 'do-nothing' situation or the road network prior to any proposed changes. The second consisted of one, or a number of, 'do-something' options, although for the moment discussion will be confined to the consideration of a single road network 'improvement'. In both cases, the road network was typically extended to include all links whose traffic flow was 'likely to be affected by the proposed scheme under evaluation'.[41]

Given that the above networks had been adequately described, the COBA program calculated the difference in user costs between the existing network and the network embodying the proposed improvement. This difference or benefit consisted of time savings to vehicle occupants, savings from the reduction of vehicle operating costs and savings from fewer accidents. Each of these categories of benefit were calculated by simulating 'the movement of a complete year's traffic on each network'.[42] This was done for each year of the road project's assumed lifetime (30 years) on the basis of traffic flow projections. Then annual user benefits were aggregated using a 10% discount rate to yield a total user benefit. Finally, the program calculated the ratio of the Net Present Value of the

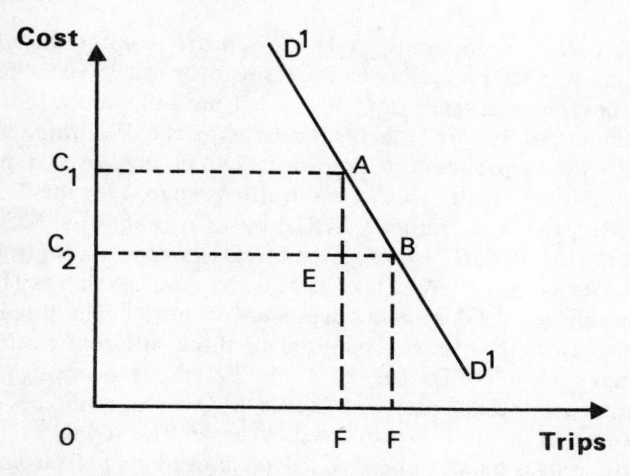

Figure 4.1 Consumer's surplus in COBA. Source: Department of the Environment, *COBA: A Method of Economic Appraisal of Highway Schemes*, Section 3.1.1.

project to construction costs of the proposed improvement as a criterion for project appraisal.

A number of points should be brought out concerning the foregoing series of calculations. First, the designers of COBA argued in the conventional way that the change in the community's welfare upon the introduction of a road improvement scheme can be approximated by aggregating the consumer's surpluses that accrue to individuals as a result of the improvement. On the assumption that the price for a trip is determined by vehicle operating costs and time losses, they constructed a demand curve for travel (see Figure 4.1). Under normal circumstances the area C_1ABC_2 would be taken as the total consumer's surplus accruing to an individual arising from a fall in the price of a trip from C_1 to C_2. However, in order to simplify benefit estimation (and because the shape of the demand curve for a particular scheme is seldom, if ever, known) the COBA program assumed that the demand curve was inelastic or vertical. Users' benefit was, therefore, obtained by multiplying the change in trip costs by the number of vehicle trips. The adoption of this procedure meant that the networks under consideration in any COBA evaluation had to be sufficiently small and sufficiently rural[43] that they could be assumed to approximate a 'fixed trip matrix'. A corollary of this was that COBA proved 'most suitable for use in evaluating road improvement schemes of the inter-urban alignment and junction improvement or capacity increase type, and small town by-pass projects'.[44]

One of the central tenets of the COBA system was that the benefits of a road improvement accrued over a number of years. It, therefore, incorporated 30-year discounting. This, in turn, required that COBA embody a method for predicting traffic levels over the 30-year life of the project. From the emergence of COBA 6 M1 until the publication of the Leitch Committee Report, the Department of the Environment, and subsequently the Department of Transport (DOT), employed a modified version of the forecasts of vehicles and traffic prepared for the Transport and Road Research Laboratory (TRRL) by J.C. Tanner in 1975.[45] This included three sets of forecasts of traffic levels (an upper, a central, and a lower) for four classes of vehicles (cars, heavy goods vehicles (HGVs), light goods vehicles (LGVs), and buses and coaches).[46] The three sets of forecasts for traffic levels corresponded to three different assumptions about annual growth in GDP (3½%, 3% and 2½%, respectively). Owing to uncertainties in these forecasts, COBA 6 M1 employed indices derived from the lowest of the three sets of forecasts for traffic growth.[47]

The traffic census data required to calculate users' benefit from a road improvement in the base year and each year of the project's 30-year life were provided by the COBA user in the field. These were generally collected in the form of 16-hour daily traffic flows measured during the month of August.[48] However, this format was not appropriate for the calculation of annual user costs along the existing and improved networks. Therefore, the COBA program incorporated a set of statistics for converting August 16-hour flows to mean hourly annual flows, and then for breaking the latter down into the hourly flow levels for the four vehicle categories cited previously. A crucial element in these calculations was the Annual Traffic Multiplier (M), commonly referred to as the 'M factor'.

As mentioned earlier, the COBA program had a traffic engineering basis. For example, the calculation of time savings for vehicle occupants required some measure of the speeds attained on existing and projected road networks. In the case of rural roads the COBA program employed a set of relationships between speed and flow prepared by TRRL. These relationships were based upon the physical characteristics of the road in question (carriage width, hilliness, bendiness) rather than on-site observations. In the case of semi-urban roads speed flow relations were taken to be site-specific, and users were expected to take on-site observations.[49] In contrast, the program incorporated fixed population-dependent speeds for journeys through central business districts and non-central business areas of towns. Finally, COBA included a positive speed trend on rural and semi-urban roads (1.5 kilometre per hour per year on rural roads to 1980 and 0 thereafter; and 0.75 kilometre per hour per year on semi-urban roads).

The COBA program also embodied a series of junction delay formulae. A large proportion of COBA benefits arose from the relief of congestion through the reduction of junction delays, and, hence, it was important that the treatment of junctions be as plausible as possible. The program recognized four general types of junctions: priority junctions, roundabouts, signal junctions and gates or swing bridges. For priority junctions users were required to specify the junction layout (such as whether it was a 3- or 4-way junction) and the minimum gap in the traffic stream commensurate with safe turning. In the case of roundabouts they had to supply a number of geometric measurements. For a signal junction users were expected to provide a figure for lost time per cycle of the lights and saturation flows for each approach link. Lastly, delay calculations for gates and swing bridges required users to provide the number and duration of closures in a 24-hour period. In all cases junction delays were calculated using formulae derived from the considerations of equilibrium queuing theory and the geometry of the junction.

In order to deal with saturation traffic levels, the computer consultants who revised the original program in preparation for operationalization added a number of 'beyond-capacity' features to COBA. In particular, flows beyond capacity on road links were assigned a constant speed for cost calculation purposes. Also, a maximum delay was assigned to each junction in a network (generally set at 300 seconds per vehicle). Otherwise, delay costs would have become infinite as the physical capacity of a junction was exceeded.

Two categories of user benefits were calculated from the traffic simulations based upon the forecasts, statistics and engineering relationships described above. The first was the time savings benefit to vehicle occupants. This was obtained by subtracting transit (i.e. travel time) costs on road links and delay costs at junctions on the improved network from those on the existing network. The costs in question were calculated by multiplying travel times on links and delay times at junctions by national averages for the number of occupants per vehicle and standardized values of time for various categories of travellers. The second type of user benefit was posited to be a reduction in vehicle operating costs arising from road improvement, evaluated in the COBA case using a formula for standard vehicle operating costs developed by TRRL.[50]

COBA also calculated a third type of benefit from road improvement – some of which accrues to parties other than the network user. This was the cost savings associated with the fact that improved networks generally have lower accident rates than unimproved ones. Accident rates on existing roads were calculated using data available from the police averaged over three years.[51] For improved roads the Department of Transport used results derived from studies of representative types of road provision. Accident savings were calculated through multiplying both rates by standard costs per accident and subtracting the costs of accidents on the improved network from those on the existing network.

In summary, then, the COBA program consisted of a number of discrete procedures, each of which yielded an end-number. The end-numbers from the various sections of the program were aggregated to yield total annual costs on the existing and improved road networks. These were then discounted, and aggregated, giving total costs on each part of the road network for the 30-year life of the project. The difference between total costs on the existing network and total costs on the improved network was the total benefit from the improvement scheme, or its Net Present Value (NPV). This, in turn, was divided by the discounted cost (NPV/C) to yield the criterion for project appraisal. The COBA user had to supply at least two network descriptions in the form of road link and junction data (e.g. alignment data, junction geometry, accident records for existing links, construction costs and any future traffic reassignment) plus figures for 16-hour August daily flow and the proportions of different types of vehicles on each part of the two networks. Nevertheless, the technical relationships characteristic of COBA were in large measure fixed. Thus, rural speed/flow relationships, junction delay formulae, the vehicle operating cost function and the equations for calculating annual flow from 16-hour August flow and the percentage of HGVs in traffic flow were built into the program. In addition, many of the parameters employed in calculating the NPV/C ratio were fixed at national averages (e.g. values of time, accident rates on certain types of improved roads, accident costs, rates of traffic growth, speed flow trends).

The end-product of a COBA analysis was an NPV/C ratio. If this ratio proved negative, departmental staff had to inform the Treasury and Treasury approval was required before such a scheme could proceed. Alternatively, if the value of the ratio was found to be zero or greater, there was no immediate requirement to consult the Treasury. As explained by one senior civil servant, even an NPV/C ratio of zero could be regarded as highly attractive by comparison with private sector returns. Given COBA's 10% discount rate and, hypothetically, a 10% inflation rate, an NPV/C ratio of zero corresponds to a healthy financial rate of return.[52] Schemes were assigned priorities, in part, according to the magnitude of their ratios, but the treatment a scheme received was also a function of its political status and its likely environmental impact, to name two of the more important other considerations influencing road ranking. Thus, for example, a scheme with a negative NPV/C ratio could still have proceeded if the Treasury judged that environmental considerations justified construction, and the Department concurred.[53]

In addition to its use as a means of distinguishing between the economic merits of different trunk road schemes, the NPV/C ratio has also been employed in evaluating alternative 'do-something' scenarios for a single

No	Description	Diagram	Cost	NPV	Cost	NPV/C	Err%
1	Single carriageway throughout at grade junction at old A47. Roundabout at A1065		1,510,134	-91,126	649,132	-0.1405	5.9
2	Dual carriageway from grade junction at old A47. Grade separation at A1065	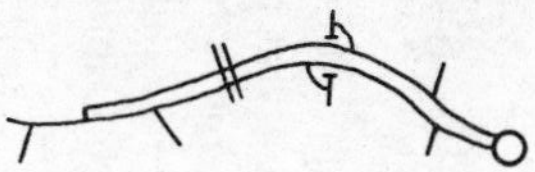	2,101,823	-30,121	903,470	-0.0333	6.3
3	Dual carriageway with grade separation at old A47. Grade separation at A1065	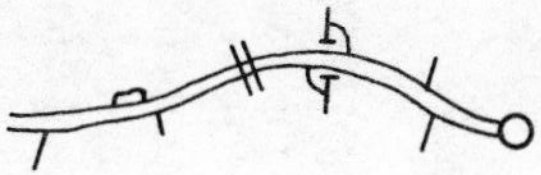	2,113,860	260,756	908,638	0.2870	8.3
4	Dual carriageway with grade separation at A1065	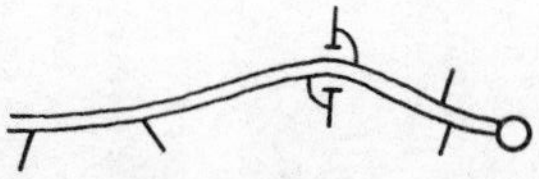	2,339,019	125,411	1,031,219	0.12616	7.1

Figure 4.2 Designs for the Swaffham Bypass. Source: Department of Transport, *Report of the Advisory Committee on Trunk Road Assessment* (London, HMSO, 1978), Table 15.1, pp. 70–1.

scheme. COBA users were urged to investigate the economic merits of a variety of alternatives in the design of road network improvements. *The Leitch Committee Report* cites one instance (the Swaffham Bypass) in which a COBA evaluation was undertaken for each of twenty different variations upon one road alignment.[54] This type of detail in the evaluation of prospective road provision for one route (in this case, a small town bypass) was exceptional. However, an examination of four of the options that were considered in this instance will illustrate how COBA has been employed as a design tool.

Figure 4.2 shows four of the alternative designs that were considered in the evaluation of the Swaffham Bypass, together with their corresponding construction costs, NPV/C ratios and First Year Rate of Return (ERR) figures. The third design in this series was the preferred one. In appraising different designs the Department employed what is called incremental analysis. This procedure involves ranking the design alternatives in order of increasing discounted construction cost (as in Figure 4.2). Then, beginning with the next to least costly scheme, each scheme is compared with its predecessor in the rank in order to determine whether the incremental NPV/C is greater than some 'cut-off' point chosen in accord with general levels of capital scarcity.

To illustrate:

$$\frac{\Delta \mathrm{NPV}}{\Delta \mathrm{C}} \text{ (Scheme 2 − Scheme 1)} = \frac{\mathrm{NPV}(2) - \mathrm{NPV}(1)}{\mathrm{C}(2) - \mathrm{C}(1)} = 0.240$$

In this case the incremental NPV/C is greater than the departmental 'cut-off' point in force when this calculation was made. Thus, Scheme 2 was preferred to Scheme 1. The best scheme was the one 'with the highest capital costs having an acceptable incremental NPV/C ratio'.[55] However, from COBA's inception until the Leitch Committee investigation the 'cut-off' point for incremental analysis was zero, which is equivalent to stating that the scheme with the highest NPV value is preferred. In view of this, the Leitch Committee recommended that the complexities of incremental analysis be eliminated from the program.[56]

The type of analysis outlined was employed in other circumstances. COBA Advice Note No. 1, for example, is concerned with the evaluation of proposals for staged dualling on new and existing road alignments.[57] More generally, COBA could be used to evaluate the merits of phasing a variety of aspects of road construction, especially if major changes in traffic flow patterns were anticipated at some future date. In addition, incremental analysis has been employed in attempts to structure arguments about choices between road options in, for example, cases in which an expensive route option with environmental benefits is juxtaposed against a relatively cheaper route option without environmental benefits.

In these latter instances, COBA users were advised to calculate the minimum value that had to be placed upon environmental effects in order to justify choosing the less economically advantageous route over the more economically advantageous route. Once this value had been determined, correct COBA practice required that the evaluation of environmental benefit should be treated as a 'separate issue'.[58] One means of assessing environmental benefit was to consider the number of properties affected by a proposed road improvement. If, for example, the NPV for a Scheme Y *without* environmental benefits exceeds that for a Scheme Z *with* environmental benefits by £30,000 *per annum*, but only five properties are affected, this approach implies that the price of environmental benefit is £6000 *per annum* per house. COBA Advice Note No. 15 suggests that such a price might be considered too high, in which case the scheme without environmental benefits would be favoured over that with such benefits. Thus,

> Incremental analysis consists of comparing *DIFFERENCES* in economic and environmental performance between scheme options and should be applied once the options have been narrowed down to a limited number of simple alternatives. It will not actually provide a solution to the problem of trading off economic and environmental factors. It will however, enable the important issues to be identified and the relative significance of factors to be weighed in the scheme appraisal.[59]

The COBA management system

From its beginnings COBA was more than a methodology for evaluating inter-urban roads. It was also the centrepiece in a nationwide road management system.

The central purpose of the COBA system of evaluation as articulated by those responsible for the methodology's development and implementation was the regularization of the economic assessment of trunk roads. The trunk road programme of the late 1970s consisted of a large and diverse collection of projects at various stages of completion within a ten- to twelve-year 'life span'. Local and regional variations in topography, traffic flow patterns and economic and environmental conditions required decentralized project drafting and review, and each of the approximately 400 trunk schemes then under active consideration was, therefore, primarily the responsibility of a regional office of the Department (whether it be a Road Construction Unit or the office of a Regional Controller). But delegation of authority to the regions did not guarantee consistency or uniform standards of evaluation, and EcHF staff argued with effect that the COBA methodology provided an economical means for Headquarters staff to supervise the activities of the regional offices in the interest of maintaining consistent levels of road provision throughout the country and, concomitantly, of preventing overly ambitious, excessive or in other ways faulty projects in particular areas.

Other management-related advantages have also been attributed to COBA. For example, owing to the detailed procedures that had to be followed in drafting and evaluating road schemes, many of the choices with a significant impact upon ultimate levels of provision were taken by relatively junior personnel. COBA served to encourage the application of standard procedures amongst these junior staff, and it allowed Headquarters staff to check their assumptions, data, and methods in a rapid and relatively comprehensive manner. In addition, in comparison with previous manual methods of economic evaluation, COBA led to a reduction in the number of calculation errors associated with scheme assessment.[60]

Thus, the regularization of the economic assessment of trunk road schemes through COBA enhanced the knowledge at Headquarters of regional activities and, hence, its capacity to intervene in a selective manner in order to avoid abuses. However, the regularization of economic assessment under COBA also contributed to other ends within the Department. As noted earlier, the originators of COBA were responding to Treasury pressures for the development of more sophisticated tools for the control of the road programme. Moreover, Treasury interest in COBA as a device for economic management and control persisted, witness the procedures for the treatment of schemes with negative net present values. Therefore, COBA constituted one means for Department of Transport officials to persuade the Treasury that the Department was continuously engaged in monitoring road expenditure down to the single project level. Yet, significantly, discretion in the development and application of COBA remained with EcHF staff at departmental Headquarters, for Treasury officials vetting road evaluations were junior and tended to rely heavily upon EcHF staff for interpretation of the COBA methodology and user printouts.[61]

The COBA management system centred upon the EcHF Division within departmental Headquarters. The staff at Headquarters, including economists, engineers and scientists, performed essentially two functions. First, they were responsible for the development and updating of the methodology. The Division retained personnel working on the value of time, vehicle operating costs, construction costs, taxation and a variety of other areas that are central to the COBA methodology. In addition, under a set of administrative arrangements that came into effect in 1976 EcHF staff acquired responsibility for reviewing COBA evaluations before schemes were entered into the Firm Programme. Before this change the Division had only seen a certain percentage of scheme evaluations (generally those that were voluntarily forwarded to

Headquarters by personnel in the field seeking advice). However, in the wake of the new arrangements, all users had to forward their evaluations to Headquarters for review. EcHF staff examined each scheme evaluation to ensure, for example, that link transit and junction delay benefits were plausible, that users had avoided double-counting and that modelled or synthetic traffic data was at a minimum. If they were dissatisfied with the way in which a scheme had been modelled or with some aspect of the subsequent evaluation, EcHF staff first presented their objections to the users in question. In the event that agreement could not be achieved between Headquarters and the users, both had the option to appeal to the Finance Division. Finally, in cases in which the net present value of a scheme was negative, EcHF personnel acted as expert advisers to the Finance Division and the Treasury concerning the economic validity of the scheme at issue.

There were, of course, limits to the scrutiny that EcHF could exercise. In general, the Headquarters staff were not encouraged to investigate every detail in the presentation of a scheme, for this would have constituted replication of the tasks of those in the field. In addition, the Division did not suggest alternative options for consideration beyond those that had been presented by the region. It was not considered to be the Division's place to override the mixed road-building expertise located in the field.[62]

In the regions COBA evaluations were the responsibility of two types of regional offices: the Road Construction Units and the Regional Controllers (Roads and Transportation), and trunk road schemes were allocated between these two types of offices according to total construction cost. Schemes costing over £3 million were automatically assigned to the Road Construction Units. Schemes costing less than £1.5 million were automatically processed by the offices of the Regional Controllers, but schemes costing between £1.5 million and £3 million were subject to negotiation between both types of regional offices and Headquarters.[63] However, not all of these projects were evaluated using COBA. Small schemes (those valued at between £50,000 and £500,000) were evaluated by another, simpler method (known as TR 502) that was based upon a series of matrices summarizing a number of types of economic and environmental choices relating to evaluation.[64] In addition, large schemes were not considered amenable to COBA evaluation for reasons cited previously. Finally, many schemes that were judged eligible on technical grounds for COBA evaluation were not initiated into the system because of difficulties associated with time, manpower and resource scheduling. When COBA was first introduced there were many more schemes eligible for COBA treatment than the system could accommodate, and even in 1976, three years after COBA became operational, only about 180 of approximately 360 eligible schemes were 'rated'.[65] Moreover, the rated schemes had been subjected to widely divergent degrees of analysis. Some had been evaluated using the full COBA program. Others had not been taken further than the 1st Year ERR format. Nevertheless, despite the above exceptions and difficulties, some 85 per cent of the schemes in the trunk road programme (accounting for about 70 per cent of expenditure) were *potentially* eligible for COBA analysis.[66]

Within the regions work connected with COBA was allocated as follows. In the case of the Regional Controllers (R&T), the offices were sub-divided into units responsible for the review of road developments within administrative areas congruent with the areas served by the various county and metropolitan councils within the region. The counties were the agent authorities (AAs) for the RC (R&T) on trunk roads, and they took charge of planning road developments, including the performance of COBA evaluations. Staff within the RC (R&T) were responsible for directing the work of the agent authorities and coordination between the AAs and Headquarters. In an analogous manner Road Construction Units allocated work connected with road planning, including economic evaluation, to their sub-units or consultants. However, there was a major distinction between RC (R&T)s and RCUs in that the latter were not involved in local transport matters. RC (R&T)s consulted closely with Local Authorities concerning Transport Policies and Programmes (TPPs) in the main through discussions with county surveyors and county planning officers in order that trunk roads best served local as well as regional or national needs and were well integrated into the local environment.[67]

In general, in both the RCUs and RC (R&T)s, COBA evaluations were undertaken by engineering staff, although the specific training these engineers possessed varied from regional office to regional office. After COBA was fully operational most new engineering personnel acquired their familiarity with the methodology through perusal of the COBA manual, discussions with colleagues and the experience of performing a series of evaluations. Originally, however, the methodology was conveyed to regional personnel through training sessions in which Headquarters staff presented the general features of COBA and then guided regional staff through a programming session designed to acquaint the latter with the types of modelling and analytical problems frequently encountered in operating COBA.[68] Those Headquarters personnel who were involved in training found that the engineers in the field first appeared to have little difficulty in assimilating the central tenets of COBA and in performing the quantitative tasks required to operate the COBA program. However, subsequent evaluations from the field often departed quite markedly from the 'correct' practice outlined in the training sessions. Engineers in the RCUs and RC (R&T)s were not loath to assert their form of expertise against that of the economists and other professionals at Headquarters. Indeed, in the years following COBA's introduction much of the effort of Headquarters staff was devoted to dissuading engineers in the field from tampering with the COBA methodology or using it in ways in which it was not intended to be used. The distance between the approaches of the two groups narrowed considerably over time, but the potential for conflict was always there.

What, then, was the balance of influence inherent in the COBA management system? Perhaps the most important point to note in responding to this question is that COBA represented an assault, if a limited one, upon the traditionally strong position of the highway engineers within the field of public sector transport. This is evident in the resistance highway engineers mounted against COBA when it was first developed,[69] in the conflicts between Headquarters staff and engineers in the field that have been an integral part of COBA's history, and even in certain tensions between EcHF economists and EcHF engineers supervising the operation of the COBA system (the economists, while recognizing that the engineers were indispensable to effective COBA monitoring, sometimes suspected that the latter identified too closely with the concerns of the engineers in the field or did not fully understand the economic aspects of COBA). Helped by a number of engineers who, at least to some extent, accepted the dictates of economic rationality, buttressed by support from the Treasury, and, finally, mindful of the requirement that senior administrators in the transport field be able to justify expenditure to Ministers and Treasury officials, Headquarters economists succeeded in making highway engineers accountable in an economic sense for the way in which they designed certain types of inter-urban roads.

Several interrelated sets of circumstances aided transport economists in this. By the early 1970s the highway engineers, while apparently in a very strong position within the then Department of the Environment, were actually becoming more and more vulnerable to challenges from other groups within the Civil Service. During the 1960s the discretion and prestige of the highway engineers was enhanced by ever more massive annual allocations of public moneys to road building, but after 1970 the road programme increasingly fell victim to doubts spawned by its previous success. The Heath Government adopted the approach to road building contained in Labour's *Roads for the Future* (eventually committing Britain to a 4500 mile strategic network of motorways and trunk roads to be ready by the 1990s), but, in view of the large sums involved, it also placed considerable emphasis upon making the 'best use' of the essentially stable road allocations of the 1970–4 period (e.g. through building roads to the principal ports, relieving congestion in towns).[70] This policy enhanced the position of the economist as the economizer of the nation's resources, while casting some doubt upon the ability of the highway engineers to manage the road programme without assistance from other professionals.

Then, the Arab oil boycott of late 1973 and the subsequent OPEC price rises served to highlight the necessity for caution in the field of road transport. Ministers, senior officials and the public at large began to ask whether extensive road building in the present could be justified in an energy-poor future. Concerns of this kind, together with the downturn in general economic indicators in the years following the oil crisis, prompted Labour to announce a significant slowdown in road building in 1974–5. Moreover, this was only the first product of a general re-evaluation of roads leading to the 'cuts' in the road programme announced in the December 1976 mini-budget and the restrictive approach to roads taken in the 1977 White Paper on transport policy and the 1978 White Paper on roads policy.[71]

Of course, the highway engineers and the myriad road lobbies that supported them found it difficult to adjust to the new policy regime, but their protests did not prevent Ministers and officials from increasingly de-emphasizing roads during the development of transport policy. Their objections served, however, to confirm a widespread public belief that highway engineers are technocratic 'empire builders' (a term, incidentally, that engineers have often applied to economists). Moreover, the less than salutary reputation the highway engineers acquired outside government served to strengthen the economists' hand. In the first place, it confirmed the need for evaluative systems like COBA. It also served to deflect criticism away from the 'technocratic' aspects of economic evaluation. In most instances, road objectors have focused their protests upon the contribution of highway engineers and certain scientists to road building. This has meant that transport economists have been relatively immune from public criticism.[72]

Thus, the decline in the stature of the highway engineers within DOT and its predecessors provided the context for an expansion in the role of the transport economists within the road programme. Moreover, by the late 1970s their influence had been consolidated as a result of the fact that DOT economists recognized the *limits*, as well as the opportunities that evaluative systems like COBA embodied. Economic rationality may serve to organize and reconcile various facets of highway engineering expertise and to determine both the absolute and relative merits of particular road projects, but the foregoing functions would be redundant if the road programme were to be seriously disrupted or even discontinued. Accordingly, COBA was seldom instrumental either in delaying a road scheme or in preventing one from being built.[73] Rather than attempting to convince engineers and administrators to drop weak schemes from the road programme, COBA operators generally concentrated upon *improving* the road proposals, good or bad, forwarded from the field.

Lower work volumes stemming from contractions in the regional centres were also not deemed advantageous. While Headquarters economists often stated that COBA evaluations would have been better performed if the work involved were to have been centralized, no major steps were taken in this direction. Instead, EcHF staff encouraged engineers in the field, especially the younger ones, to explore as many aspects of the COBA methodology (and, particularly, incremental analysis) as was feasible given the constraints of time and resources available. In doing so, EcHF staff ensured that the position of the engineer in the field was not seriously jeopardized, while still maintaining a patron–client relationship between Headquarters personnel and staff in the regions. Like the public participation procedures introduced by Geoffrey Rippon in 1973,[74] COBA was instrumental in ensuring that the workloads in the field did not fall as the road programme slowed down or contracted,[75] and there were few highway engineers, especially among the younger men, who did not recognize this. At times engineers in the field attempted to circumvent the dominance of Headquarters staff in this regard by 'supplementing' or 'improving upon' COBA,[76] but organizational arrangements within the Department of Transport did not encourage this type of initiative.

A COBA assessment

Space prohibits a full evaluation of the COBA program and the management system associated with it, but it is possible to analyse some of their leading features. Perhaps the best way to proceed in this connection is to examine a series of interrelated problems that have arisen during the operation of the COBA program and the COBA management system and then to review what these problems indicate about the nature of the COBA system as a whole.

The boundary problem

COBA users in the field and EcHF staff continuously confronted a variety of difficulties relating to what one might call the 'limits' or 'boundaries' of the COBA system. As noted earlier in this chapter, the COBA program is strictly only applicable to schemes that are small enough and rural enough that they can plausibly be said to approximate a fixed trip matrix. In accord with this, the standard COBA program (1973) could handle a maximum of 100 links and nodes, and users were advised that it was not applicable to major long-range new routes and improvements concentrated in urban areas.

However, as their familiarity with COBA increased, staff in the regions began to press for greater program capacity (so that they could evaluate larger networks) and more leniency in deciding what was and what was not urban. In the wake of this, experimental versions of COBA were developed. These were capable of handling up to 1000 links and nodes.[77] EcHF staff were not especially enthusiastic about developments of this kind, fearing as they did that a marked expansion in the capacity of the COBA program or an increased tendency among users to apply COBA to relatively urban situations might bring into question the validity of the economic assumptions upon which the program was founded, and, therefore, jeopardize its credibility. However, their resistance to these threats to the integrity of COBA was relatively low because when no information is available about how demand for trips varies with trip cost in the area of a projected scheme (as was almost always the case), the modelling techniques and economic principles underpinning COBA provided no indication as to how large or how urban the scheme could be before it was 'too large' or 'too urban' to be evaluated using COBA. Thus, while EcHF staff asserted the COBA is probably inapplicable when about 10 per cent or more of traffic changes destination or a town in the immediate vicinity of a scheme has a population of 100,000 or more, in practice the 10 per cent figure was deemed very arbitrary and on occasion COBA was used to evaluate schemes bordering on cities of 250,000.[78]

Another set of difficulties relating to boundaries centred upon what to include and what not to include in a COBA network. In COBA Advice Note No. 4 EcHF staff recommended that if a user had a large network to evaluate (i.e. over 100 links and nodes) he should consider dividing it into two or more units for analysis.[79] However, it was by no means clear what criteria were to be adopted in doing this, even in instances in which a large scheme broke down naturally into two or more units. Consider the case of two consecutive town bypasses (see Figure 4.3). The bypasses can be analysed separately or together. If they are analysed separately one bypass may turn out to be economically viable while the other is not. In these circumstances, when the bypasses are analysed together, the result may be positive or negative, depending upon the relative economic merits of the separate schemes. Note also that if both bypasses are to be built, there may be a need to improve the stretch of road connecting them, in which case the alternative of building a longer stretch of road to bypass both towns at once should perhaps be considered. The important point is that COBA provided no guidance about how schemes should be aggregated or disaggregated and what should or should not be included in an evaluation.[80]

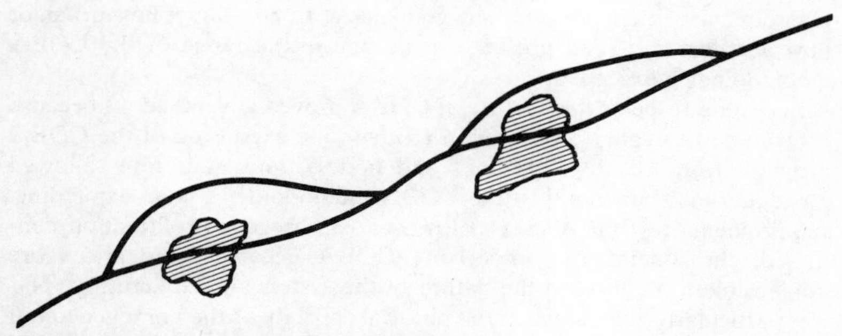

Figure 4.3 Two consecutive town bypasses

A further set of boundary-related difficulties was associated with the 'beyond-capacity' features of the COBA program. As noted earlier, the computer consultants who made COBA modular were concerned that delays should not go to infinity as traffic flows exceeded the capacity of links or junctions. They, therefore, introduced 'MAX DELAY' devices into the COBA program. These simply cut off the delay–flow curves for links and junctions as they rose to infinity, thereby, fixing a maximum delay figure for each part of the network.[81] However, these devices created almost as many problems as they solved. To begin with, as A.J. Harrison has put it, when attempting to fix the cut-offs 'it is difficult to argue for one level rather than another'.[82] In addition, as soon as the maximum delay level was activated in the running of the COBA program, huge delay costs were generated. This was a particularly acute problem in the case of junctions. Given that COBA did not incorporate any type of relaxation modelling, a very few closely spaced junctions could lead to double-counting and, therefore, enormous delay costs. There were schemes submitted to EcHF in which 96 per cent of benefits stemmed from delay savings associated with two or three junctions. Moreover, users rapidly came to recognize the advantages of activating the MAX DELAY devices for junctions, and many engaged in a practice called 'junction hunting' until it was discredited by too many questionable results.[83]

The three categories of boundary-related difficulties described above were associated with the arithmetic format in which the COBA program was cast, the format that united the economic and engineering expertise embodied in COBA. Arithmetic modes of analysis – focused as they are upon discretely distinct, relatively quality-less entities – do not recognize qualitative variations in the systems to which they are applied. Thus, COBA did not embody any criteria for distinguishing the categories 'one', 'some' and 'many', or 'not urban', 'more urban' and 'very urban' and, as well, none for differentiating one phase of a road project from another.

Consequently, it did not offer any guidance as to how large, how urban or how aggregated a road project can be before the range of the COBA methodology is exceeded.

In certain respects this feature of COBA proved advantageous because it facilitated category proliferation (witness the expansion of the COBA program from 100 to 1000 links and nodes), and, therefore, allowed Headquarters staff to adjust the COBA methodology to the 'expanding' requirements of COBA users. However, as category proliferation continued, the assumptions underlying COBA became more and more implausible in relation to the nature of the systems under scrutiny. This was particularly evident when the physical capacity or the homogeneity of a road network was at issue. COBA would have been rapidly discredited if Headquarters staff had allowed delay times on a network to go to infinity as traffic flows increased or if they had condoned 'junction hunting'. Yet the system did not incorporate any indications as to the level at which the MAX DELAY cut-off should be made or any guidance for positing 'how many junctions, how closely spaced' represent 'too many junctions, too closely spaced'.

There was a final, and very important, boundary-related effect associated with the arithmetic character of COBA. COBA managers and users made very few attempts to integrate their method of evaluating roads with those employed by land use planners and other professionals with an interest in how man shapes his environment.[84] This was not surprising given that COBA did not recognize the 'surroundings' in which road construction proceeds. It assumed that road networks constitute self-contained homogeneous 'technologies', which, if they do not merge with their surroundings, are relatively inconspicuous within them. Moreover, fortunately for those who developed and employed the COBA program, this view of road networks has a fairly high degree of plausibility, not because roads are, indeed, self-contained, homogeneous and inconspicuous technologies, but because, until relatively recently, road construction, especially of the inter-urban type, was perceived to have only a limited and fairly sporadic impact upon small numbers of people (mainly those directly affected through property expropriation). Even when, in the late 1970s, road construction became a highly controversial issue, few road objectors had the time or the resources required to scrutinize the full implications of the COBA methodology for the assessment of a particular road project, much less the evolution of the road programme. The result was that the way in which COBA portrayed road networks remained largely unchallenged in the 1970s.[85]

The numbers problem

Much of the content of the COBA format was fixed, either as set relationships between variables or as national averages for various parameters, and, therefore, the credibility of the results from the COBA program depended crucially upon the validity of the fixed relationships and averages built into it. The fact of the matter was, however, that a great deal of the fixed material in the COBA program was theoretically and empirically inadequate. What is more, in private, those who developed and managed the COBA system acknowledged this to be so.[86]

Many of the theoretical and empirical inadequacies of the fixed material in the COBA program stemmed from the way in which the program was first designed. While the logic that integrated the various facets of the COBA methodology was economic, the 'heart' of the COBA program consisted of a series of traffic engineering relationships that, taken together, were used to model the way in which several classes of vehicles traverse different types of road networks. The original designers of COBA attempted to provide it with a sound foundation in traffic engineering by assembling the best bits and pieces of engineering theory and engineering data then available relevant to the problem of modelling traffic flows on do-nothing and do-something road networks. However, the quality of the best engineering material at hand for each modelling task varied enormously. Also, the original COBA designers, anxious as they were to complete the outline of the entire evaluative system, devoted relatively little attention to how the various bits and pieces of theory and data incorporated into COBA would fit together.

As a result, the final product was highly uneven. Some aspects of the completed COBA program were genuinely relatively sophisticated for their time (e.g. the junction delay formulae). Others rested on theoretical and empirical quicksand. This is particularly true of the traffic statistics employed in the program. In one case a statistical conversion table was incomplete. In several others, those familiar with COBA suspected that supposedly consistent statistics were derived from different and inconsistent data bases, although often they had no means of confirming their suspicions because the source data could not be traced. In still another case (specifically, the statistics used to calculate hourly flow groupings for four vehicle categories from mean annual hourly flow) the origin of the figures that appeared in *The COBA Manual* was unknown. However, it was the M factor that constituted the most blatant symbol of COBA's theoretical and empirical difficulties.

The M factor, the ratio between annual traffic flow and August 16-hour flow, was the most important statistic in COBA in that all benefit calculations depended upon its validity, but there was little in the history of its derivation to inspire confidence. *The COBA Manual* set M equal to

233 – 5.2 H where H was the percentage of heavy goods vehicles in the August 16-hour flow. This relationship was based upon data from an all-country exercise conducted in 1966, and was the result of a regression analysis performed on an M-H distribution for that year, but few who were familiar with COBA placed much faith in the relationship obtained from the 1966 exercise. To begin with, it stemmed from what one engineer described as a 'Dalmatian' M-H distribution. Furthermore, the M-H equation has an intercept of 233, indicating that the M factor cannot be less than that figure, but it was known empirically that many roads have an M factor as low as 100. Also, the base date for the relationship was ambiguous. COBA managers knew that the M factor equation (derived as above) varied over time, and, therefore, all HGV data that users collected had to be backdated to 1966 in order that the M factor for each stretch of road could be calculated. However, the HGV data upon which the 1966 expression was based were actaully from 1968. Finally, after the 1966 M factor had been in use for some time, COBA managers discovered that the expression was only supposedly valid between 5 and 25% H. This was significant given that certain users had been attempting to improve their COBA results by raising their % H figures to as high as 30% (the M factor equation was fairly easy to manipulate; users could raise % H by the elimination of LGVs and buses as vehicle categories, as well as other strategies). However, cut-off devices for % H were not a feature of the COBA program.[87]

Given the many number-related weaknesses inherent to COBA and the fact that most COBA managers recognized these weaknesses, the obvious question to pose is: were there sustained efforts to remedy the inadequacies of COBA? The answer is yes and no. Statisticians, engineers and outside consultants made attempts to improve the traffic-engineering, and particularly the traffic-statistics, basis of COBA, but often their efforts ran aground as a result of the fact that the results they obtained were seen to threaten the integrity of the COBA system.[88] The important point in this connection is that the traffic-engineering components of COBA, and especially the 'numbers' that they yielded, were the focus of sometimes covert, sometimes overt conflict between engineers in the field, often supported by engineers at EcHF, and the government economists in charge of COBA. Quite naturally, COBA users, most of whom were engineers, were convinced that they were best equipped to assign values to engineering varables. Up to a point, the COBA system recognized and exploited the engineering expertise of users in the field, permitting as it did regional and local discretion in the design of road networks, the generation of traffic data and the traffic assignment. At the same time it denied users the authority to manipulate a wide variety of other engineering variables, many of which were central to a COBA evaluation, and economists at Headquarters were very reluctant to cede discretion over these variables to personnel in the field. A corollary of this was that they were reluctant to accept suggestions for modifying the traffic-engineering components of COBA even from Headquarters engineers and statisticians unless it could be clearly demonstrated that the proposed modifications would not substantially alter their control over COBA variables or change long-run results.

The two sides of the conflict between engineers and economists are perhaps best illustrated by considering the case of the M factor. Like all the fixed relationships and parameters in COBA, the M factor was national in scope. As such, it subsumed all regional and local variations in the relationship between annual and August 16-hour flows, and could, therefore, be as much as 40 per cent out for any particular scheme evaluation. Engineers both in the field and at Headquarters argued that the determination of M factors for roads should be localized, especially since efforts to produce national statistics in this area proved unconvincing.[89] Headquarters economists responded by arguing that the engineers' suggestions concerning the M factor were too particularistic and that locally derived statistics would undermine the consistency of the COBA methodology, thereby threatening the ability of Headquarters to make 'correct' resource allocation decisions. They also noted that the national M factor, despite its weaknesses, was given engineering approval when COBA was first developed, and appealed to the desirability, if not the necessity, for continuity in the operation of the COBA system.[90] Moreover, the economists for the most part won the day with arguments of this type. In the end, engineers in the field conceded that it was the last page of the printout containing the results that was the really important part of the COBA evaluation for them, and, if the values derived from the national M factor expression were high enough that most of their schemes were approved, they were generally content to use it, despite its many weaknesses.[91] The result was a failure to undertaken a serious review of the M factor as an engineering variable. Even when, just before the Leitch Committee was established, EcHF decided to re-examine the M factor, the research it commissioned was devoted to generating M factors for every month of the year despite the fact that Headquarters personnel knew that M factor variation is much greater between sites than it is between months.[92] Rather than debate the structure of this variable, COBA managers and users focused upon the numbers that the M factor expression generated and their contribution to the average level of benefit across a variety of schemes.

Multiplied across many engineering variables and many schemes, the type of influence that Headquarters economists wielded in the case of the M factor has also had another major effect upon the way roads are evaluated. Like many cost–benefit methodologies, COBA was designed to assist choice, in this case the choice between options for a single road project and the ranking of different schemes, but the interpretation that the concept of choice received in COBA was limited. As noted earlier, COBA was used to distinguish the merits of various types of road provision and junction layout on one road alignment. It was also employed to distinguish the merits of different alignments. Economists treat each kind of road proposal as a discretely distinct, homogeneous option, but this was seldom the way in which proposals were seen in the field. Engineers frequently favoured one road proposal over another for reasons that, while apparently sensible, find no expression in COBA. For example, one scheme could have had a higher NPV than another because nearby urban areas meant that traffic flows on the first were greater than those on the second. At the same time, traffic on the first was more likely to disrupt and be disrupted by the urban environment than traffic on the second, with the result that, from an engineering standpoint, the second was the preferable scheme. In another case, an engineer might have been tempted to favour one scheme over another because, regardless of their respective NPV levels, the first had less effect upon land prices in the immediate vicinity than the second. This consideration was important for small town bypasses in that the alignment chosen often had a substantial effect upon town boundary planning and, therefore, land prices. Moreover, increasing land prices in specific areas could threaten the 'economic' viability of small junction upgrading schemes and the like in that their costs were highly dependent upon the availability and price of land near the proposed improvement.[93]

Engineers in the field were seldom able to persuade EcHF staff that considerations of this kind should be a major concern in the evaluation of a scheme, and, therefore, it may be said that even with respect to the concerns of its immediate users the COBA system moulded or formalized choice. Certain options were not considered. Certain scenarios remained unexplored. Those options and scenarios that were reviewed were seen as simple, homogeneous and separable. The early, problem-oriented COBA instruction sessions, the highly explanatory nature of the COBA manual and program and contacts between EcHF staff and users were all employed to convey the economists' view of choice and road evaluation generally to engineers in the field.

However, contradictions emerged in this process. Each COBA evaluation was a relatively complex task for the user and one that could not be fulfilled well (even from the economist's standpoint) through following instructions by rote. The modelling aspects of the evaluation required that the user be aware of the limits of the COBA format (i.e. the fact that it could not accommodate closely spaced junctions).

Furthermore, 'good economic practice' required the user to be judicious in his assessment of the appropriateness of input data and the results that a COBA run yielded. (One EcHF staff member remarked that it was sometimes difficult to impress upon users that an NPV/C ratio of 6 or 7 constitutes a capitalist's 'dream' and is, therefore, an inappropriate COBA result.)[94] In these circumstances, EcHF could not exercise 'total' control over each COBA evaluation, and, therefore, as mentioned earlier, COBA operations were punctuated by attempts by users to exercise engineering judgement in the evaluation of roads. In nearly all cases, however, these attempts were frustrated when Headquarters staff reviewed the schemes in question.

Finally, it should be noted that Headquarters economists were subject to none of the restrictions that applied to COBA users. The economists in EcHF worked as a team of equals to ensure that the COBA treatment of 'economic' issues like construction costs (including differential inflation), taxation, growth assumptions inherent to traffic forecasts, values of time, vehicle operating cost and incremental analysis was as 'plausible' and up-to-date as possible. Moreover, they displayed little reluctance to incorporate their findings into COBA (most of the COBA Advice Notes were concerned with economic, rather than engineering issues), at least where these did not have a significant impact upon the number of schemes that qualified as economically viable. Indeed, changing the economic 'rules' of the game was seen to be an integral part of the COBA management function.[95]

The problem of purpose

A very prominent aspect of both the COBA program and the COBA management system – and one that is frequently overlooked – is that they are rife with anomalies connected with the purpose of COBA's existence. For example, COBA was initially developed in response to the problem posed by traffic congestion in small historic towns, but its originators made no attempt to assess the specific nature of this problem. (That is to say, does congestion in towns stem from too much traffic, traffic of a particular type such as lorries, too many traffic entrances along the through-town route, too many junctions, etc.) Indeed, the analytical apparatus inherent to COBA only became applicable when one, and only one, solution to the congestion problem – specifically, a bypass – had been chosen. Furthermore, especially in its early history, COBA was said to be applicable when a town confronted environmental difficulties as a result of traffic, but the methodology dealt with environmental issues only indirectly – and even then in the context of strictly economic benefits and costs.

Other anomalies arose in connection with the way in which COBA measured the economic gains and losses associated with various road proposals. As one would expect given the nature of COBA's do-nothing–do-something model, final outcomes were heavily dependent upon: the configuration of the road networks (how many junctions they had, etc.), traffic assignment (that is, the level of traffic flow assigned to each link in the road networks under consideration), grossing up procedures including traffic forecasting and that involving the M factor, the numbers assigned to values of time, accident costs and the like and estimates of the road construction costs. It is significant, therefore, that when COBA was discussed within the Department, or even in more public forums, these elements of the COBA methodology were not given equal attention.

To illustrate, traffic assignment, especially on the do-something network, was absolutely crucial to COBA outcomes, and COBA managers were constantly involved in reviewing assignment decisions made in the field.[96] Yet assignment practices were rarely discussed overtly. *The COBA Manual* and the COBA Advice Notes did not contain any mention of the topic, and *The Leitch Committee Report*, while it mentioned assignment on two occasions, did not investigate the adequacy of the assignment practices that COBA practitioners and managers have condoned.[97]

Similarly, as we have seen, the adequacy of the M factor did not receive serious examination within DOT, although COBA users and managers readily admitted that, from their experience, it played a very important role in determining absolute and relative NPV levels across the road programme. Moreover, *The Leitch Committee Report* did little to promote in-depth discussion of this parameter.[98]

In contrast, public and professional doubts concerning the validity of the DOT's vehicle and traffic forecasts obliged officials to scrutinize the Tanner forecasting methodology at some length. Furthermore, *The Leitch Committee Report* strongly urged the Department to abandon the extrapolatory approach to forecasting inherent to Tanner's work in favour of causal forecasting models. The argument was that the latter would be more sensitive to changes in the environment in which roads are constructed because they are geared to alterations in variables like car prices, fuel prices, incomes and so on, rather than, as in the case of the Tanner 'model', simply to the passage of time.[99]

The numbers assigned to values of time and accident costs also sparked controversy outside the Department with the result that officials were obliged to defend departmental practice with respect to issues such as the value of small time savings and the economic cost of the pain, grief and suffering following accidents. *The Leitch Committee Report* recommended a few changes in this area (including a substantial increase in the pain, grief and suffering allowance associated with accidents), but broadly confirmed the approach to time and accident valuation embodied in COBA.[100]

The very different treatment accorded to the various elements of the COBA methodology suggests that COBA practitioners and managers, and even COBA's critics, failed to see the different aspects of the COBA methodology in terms of the whole; that is to interpret each of the methodology's parts in the light of the overall purpose that COBA served. To be specific, the Leitch Committee's recommendations for improving the forecasts used in COBA were of limited value because the serious inadequacies of the M factor were neglected. Indeed, the lack of interest in the adequacy of such crucial elements of the COBA methodology as the M factor and traffic assignment practices indicates that the COBA system bore less relation to the goal of providing credible evaluations of individual road proposals than to that of generating end-numbers (NPV/C ratios) that were not out of line with the economist's conception of what the rate of return on an inter-urban road proposal should have been. Moreover, this contention is given added weight by the fact that EcHF emphasized sensitivity analysis rather than on-site or even before–after studies in assessing the COBA methodology.[101] Under this type of regime a parameter is judged, not according to its theoretical and empirical support, but according to the importance of its contribution to overall results.

Thus, in an important sense the development of the COBA system tended to ignore the problem of purpose. This was especially evident in the case of vehicle operating costs. Vehicle operating cost savings made a negligible contribution to average COBA earnings, yet from the outset vehicle operating costs were the object of continuing technical investigation.

Accident costs provide another example of the same phenomenon. By the late 1970s, knowledge of the frequency, type, and situation of road accidents in Britain was quite extensive (witness the data presented in the annual series *Road Accidents in Great Britain*).[102] Debate continued, however, over whether or not road accidents should be costed for purposes of economic evaluation, and, if so, how. Drawing upon the work of Reynolds and, more importantly, Dawson, DOT personnel costed road accidents by dividing their effects into two components.[103] The first rested upon the assumption that if an accident is prevented certain fairly concrete savings accrue to society, including avoided medical, police and administrative costs, avoided damage costs to vehicles and other property and lost output owing to any injury or fatality associated with the accident. The second component consisted of the pain, grief and suffering avoided by preventing accident-induced fatalities. This was assigned a notional and very much minimum value by discounting the future consumption of an average non-productive person.

Although DOT analysts avoided assigning an explicit value to life by calculating costs on a per-accident rather than a per-casualty or per-fatality basis, the accident costing procedures sketched above proved controversial. The Department was criticized for not basing its accident costs upon the values of life emerging from recent risk reduction studies – something with which the Leitch Committee concurred in recommending that the pain, grief and suffering allowance be substantially increased.[104] In addition, some commentators condemned the lost output or forgone consumption approaches to costing accidents. A fairly obvious solution to these difficulties – and one that was proposed on a number of occasions – was to demonetize accidents, thereby preventing them from being hidden among other variables in economic evaluations and highlighting the contribution particular projects could make to reducing absolute numbers of accidents.[105] However, DOT personnel were strongly opposed to this suggestion without being able to articulate a rationale for their opposition. In their view, the important thing was to improve the values employed in accident costing, not to remove the monetization process.

The continued investigation of vehicle operating costs, despite their minimal contribution to COBA outcomes, and the strong opposition displayed by DOT personnel to the demonetization of accidents (like all of the anomalies connected with the 'why' of COBA's existence) suggest that the COBA methodology was devoid of purpose at the cognitive level. Moreover, it can be demonstrated that this lack is inherent to the structure of the COBA model.

To begin with, it should be noted that there are essentially two methods for describing and/or evaluating the nature of a transport network.[106] In the first, zones of activity are defined and a matrix is derived that describes the number of trips between zones according to trip purpose (recreational, journey to work, etc.). The object of this method is to generate a matrix that will provide information as to the consequences of, for example, improving transport links between zones. The second method, of which COBA is an example, is to assume some form of average trip taken, and, having done so, to specify in detail the types of networks that are available to accomplish the trip (either actual or projected). The object in this case is to establish which network best facilitates the average trip.

The two methods differ in many senses, but, for present purposes, the most important are as follows: the first is concerned with trip purposes and, therefore, uses estimates of behavioural costs, while the second assumes a fixed trip matrix and deals with resource costs. In the first method values of time and other parameters can be geared to journey purpose, while in the second these parameters are designated as sets of averages because of the lack of concern, relatively speaking, for why trips are undertaken. Another crucial point is that although both methods attempt to arrive at an absolute value for the economic worth of a particular scheme, only the second can be used for *ranking* schemes because behavioural costs are non-comparable, scheme to scheme. Thus, while it is the most useful from an economic standpoint because it permits comparisons between schemes, the fixed trip matrix approach to describing and evaluating transport networks ignores the reasons for travel, indeed, the purpose of transport facilities generally. This was at the root of certain tensions between the economists of EcHF and a number of analysts with scientific training who were engaged in work on the value of time and other issues. The concern of the latter for the reasons why drivers act as they do contrasted sharply with the behavioural agnosticism, relatively speaking, of the economists managing COBA. However, the models produced by considering behaviour could not rival the simplicity of COBA.[107]

If, then, COBA did not accommodate or recognize purpose, how was it justified and, thereby, sustained as an evaluative system? The answer, given in part earlier, is that it *regularized* the assessment of roads. Through COBA, economic expertise was brought to bear upon myriad engineering activities in the field with the result that they were organized and reduced to a common, monetary denominator. In the process, choices regarding levels of road provision were formalized, the excesses to which highway engineers appeared prone were curbed and the various groups participating in the road programme were induced to adopt one understanding of the way in which road projects of a certain size and type should be analyzed and evaluated. It is in this social context that a number of the anomalies described earlier make sense. For example, DOT personnel opposed the demonetization of road accidents because it constituted a threat to the unity of approach to road assessment that COBA afforded and, therefore, to the status of those, including the staff producing the accident cost figures, who adhered to the economic logic inherent to COBA. In addition, vehicle operating costs received considerable attention, despite their relative lack of importance to COBA outcomes, because they fell within the economists's range of expertise, and, hence, constituted a significant symbol of the dominance of economic logic within the COBA program and the COBA management system.

Local variations in the situation of roads, political pressures and, frequently, personalities prevented the review of inter-urban roads from becoming completely self-contained, completely routine; but certainly the central thrust of the COBA methodology and the COBA management system was in that direction. This is perhaps most evident in the way in which they contributed to the development of the road programme as a whole. The primary objective of COBA practitioners was to evaluate the economic worth of particular schemes by determining their NPV/C ratios, but COBA was also employed as a guide to assigning priority to road projects as they progressed through the various stages of implementation. Moreover, average COBA outcomes came to be used during broad road-policy discussions as a general indicator of the kind of benefits that could be expected from inter-urban roads. Thus, COBA played a role in the evaluation of roads, in the implmentation of road projects and in the broad development, or formulation, of road policy. The significant point about these three phases of COBA usage is that COBA practitioners rarely distinguished between the premises inherent to each. One example will suffice. Typically, 80 per cent of average COBA benefits were of the time savings type, and, from this, it became an unwritten assumption affecting much *policy development* that a new road is meant primarily to move people and goods from place to place more easily than was possible before the road was built. As a consequence, all schemes with high accident benefits (say 30 to 50 per cent) were scrutinized carefully during the course of *evaluation*, more carefully than other types of schemes, and schemes designed specifically to minimize accidents did not receive *implementation* priority.[108] Hence, to all intents and purposes, policy formulaiton, implementation and evaluation were collapsed under COBA, with the result that the integrity of the COBA methodology and management system was seldom questioned and responses to most problems became a matter of course.

Conclusions

The forgoing analysis indicates that the COBA methodology and management system together have closely approximated the rationality-based administrative system described in Chapter 1. The application of economic expertise to the problem of evaluating inter-urban roads has yielded an arithmetic structure in which knowledge from a variety of sources and covering many different subject areas has been synthesized. Each of the many components of the COBA system was designed to produce an end-number. The end-numbers for the components were then fed into a calculating mechanism founded in economic rationality and upheld by those committed to an economic ethos, whether economists or engineers. The system, furthermore, clearly had no difficulty in accommodating a large number of analytical categories, with the result that

COBA practitioners have been able to treat road networks of considerable size and complexity, and organizational diversification has presented relatively few difficulties.

The dominance of economic logic within the COBA system lent it certain strengths. Its extreme pragmatism with regard to subject matter and the number of categories it was able to encompass were cases in point. Also, the focus on numbers that it encouraged meant that conflicts between the different professionals involved with COBA, while often long-lived, seldom jeopardized the system's operations. Moreover, the COBA system was rarely disrupted by attempts to recycle through the phases of the policy problems associated with inter-urban roads, for its logic served to liaise the processes of policy formulation, implementation and evaluation. But, for all this, the system had its weaknesses. It was characterized by a variety of boundary-related problems. Many of its fixed relationships and parameters were theoretically and empirically inadequate. Most importantly, the COBA system remained divorced from the concept of purpose.

Nevertheless, in the face of the criticisms of the road programme and its underpinnings that came to the fore in the late 1970s, the COBA system proved to be remarkably resilient. Components of the methodology, particularly the traffic forecasts, came under attack, but the methodology as a whole remained relatively unscathed. The Leitch Committee recommended that COBA be supplemented by a comprehensive programme of environmental appraisal (a more elaborate version of the type of environmental assessment described in this chapter),[109] but found the overall system of economic appraisal to be 'basically sound'.[110] Moreover, in the words of a 1978 White Paper on roads:

> Value for money will remain an essential objective in the planning and building of roads.[111]

Thus, COBA or COBA-type methodologies appear to have an ongoing role to play in shaping road provision. Yet, when the COBA system is examined in detail, it is clear that its overall effect has been to promote road building that, while incremental, is also undirected and potentially limitless.

5

The evaluation of investment in human resources

Unemployment and human capital

Unemployment was among the most prominent political issues of the 1970s in Britain. The upward progression in unemployment rates, which led to over 3 million unemployed in Britain by the early 1980s, assumed major political proportions in the mid-1970s. In each of the intervening years the debate over the meaning that should be attached to the unemployment figures intensified, especially as unemployment figured prominently in discussions about the overall viability of the British economy. Cabinet statements, rebuttals from the Opposition, interventions from the TUC and CBI, and extensive media coverage drew public attention to various facets of the unemployment problem. Successive governments responded to the political imperative to be seen to act in a field in which waste and distress are so obvious. The resulting government initiatives prompted, in turn, widespread discussion of the causes of unemployment and the suitability of the remedies proposed for its alleviation.

From the outset the economics profession took a great interest in the unemployment question. Many of its members, particularly those who specialized in macroeconomic problems, played a prominent part both in attempting to specify the nature and causes of the rapid rise in unemployment levels Britain experienced during the 1970s and in providing advice about appropriate means for lowering the numbers of unemployed. These economists were for the most part concerned with interpreting the month-to-month, year-to-year, fluctuations in the employment statistics and other macroeconomic indicators in an effort to forecast short to medium term changes in these series and, on that basis, provide advice about how fiscal, monetary and other instruments could be deployed to best effect in the employment field. The analysis of employment and unemployment was an important facet of the work of a macroeconomic forecasting industry, based in large part upon economic expertise, whose ranks included the National Institute of Economic and Social Research, the Cambridge Economic Policy Group, the Henley Centre for Forecasting, the Economic Models group, the London Business School and private groups like Forex, Phillips and Drew and Kemp-Gee. The assessments of these groups vied with those of the Treasury, the Bank of England, the Department of Employment and other public sector bodies that employed economists to report upon and study changes in levels of employment and other macroeconomic developments.

The British forecasting industry produced large amounts of documentation annually, but even these sizeable analytical efforts could not stem what was by then a long-term decline in the credibility of the economics profession in the macroeconomic sphere. In no case was this decline more evident than in the study of employment and unemployment.[1] To begin with, the split in the economic ranks between Keynesians and monetarists yielded differing interpretations of existing statistics and differing forecasts. More importantly, a large proportion of conventional macroeconomic advice regarding unemployment became inoperable during the 1970s. The traditional Keynesian response to unemployment was to stimulate demand, but as the 1970s advanced reflation came to be viewed as a less and less viable policy option owing to IMF restrictions and a general wish to avoid another round of severe inflation. This was reflected in Labour's partial conversion to monetarism after 1976, but the monetarist emphasis upon curbing inflation even at the expense of higher unemployment was not consistent with the long-run objectives of the Labour Governments of the late 1970s. Other Keynesians, notably those who adhered to cost-push explanations of inflation were more in tune with both Heath's Conservatives and Labour in their advocacy of incomes policy as a means of achieving lower rates of inflation and higher levels of employment. However, their analyses of the relationships between employment, inflation and productivity continued to present profits as the motive force for the economic system. They were, thus, unable to address the equity issues government confronts in attempting to restrain wages and salaries in the absence of effective restraints on prices and profits.

As their credibility in the macroeconomic sphere ebbed, economists explored other ways of addressing the unemployment question. Some turned to the examination and espousal of what were termed 'structural measures' in the employment field. During the late 1970s it was fashionable in some economic quarters to argue that high unemployment levels had resulted in large measure from work disincentives connected with the combined effects of the British tax and social security systems. Unemployment levels, it was asserted, would be reduced much further by raising the tax threshold than by job creation schemes. However, this proposal rested upon the assumption that the level of unemployment and social security benefits, when compared with after-tax income from employment, removed the incentive to find and remain in work. Under Labour this contention met with little sympathy, although in the wake of the 1979 Thatcher victory structural approaches to the unemployment question gained greater credence, together with a reinvigorated monetarism – again with little success as far as unemployment was concerned.

Another, and much more auspicious, way for economists to avoid the dilemmas inherent in the macroeconomic approach to the unemployment problem was to abandon the latter altogether and focus, instead, upon the microeconomics of labour. This is a relatively new area of economic specialization in Britain. For example, in 1972 Thirlwall, a former economic adviser with the Department of Employment, noted that despite the 'considerable amount of public money and resources' then being devoted to manpower policies there were virtually no British studies devoted either to the microeconomic evaluation of these policies (costs, benefits, etc.) or to their effects, if any, upon reducing labour market disequilibrium.[2] Fisher has explained the lack of work in the microeconomics of labour prior to 1970 by noting that the neglect was 'in step' with the eclipse of price theory generally during the period when the most important aspects of Keynes's work were being assimilated and theories of monopolistic competition emerged.[3] The area also suffered with respect to other specialities because many economists considered it to be dominated by institutional factors and, therefore, not amenable to standard types of analysis.[4] Furthermore, the speciality probably failed to attract attention because the problems of the labour market were not traditionally accorded the same prestige as those of industry, the financial markets and government, and it was only with the relatively recent use of incomes policy as a means to control inflation that this bias was shown to be dated. However, with the emergence of inflation and unemployment as major political and economic problems, and as the weaknesses of macroeconomic theory in the employment field became increasingly apparent, the microeconomics of labour experienced a revival, especially after 1970.

The theoretical inspiration for this revival was largely American. During the 1950s and early 1960s developments in consumer analysis primarily associated with Milton Friedman and the Chicago School restored the discussion of competitive markets and the conditions characteristic of market equilibrium to the centre of the economic stage. In the wake of this, economists like Schultz began to emphasize the competitiveness of labour markets and to speculate about the mechanisms involved in the individual's choice of work, as well as the nature of labour market equilibrium. The most notable result of this renewed interest in labour markets was the theory of human capital pioneered by Schultz and his colleagues and developed by Becker and others.[5]

Human capital theory consists in the application of standard capital theory to the problem of how individuals equip themselves to compete in the labour market. As such, its novelty lies not in the originality of its logic, but in the apparently unorthodox nature of its many potential uses. Stated simply, the theory asserts that individuals, acting in their own interests, enhance their capabilities as producers, and, hence, their projected incomes, by investing in themselves. The investment in question can take many forms ranging from health care through vocational training and higher education to marriage and family planning. In each case, however, the assumption is that the individual justifies sacrifices in the present by orienting himself towards future rewards (pecuniary or otherwise) rather than immediate enjoyment.

Since its emergence in the early 1960s the appeal of the human capital research programme has been compelling, both in the United States and elsewhere. As Blaug has observed, it spawned an immense literature, both theoretical and applied, in which may be included much of the worldwide output of some of the fastest growing economic specialities of the 1970s as measured by numbers of articles in the major economics journals (e.g. the economics of education, and health economics).[6] Part of the programme's attraction lay in the relative simplicity of its logic and in the way in which it unified the study of areas that, before its inception, were considered widely divergent (for example, the economics of education and training and the economics of the social services). The programme also acquired adherents because of the parallels it establishes between physical investment and investment in education and social services, parallels that facilitate the extension of evaluative methodologies such as cost–benefit analysis to social programmes. The logic of human capital theory is such that the rate of return on an investment in education or health, for example, can be construed as the ratio of the future rewards the investment brings to the individual (its economic benefits) to the present sacrifices it entails (its economic costs).[7] Indeed, a large proportion of the human capital research programme has been devoted to calculating exactly such rates of return.

Given its many advantages as an analytical format (especially in applied contexts), the human capital approach to the problems of education and social services has flourished. This is not to say, however, that the approach is without difficulties or contradictions. For example, there is the question of its empirical support. Although human capital theory has a logic that resembles that of cost–benefit analysis, it is not a welfare theory and, therefore, its practitioners cannot evade the question of its empirical validity by claiming that it is normative in character. As formulated originally by Schultz and Becker, human capital theory embodied assertions about the behaviour of individuals confronted with choices concerning whether or not to invest in education, training and other forms of human capital that are, in principal, testable.[8] Attempts have been made, largely in the United States, to substantiate the theory empirically, but Blaug's 1976 review of the relevant literature found that the methodological weaknesses of these efforts and the contradictory results they have often yielded give the economics profession few grounds for confidence in the theory's validity.[9]

The failure of American economists to substantiate human capital theory empirically did not result in extensive questioning of the human capital approach,[10] but it has set into relief other difficulties that have plagued the theory from its beginnings. For instance, empirical studies in this area have generally been confined to the United States, largely, it would seem, because economists feel that human capital theory, founded as it is upon the sovereignty of the individual, can only be adequately tested in countries with a market-oriented approach to investment in the individual both in terms of supply and demand. This raises the question of the theory's relevance to countries like Britain where access to services such as education and health care is largely determined by government. In practice, there has been a tendency among British economists affiliated with the human capital approach to ignore the differences between the American and British systems for the delivery of social services, as indicated by, for example, their failure to distinguish between costs paid by the individual for some service and costs borne by the state to provide the same service on behalf of the individual. Although there are many precedents for this type of elision in the economic literature, the distinctly American flavour of human capital theory has meant that the theoretical ambiguities associated with it are more prominent in the case of human capital research than in other areas of microeconomics.

One cannot conclude a sketch of the difficulties and contradictions associated with human capital theory without mentioning the aversion that many outside the economics profession, and some within, have to the way in which it groups plant, machines and men into one category.[11] In its name, and in each of its postulates, human capital theory flies in the face of the widely held assumption that the processes of educating and healing cannot be equated with each other, much less with investment in bridges, roads or industrial plant. Moreover, in doing so, it makes little attempt to explain in detail in what ways these processes are similar.[12] Rather, the theory reifies a quantity called human capital in the conviction that in some circumstances (although these are not clearly delineated)[13] individual spending constitutes investment instead of consumption. As already noted, this approach has the effect of apparently unifying many otherwise disparate efforts under one heading, but there is always the danger that the enterprise will appear too reductionist to be credible.

Yet, despite the difficulties outlined above, the human capital research programme gained many adherents in Britain. The programme is centred upon the economics of education, but also embraces parts of the economics of vocational training, health economics and what has come to be known as the 'new theory of voluntary unemployment'. Taken together, these branches of the human capital research effort aspire to offer 'an almost total explanation of the determinants of earnings from employment'.[14] As such, they have been central to a revived micro-economics of labour, and it is this new form of specialization that has permitted members of the economics profession to make a significant contribution to the industry-specific, and, very often, group-specific approaches to the problems of employment and unemployment that have become increasingly common in government under the general heading of manpower policies.

Training for skills in Britain

The catholic nature of the human capital research programme has assisted many economists in gaining entry to fields of social policy that, in its absence, might have appeared beyond the range of the profession's expertise. This was particularly true, moreover, of areas of social policy that, while not fully governed by the market, are at least circumscribed by market transactions. Vocational training is a case in point. From the economist's standpoint, the individual's decision to seek training may be viewed as a response to market conditions. Moreover, there is a market-dictated opportunity cost in undertaking training. After training the individual concerned faces the market again in an effort, it is to be hoped successful, to employ new skills. The question at issue is 'What is the return that can be expected from this state-subsidized investment in human capital?'

Vocational training was, however, not always seen in this light. Traditionally, British policies were founded upon social rather than economic rationales. In general, until the late 1950s and early 1960s, training was viewed as primarily an industrial responsibility, and government only became extensively involved in training when extra-ordinary circumstances such as war disrupted normal training and work experience patterns, thereby creating an immediate social problem. Thus, the first government training programmes were established in 1917 in order to assist disabled veterans and, later, engineering workers whose training had been interrupted by the war, to retrain, but by 1926, when most veterans had been resettled in civilian occupations, the programmes had been run down. Similarly, while the first modern Government Training Centre (GTC) came into existence in 1925, the GTC programme did not make a significant contribution to training until the Second World War when it was vastly expanded to train men and women for the armaments industry and, later, to retrain ex-servicemen for civilian employment. Again, as after the First World War, the number of training centres and training places contracted markedly when most World War II veterans had been resettled.[15]

This pattern of government training development ended as a result of the British economy's failure to achieve sustained growth during the late 1950s and early 1960s when many European nations were experiencing unprecedented economic expansion. A variety of explanations were advanced for this failure. Some centred upon the economic constraints associated with Britain's international obligations, especially those stemming from sterling's role as a reserve currency. Others pointed to the structural weaknesses of the British economy, including the lack of an adequately trained, well deployed workforce.[16] As the 1950s drew to a close, this latter explanation of Britain's relatively poor economic performance became more compelling. The Carr Committee of 1958, for example, voiced 'a concern with the provision of an adequate volume of apprenticeships in relation to certain demographic features'.[17] In the wake of this and other indicators that industry on its own was not providing adequate facilities for the renewal of the labour force, Ministers and officials began to consider the need for manpower policies, with the result that the early 1960s witnessed the implementation of a variety of measures designed to improve training and placement. Moreover, unlike previous instances of government involvement in the labour field these measures had an explicitly economic rationale.

The two main initiatives of the early 1960s on the training front were the 1963 expansion of the GTC programme and the passage of the Industrial Training Act in 1964. The GTC programme was enlarged in order to encourage unemployed workers to retrain and employed workers to upgrade their skills. This expansion was accelerated in 1973 when the Government Training Centres – subsequently renamed Skillcentres (SCs) – were integrated into a wider training programme known as the Training Opportunities Scheme (TOPS) which encompassed vocational training in colleges of further education and employers' establishments as well as in Skillcentres.[18] The Industrial Training Act of 1964 initiated the establishment of thirty Industrial Training Boards (ITBs) with responsibility for planning the provision of training facilities within their respective industries, notably by sponsoring training to relieve skill shortages.

Despite their subsequent importance, however, these were but the major parts of a manpower package including the Selective Employment Tax (designed to shift employment from the service industries to manufacturing). Resettlement and Employment Transfer Schemes, Redundancy Benefit and measures intended to encourage firms to move from the crowded Southeast to less developed areas.[19] While upon first perusal these initiatives may appear disparate, in actuality they all in some degree reflected a series of overtly economic conventions that have underpinned British manpower policy throughout the 1960s and 1970s.

First, and foremost, according to the official view, policies in the manpower field had to bear some relation to the four most common macroeconomic objectives of Western industrialized countries: full employment, stable prices, balance of payments equilibrium and rising productivity.[20] Occasionally social equity also emerged as an objective in this context, but equity played a less prominent role in manpower policy debates in Britain than in other Western countries. Needless to say, in recent decades Western governments have seldom been able to pursue these objectives in a consistent, much less fully simultaneous manner. However, manpower policy formulation was usually sufficiently removed from the cut and thrust of macroeconomic debate that Ministers and officials were able to invoke as many as three or four of these often contradictory national objectives in justifying particular policy stances.

A second convention was that these policies had to be 'active' or 'positive'. Officials did not refer to policies to assist the unemployed, but to 'manpower policies'. The assumption was that as productive processes become increasingly sophisticated members of the workforce must be encouraged to prepare themselves to undertake new tasks, often in different locations. Government was seen as having a role in facilitating this type of adaptation by attempting to reduce rigidities in the labour market. This included the provision of training for those wishing to move into new work areas experiencing labour shortages, assistance for those wishing to relocate in regions with surplus job opportunities and encouragement for those planning to move from less productive to more productive employment. Obviously, the unemployed are most in need of government services of this kind, but the official view was that the problems of the unemployed in this regard are but an extension of the difficulties all members of society encounter in adjusting to changing economic circumstances. Seen in this light, the unemployment problem is not confined to those on the unemployment register. Rather, it is latent in the continuing obsolescence of all private and social enterprise. Manpower policies were, therefore, broadly directed towards enhancing the economy's 'adaptability and power of progress'.[21]

The conventions described above were reflected very clearly in training policy. British vocational training, whether it was conducted under the aegis of the ITBs, TOPS, or another programme, was intended to contribute to the achievement of macroeconomic objectives and, in particular, full employment and rising productivity. More than this, vocational training was seen as an *active* means of promoting these objectives. Its aim was not simply to reduce the numbers on the unemployment register, but to encourage the development of new skills and skills in short supply in the workforce and, thereby, improve the prospects for sustained growth.

One consequence of this activist policy orientation was the use of economic criteria in deciding who should be trained. A key assumption inherent in an activist approach to training was that training opportunities are allocated to greatest effect if they are given to those individuals most able to turn them to their economic advantage (e.g. the young, the educated and the highly motivated). Thus, the ITBs sponsored the training of those best equipped to benefit from it and, thereby, relieve industrial skill shortages, and refused to accept a mandate to alleviate unemployment generally. Furthermore, while government provided training for *both* the employed and the unemployed through TOPS, this programme too was oriented towards meeting economic, including industrial, needs, and, therefore, its organizers were reluctant to admit large numbers of older or long-term unemployed.[22] Facilities were made available for helping those like the disabled, the socially disadvantaged, displaced older workers and the generally hard to employ, who have particular difficulties in finding and keeping employment. However, in these instances what the government was prepared to offer was not training but employment rehabilitation.[23]

For present purposes the importance of the economic conventions reflected in the formulation and implementation of manpower policy lies in the way in which they have eased the entry of economists into the labour field. In the case of vocational training, great stress was given, for example, to the contribution of training to rising productivity. Moreover, this assumption prompted some obvious questions. First, is it valid? And, if so, to what extent? In the case of vocational training, the potential scope for economic analysis was illustrated in the 1970 Manpower Paper, *Cost–Benefit Aspects of Manpower Retraining*, prepared for the Department of Employment and Productivity by J.J. Hughes.[24] In it Hughes noted that the economics profession was assigning greater and greater importance to the contribution of investment in human capital to economic growth, particularly in the wake of Denison's analysis of the sources of what he called 'residual growth'. In the light of this, Hughes's immediate concern was to determine the type of rate of return one could expect from vocational training by reviewing the methodologies and results of one Swedish and a number of American cost–benefit studies of institutional training. He found that while there was considerable variation in the results of these studies:

> . . . even the most conservative estimates reveal that manpower retraining is a worth-while investment for the individual, and an even more worth-while investment for the government and society at large.[25]

On this basis, he recommended training as an effective means for improving the skill endowment of the workforce in a tight labour market and preparing for future economic expansion in a slack one. He also argued that further research designed to compare the cost–benefit ratios of institutional and on-the-job training was required, especially given the great importance of the latter within the British training effort.

By 1970 there were sufficient international precedents and enough interest within the economics profession to justify more work in the economics of vocational training. In fact, a few economists had already seen the opportunities and acted.[26]

Evaluating the profitability of GTC training

The rest of this chapter is concerned with the details of what was one of the most extensive and longest lasting government evaluations of vocational training undertaken in the 1970s.[27] This was the cost–benefit analysis of GTC (later Skillcentre) training, conducted first on contract to the Department of Employment and Productivity and subsequently taken over by economists within the Training Services Agency, later the Training Services Division, of the Manpower Services Commission (MSC). The study began in 1969, and continued in a variety of forms thoughout the 1970s. Its importance lies not only in the many precedents it established in the economics of vocational training, but also in what it reveals about the strengths and weaknesses of the economic perspective on non-physical investment programmes generally. Like the discussion of COBA in Chapter 4, the following review of the cost–benefit analysis of vocational training is, at times, quite technical, but the full character of its contribution to the evaluation of training policy cannot be appreciated without treating certain aspects of the methodology employed in some detail.

The cost–benefit analysis of vocational training in GTCs originated with discussions between the Department of Employment and Productivity and an academic contractor (an economist) in the late 1960s. Initially resource constraints prevented the Department from pursuing these discussions very far. However, by 1969 the economic effects of GTC training had assumed some prominence in internal discussions. In addition, in 1968 the Social Survey (later the Office of Population, Censuses and Surveys – OPCS) began work on a follow-up survey of 1965 and 1966 GTC trainees, and this offered the prospect of a data base suitable for undertaking an analysis of the costs and benefits of GTC training. Accordingly, the Department invited the academic contractor to submit a research design making use of the new documentation on GTCs that was then emerging. The Department received the research design in March 1969, and a year later gave official approval to proceeding with a contract on the economic effects of GTCs.

The course of the contract is set out in a series of papers submitted to the Department over the next several years. One of the first of these is well worth examining in some detail, for in it the contractor looked at the evaluative problem that adult training presents for the economist.

In 'Costs and benefits of adult retraining in the United Kingdom', the contractor advanced a simple model for GTC vocational training. In this model individuals volunteer to participate in a training programme, not because they enjoy the training process, nor because they are interested in matters like a better working environment, but *exclusively* in the expectation that the investment will yield a return in the form of increased earnings after training. The model assigns a number of simple qualities to the training process. It is characterized by finite duration and a finite result, namely the award or refusal of a training diploma. Otherwise, training is a black box into which individuals flow and out of which they emerge with or without a diploma. The task of the economist is, then, to determine the economic benefits and costs associated with training by juxtaposing the 'do-something' situation in which investment in human capital in the form of GTC training proceeds against the 'do-nothing' situation in which it does not. This task is eased by two dichotomies characteristic of training and the labour market that assist the identification of discrete costs and benefits: first, either an individual receives a training diploma or he does not; and second, either he enters employment after completing his training or he does not.

Like the COBA model, the training model compares a factual scenario with a counterfactual one, except that in the former case the factual scenario is the do-nothing option, whereas in the latter it is the do-something option. However, in other respects the training model is less elaborate than the COBA model. Using concepts and data borrowed from engineering, highway analysts were able to resolve road investment into a number of discrete components, each of which was modelled separately. They then considered which particular combination of these discrete components represented an optimal solution for the road investment problem at hand. In contrast, the representation of the investment process at the centre of the training model is monolithic. In this instance, the economic problem lay not in identifying various parts of the training process and in comparing and contrasting these to determine an optimal investment mix, but in determining whether or not the benefits of training, understood as a single entity, exceed the costs. Thus, whereas a specific view of the technique associated with road building is latent in COBA, the training model does not encompass a view of the process(es) whereby skills are transmitted to vocational trainees. Indeed, the absence of this kind of discussion is characteristic of economic evaluations based explicitly or implicitly upon human capital theory. The theory is not concerned with explicating the ways in which human beings augment their capacities through investing in themselves. Rather, it is concerned with the translation of these increased capacities into 'changes in the quantity and quality of labour'.[28]

'Costs and benefits of adult retraining in the United Kingdom' was primarily concerned with discussing the ways in which the effects of training upon earnings postulated in the training model might be measured. At the time, the standard method was to collect data concerning the employment records and earnings levels of trainees just before training and at intervals after training had been completed. Any improvement in earnings or employment experience was, as a first approximation, attributed to the training. As the paper noted, however, by the late 1960s this approach had been subjected to extensive criticism because it failed to distinguish between improvements arising from training and those that could be attributed to cyclical and other factors. The paper went on to observe that a number of American economists had attempted to avoid the difficulties associated with before–after comparisons through the use of control groups, although this approach too was subject to doubt. The main problem in the latter case centred upon the matching of controls to trainees, which can never be perfect. In particular, there was always the risk of self-selection. Trainees might well differ systematically from otherwise comparable non-trainees because of higher levels of motivation, greater tenacity and so forth.

Significantly, this first review of the evaluative problem posed by vocational training did not commit the contractor to any particular method of assessing the direct effects of training, but it was definitive about the importance of indirect effects in the evaluation of training programmes. The paper focused in particular on those indirect effects arising from situations in which trainees interact with other workers. These may be divided into displacement and replacement (or vacuum) effects.

Displacement occurs when a worker who has undergone training gains employment at the cost of another worker's job. If the displaced worker remains unemployed, then training has presumably resulted in little more than a change of faces at the Jobcentre. Alternatively, the displaced worker may be rehired rapidly, in which case the economist with an interest in indirect effects must ask whether or not the worker who has rehired displaced yet another worker from his job. If he did, the evaluation of the full ramification of training upon employment and earnings requires the examination of at least one further link in the labour market chain.

Replacement occurs when the job vacancy left by an employee who volunteers for training is filled by another worker. Under normal circumstances the earnings a worker forgoes for the duration of a vocational course are included in the costs of training. However, if the prospective trainee is replaced by an unemployed worker, costs of this kind may be said to disappear. Alternatively, if his job is filled by an employed worker, it may prove necessary to trace back through the whole chain of labour market effects in order to assess costs and benefits fully.

In addition to introducing a discussion of indirect benefits to the evaluation of training in this early paper, the contractor also gave consideration to the form the post-training benefit stream assumes. He posited three possibilities. The first was that the stream of benefits from training remains constant over the lifetime of the trainee. A second was that skills become obsolete over time. Hence, benefits taper off until eventually there is no differential in earnings between the trained and the untrained worker. Finally, it was possible that training results in upward-sloping benefit curves. Workers might enhance their ability to learn on the job through training, and thus continually improve their earnings position. The concern in each instance was that enough of the benefit stream be incorporated into the analysis to ensure credibility.

The discussions of indirect effects connected with training and of the form of the post-training benefit stream contained in this early paper had two important common characteristics. To begin with, neither was buttressed by any empirical evidence despite the existence of long-standing methodological controversies concerning the conceptual validity of replacement and displacement and the length of time over which benefits from training accrue. In addition, both discussions considerably extended the scope of evaluation in the area of training without providing any detailed justification either for enlarging the debate about appropriate normative measures or for the decision to stop at a specific point in this process. For example, the treatment of indirect benefits greatly broadened the task the analyst confronts in evaluating a training programme (particularly given the complications of generating replacement and displacement ratios) without any justification beyond the assertion that in certain circumstances these benefits may be important.

On the other hand, why stop with displacement and replacement? At one point the paper observed that indirect benefits may arise from trained workers passing on their skills to others or from instances of 'joint demand' in certain sectors of the labour market, but these 'third party' effects were not pursued.

This early effort to come to terms with the evaluative problem posed by vocational training outlined methods that were later to prove central to the cost–benefit analysis of training. Just as importantly, it indicated that the economist confronts a number of significant obstacles in any efforts to regularize data collection and economic analysis in the manpower field. In particular, simple before–after sampling was revealed to have little validity in this area because of the variability of labour markets over time and space. Moreover, it became clear that any research strategy designed to assess the economic benefits of GTC training demanded efficient and timely data collection and analysis. At the same time, however, if the approach to direct benefit evaluation embodied in the human capital treatment of training is to be credible, the time span over which follow-up surveys of trainees take place cannot fall below a certain minimum. Were this to occur, not enough of the benefit stream would be included in the training assessment. Given this, the economist cannot avoid the problems of labour market variability already mentioned in connection with before–after studies. The use of control groups is one method of dealing with these problems, but is not fully satisfactory. In the end, the contractor and other economists associated with the evaluation of GTC training largely abandoned the use of control groups in favour of another more manageable method of coping with labour market variability.

In 1969–70 the Department of Employment and Productivity came to terms with its academic contractor as to the design of a study to assess the profitability of the GTCs. The study had two objectives. First, it was to appraise the economic costs and benefits of GTC training. In addition, officials hoped that the project would succeed in developing procedures that the Department could use for appraising the economic effectiveness of the GTCs *on a continuous basis*. The intention was that the work should take place in two phases. Phase I was to be largely statistical. The research would focus upon reworking the raw data collected by the Social Survey in its follow-up studies of 1966 GTC trainees. The reworked data were then to be combined with the relevant cost estimates so that preliminary profitability levels could be calculated. On the basis of these results, a few specific trades in representative regions were to be isolated for further analysis over a two-year period. This came to be known as Phase II. Its aim was to investigate the relationship between training and subsequent earnings and employment experience in greater depth.

In the event work on the study did not proceed as originally planned. Phase I was delayed because of data-related problems. Despite the desirability of completing Phase I before Phase II began, the contractor found himself pressed to proceed with the detailed follow-up on selected groups of trainees. In the absence of the Phase I data, he relied on his general knowledge of the training process and other data sources to select groups for Phase II. The focus was placed upon the more common trades (construction, engineering and the automotive trades) and on GTCs located in either high or low unemployment areas. The surveys consisted of an initial questionnaire circulated to those trainees still at the selected GTCs, plus follow-up questionnaires which were distributed to trainees six and twelve months after they had completed their courses. By the end of May 1972 the contractor had circulated the initial questionnaire to 1155 trainees, and 1094 of these questionnaires were completed. In subsequent months the data from these questionnaires was coded and transferred to punched cards for computer analysis. During the same period the contractor prepared six-month and twelve-month follow-up questionnaires, which were later circulated to trainees at the appropriate times.

The Phase II design that emerged during this period employed control groups. Given that a credible 'do-nothing' scenario was required for economic analysis to proceed and that the literature on the evaluation of vocational training had little to offer in the way of methodologically developed alternatives to control groups, there were few options in this regard. However, almost immediately this choice of methodology began to pose difficulties.

The Phase II control group consisted of applicants for training who had passed the GTC selection panels and been accepted but subsequently withdrew their applications. Although these controls were presumably well matched with those applicants who did enter training, the numbers were small. High levels of unemployment in 1972–3 had tended to reduce the GTC withdrawal rate and, therefore, the number of potential candidates for the control group. In addition, the control group survey was characterized by a low response rate because the contractor had had to rely on a postal questionnaire. The low yields associated with the withdrawal method of selecting controls exacerbated the contractor's previous doubts about control group methodology, with the result that throughout 1972 he devoted considerable effort to the development of an alternative 'do-nothing' scenario. A progress report submitted to the Department of Employment in July 1972 noted that 'much attention' was being given to a probabilistic model that could be employed in lieu of control groups during the evaluation of GTC training. Then in February 1973 officials received a detailed review of the use that might be made of a Markov chain model in the assessment of GTC profitability.

Probabilistic modelling in the assessment of training benefits

The 1973 Report, entitled 'A Markov chain model of the benefits of participating in government training schemes', began by noting that the expansion of the GTC programme and the creation of TOPS (both of which were announced in the Department of Employment's *Training for the Future*, 1972) added an extra degree of urgency to the task of determining whether or not vocational training of the GTC type had been worthwhile for those undertaking it in the past. It then went on to illustrate the use of a stochastic model, instead of a control group, in the evaluation of the benefits accruing from GTC training in Scotland without, however, discussing why this approach was superior to control group methodology.

The new model for the labour force experience of workers who do not undergo training assumed that the probability of movement from one employment state to another (for example, from unemployment to employment) in a given period is known and depends *only* on the employment status in the preceding period. Taking employment state transitions to be approximated by a first-order regular Markov chain, the Report presented a transition probability matrix which, as finally formulated, involved five unemployment states and two employment states (each of which represented different lengths of time out of or in a job). Total numbers of employed and unemployed among those who did not undergo training could be simulated for each period after the start of the GTC course, according to the paper, by multiplying an initial employment state vector L_0 and the transition probability matrix P' to yield the employment state vector in the first period L_1, multiplying L_1 by P' to yield the employment state vector in the second period L_2, and so forth.

Having developed the new model, the paper set out to apply it to GTC training in Scotland using unpublished data from a survey of 258 Scottish GTC trainees undertaken at Heriot-Watt University. The first task was, thus, to estimate the cells in the transition probability matrix. Two alternative sets of transitional probabilities were employed to fill the matrix in order to facilitate later sensitivity testing. The first set of probabilities was derived from a study of the unemployment register by Fowler.[29] The second came from a study by MacKay of engineering worker redundancies in the Midlands.[30] The probabilities derived from Fowler gave a faster response time and higher steady-state employment than those from the MacKay study. The second task was to estimate the cells of the initial employment state vector L_0. This was done on the basis of dates relating to previous employment (available for about a third of the Scottish trainees) and information indicating which trainees were in employment before training.

The paper employed two initial state vectors, one for those who had been employed before training and another for those who had been unemployed. These vectors in combination with the two transition probability matrices led to four simulations which were, in turn, used to calculate average earnings in the absence of training.

The results of the simulations, together with the post-training earnings data for the Heriot-Watt cohort were used to calculate the direct benefits of GTC training. These were then discounted and juxtaposed against the costs of training. (It should be noted that the analysis excludes any consideration of indirect benefits like those reviewed in the earlier methodological paper.)

The 1973 analysis had a number of features that deserve to be brought out at this juncture. First, and foremost, the stochastic simulation model did not answer the earlier objections to control groups. The first foray into methodology had recognized that a 'black-box' approach to the evaluation of training cannot subsume all qualitative distinctions between trainees, if only because it fails to explain why some enter training and others do not. However, if control group methodology is inadequate compensation for the weaknesses of the 'black-box' approach, a simulation model that assumes that employment status in one period is dependent only on employment status in another must be more so. However, by 1973 considerations of this kind seem to have receded into the background. Practical difficulties in isolating control groups of sufficient size had rapidly precipitated an effort to regularize the calculation of earnings in the absence of training (and, therefore, direct training benefits) even if this meant removing the human element from an important part of the training evaluation.

The second prominent feature of the 1973 analysis was its extensive resort to sensitivity testing. For example, like its predecessor, it presented no empirical basis for one time horizon over another in the evaluation of GTC training. Consequently, the simulations were run for several different time horizons up to ten years, thus presumably enabling the reader to make his own assumptions about the period over which benefits accrue and demonstrating the sensitivity of the results to the time horizon chosen. The paper also resorted to sensitivity testing in the case of the transition probabilities employed in the simulation model. In the absence of empirical standards, the simulations were run first with a faster and then with a slower transition probability matrix so that the reader had the benefit of four simulations in evaluating the economic impact of the Scottish GTCs under scrutiny. The important point about both this procedure and the sensitivity testing applied to the choice of time horizon is that they were essentially devices for coping with ignorance. The paper had no guidance to offer concerning the most appropriate choice either of time horizon or of transition probabilities; the solution was to throw the weight of judgement upon the official audience.

Finally, the 1973 paper was distinguished by a tendency to conflate analysis and evaluation. One of the more evident cases of this was associated with the sensitivity testing undertaken in connection with the time horizons. As mentioned above, the paper presented cost–benefit ratios for different time horizons up to ten years after the start of training. However, only those ratios for the first eighteen months after training were derived directly from the Heriot-Watt earnings data and the simulation model. The contractor provided earnings figures and, hence, cost–benefit ratios for the remainder of the ten-year period by assuming that the level of unemployment that obtained among non-trainees and trainees at eighteen months after the training period would remain constant over the next eight and a half years and that the real earnings of employed workers would rise by 3 per cent per annum. Given that beyond the first eighteen months changes in the cost–benefit ratios for training were fully predictable from initial assumptions, it is difficult to construe what was being 'tested' by varying the time horizon.

Conflation of analysis and evaluation was also evident in the summary of the results for the assessment of training in Scottish GTCs. The paper found that the two sets of transition probabilities led to very different results for the unemployed. The Fowler simulation yielded considerably lower NPVs than the MacKay simulation. Alternatively, for those employed before training the results from the two sets of transition probabilities were quite similar. In addition, the NPVs for these latter simulations were generally somewhat higher than those resulting from the MacKay simulation for the unemployed. From this, the conclusion was that GTC training was more profitable for those joining the course from employment. However, this inference stemmed from a serious confusion of categories. True, the two simulations run for those employed before training yielded relatively high cost–benefit ratios. But these were no more than simulations, and their validity, the merits of the methodology aside, hinged upon the legitimacy of the transition probabilities employed. Thus, for example, if the MacKay probabilities were legitimate then training the unemployed might have yielded as much, if not more, benefit as training the employed, depending upon the time horizon chosen. As it happened, there was no means of deciding which set of probabilities was legitimate (if any). Furthermore, there was no basis for inferring that the spread of the simulation results had any bearing upon the relative economic merits of training the employed versus the unemployed.

The paper on stochastic modelling received a mixed reception in official circles. Its complexity proved somewhat daunting. Moreover, those supervising the contract were concerned about the lateness of the report for Phase I and the fact that the Markov chain analysis bore no relation to the type of report they had expected would emerge from Phase II. They were, therefore, gratified when the Phase I Report arrived in March 1974.

First results

The Phase I Report, entitled 'Costs and benefits of manpower training programmes in Great Britain' demonstrated once again the contractor's determination to substitute simulation models for control groups. The paper contained a lengthy, non-technical discussion of the model developed in the 1973 paper, the one major difference being that only the Fowler probabilities were employed in analysing the Phase I data, although no explanation was offered for dropping the MacKay probabilities. The paper then proceeded to a description of how cost–benefit ratios and profitability levels could be calculated for Phase I using the results from the simulation model, conventional estimates of the direct resource costs of training and post-training earnings data for the 1965–6 GTC trainees surveyed by OPCS.

As was apparent from even a cursory examination of the results, the levels of profitability calculated for Phase I differed markedly from those calculated from the Heriot-Watt data. In the latter case, the Fowler simulations suggested that GTC training became profitable in cost–benefit terms within the first two and a half years after completion. In contrast, only one of the Phase I training trade groups broke even in cost–benefit terms by the *eighth* year after completion, and the results for all trades suggested that the benefits of training only exceed the costs in the *tenth* year after completion. Furthermore, another training trade group (miscellaneous trades) apparently imposed societal losses for the duration of the evaluation's ten-year time horizon (as indicated by cost–benefit ratios considerably less than one).

The marked differences between the Phase I results and the Heriot-Watt results (calculated using the same methodology) deserved explanation. However, the paper did not address this issue. Rather, it proceeded to argue that the direct results underestimate returns from GTC investment because they do not take indirect benefits and costs into account. By indirect benefits and costs were meant replacement, displacement and what were labelled 'complementarity effects'. The latter were synonymous with the 'joint demand' of the earlier paper, and referred to situations in which an influx of workers trained in relatively scarce skills leads to the employment of additional or 'complementary' workers as skill bottlenecks are relieved. However, the Phase I Report, like the earlier treatment of indirect effects, did not pursue the implications of 'complementarity' beyond the definitional stage.

The remainder of the Phase I Report was devoted to testing the 'sensitivity of the final results to differing assumptions about externality effects'. Replacement and displacement fractions were varied, and the results calculated for all trades and, in some instances, for the three trade groups. From these calculations, it became evident that GTC training was very profitable, very unprofitable or somewhere in between, depending upon the replacement and displacement fractions assumed. However, in this case, and in contrast with the other instances of sensitivity testing that have been examined in this chapter, some guidance was offered as to what constitutes a plausible choice for the replacement fraction, 'r', and the displacement fraction, 'd'. For example, displacement fraction values greater than ¼ were not considered on the assumption that GTCs tend to direct their efforts towards trades with skill shortages. Moreover, certain combinations of values for 'r' and 'd' were judged to be unlikely.

Having presented the results for the calculations of costs and benefits including indirect effects, the Phase I Report concluded that GTC training had been demonstrated to be extremely profitable and to compare favourably with other public sector investments. Yet an examination of the figures does not support this contention. Methodology aside, there was no means of knowing which set of replacement and displacement values was legitimate. The combination, $r = 1/4$ and $d = 0$, for example, might have best represented the state of the labour market at the time, in which case the benefits of training would not have exceeded the costs until the fourth or fifth year after completion. Nevertheless, by including indirect benefits and costs in its analysis, the Phase I Report did succeed in improving profitability levels sufficiently that training could not be dismissed as an uneconomic proposition. In some senses, this was deemed more important than the calculation of exact profitability levels. The aim was not to provide a detailed account of Phase I (the data and results were very dated anyway), but to suggest the means of monitoring GTC training over the long term.

The official reaction to the Phase I Report, like that to the paper on stochastic modelling, was mixed. During the course of internal discussions administrators, economists and other specialists from both the Department of Employment and the newly formed Training Services Agency commented upon the paper. In general, these commentators seem to have accepted that the Phase I Report proved the economic value of GTC training to society. However, there was scepticism about the use of constant transitional proportions in the simulation model (several officials argued that these would vary with the level of aggregate demand). In addition, a number of commentators felt that the Phase I analysis did not give sufficient attention to the examination of objectives in GTC training and, therefore, to the relationship between objectives and the economic methodology employed in the Report. Finally, some officials were concerned that the Phase I analysis relied upon assumptions, some crucial to the results, which were not supported by any concrete evidence.

Nevertheless, officials found the Report convincing in one important respect. As far as the Department of Employment and TSA were concerned, it presented a plausible method for reviewing the profitability of GTCs on a continuous basis although, obviously, many of its features would have to be refined before it could be applied in a routine manner. Thus, in the summer and autumn of 1974 the central questions within official circles became: who was to take charge of the development of this methodology, and what arrangements would be required in order to implement an evaluative methodology of the kind that the contractor had proposed. Moreover, these questions assumed an added urgency as the result of the organizational changes that accompanied the creation of the MSC and the conclusion among officials that the contractor did not have the resources to undertake the development and implementation of such a methodology.

In 1973–4 statutory responsibility for GTC training was transferred to the newly created TSA, and consequently, in September 1974 the Department of Employment withdrew from the training contract. At this juncture, the study might well have lapsed owing to some disillusionment in official circles about the way the project had progressed. However, a number of TSA personnel and, in particular, an economic adviser on staff were interested in the possibilities that the Phase I methodology seemed to present for the evaluation of training. Their judgement was that the contractor's work deserved development because it constituted the only evaluation available in the area and, just as importantly, offered an alternative evaluative methodology which promised to turn the CBA of training into a routine monitoring device rather than a laborious research task.

The Training Services Agency did not, however, commit funds to the study without insisting upon fundamental changes in the way in which the Phase II work was to be carried out. The contractor relinquished his position as project supervisor, and agreed to transfer all of the Phase II data banks and other materials to TSA facilities. In-house economists then undertook to proceed with the Phase II analysis in accordance with the government's original requirements, including the use of a control group, although the former contractor was retained as an informal consultant to the project and, in the event, had quite a substantial influence upon the complexion of Phase II work. At the same time, though, plans were laid to develop the Phase I probabilistic model for use as a routine means of assessing the 'do-nothing' situation. For the project's civil service advocates, as for the former contractor, the way ahead led towards simulation of the work force experience of non-trainees.

From analysis to programme management: the evolution of an evaluative system

When the Training Services Agency assumed responsibility for the training evaluation project it was in the midst of coordinating a large expansion of government training facilities inaugurated by the 1972 creation of TOPS. The Agency's first Five Year Plan aimed at training 70,000 to 75,000 people a year within TOPS by 1975 compared with the 15,000 trained in government facilities in 1971, and set a target of 100,000 trainees a year to be achieved as soon as possible. GTCs constituted only one part of the operations of TOPS. Despite this, however, in 1972–3 Department of Employment officials had anticipated that the training study would yield data that might be of use in assessing the appropriateness of TOPS training targets and, perhaps, of the choice of training areas. As it happened, the Phase II data (1972–3 surveys) were not available in the 1973–5 period when they might have had most impact upon policy formulation with respect to TOPS. Nevertheless, in view of the general dearth of analytical work on training, TSA personnel felt the training study was worth pursuing.

The TSA group that took over the training study consisted of a mix of economists and statisticians. The study formed a continuing, if intermittent, part of their work from April 1975 onwards. The study was divided into a number of sub-projects. First priority was assigned to the cost–benefit analysis of GTC training using the Phase II data. In addition, an effort was launched to isolate training from other variables that might affect earnings differentials through the use of multivariate regression analysis. Finally, work began on refining the probabilistic training model in preparation for computerizing it, testing it, and, eventually, offering the completed computer package to other MSC professionals as a substitute for control groups.

In June 1976 a paper was circulated to senior officials dealing with the results from Phase II. The results were as follows. Without the inclusion of indirect benefits and costs, the social return to Skillcentre (formerly GTC) training (all trades) was negative for the 1972–3 trainees surveyed. Moreover, the losses were substantial (as indicated by benefit–cost ratios of 0.5 at a discount rate of 10%). There were some differences between trades; construction trades showed a positive return after six years, but all other trades were negative over the full ten-year time horizon. There was also some regional variation in the results. Generally, training displayed higher rates of return in the North than in the South.

However, like the earlier contractor, TSA analysts did not conclude the analysis at this stage. They also pursued the evaluation of indirect effects although in a more circumspect fashion than the original contractor. The 1976 paper varied the replacement and displacement fractions in a manner similar to the Phase I Report. Again, this had the effect of improving profitability, with the key variable being replacement. Introducing externalities did not affect the order of economic precedence among the training trade groups, but it did affect the regional breakdowns. With externalities returns to training in the South exceeded those in the North, this being a reversal of the pattern of results without externalities. The change was explained by pointing to the higher cost of forgone earnings in the South than in the North. Variations in replacement, it was argued, affected the Southern results more than the Northern results.

In the months following the initial presentation of the 1976 paper, the Phase II results were circulated to a number of groups both inside the TSA and outside through the media of unpublished papers and seminar presentations. These papers and presentations attempted to interpret not only the Phase II results, but also the results of the earlier papers on training. They gave particular attention to such issues as the relationship between training objectives and the format of economic analysis, trends in the evaluation results and the implications of the training study for training policy.

The first papers in the training study had, in line with human capital theory, assumed that the focus on earnings in training evaluation can be justified because increased earnings are a good, if not perfect, proxy for increased productivity. In circulating the Phase II results, TSA officials also argued that earnings differentials could be used as a measure in the assessment of whether or not 'objectives' other than higher productivity were being fulfilled by training. Training programmes were said to be geared to reducing unemployment, and higher earnings, therefore, constituted a measure of whether this goal had been achieved. Increased earnings were also felt to be a measure of the general success of training programmes, including, for example, their contribution to equity. Thus, earnings differentials became a proxy measure corresponding to a variety of macroeconomic objectives.

Consideration was also given to the trend in results from the training evaluations. In particular, the results from the Phase I Report and the Heriot-Watt data were compared with the results from Phase II. The view was that the results were not so different as to preclude comparison. Correcting for geographical location, rates of return excluding externalities were found to fall substantially between 1965–6 and 1968–9 and fall again, but less dramatically, between 1968–9 and 1972–3. When externalities were included, the results remained relatively stable over the time period under consideration.

Finally, the implications of the evaluation results for training policy received attention. From the TSA perspective, the results suggested that the mid-1970s emphasis on training investment and training targets should be re-examined. The positive results obtained when externalities were included were said to confirm the general value of the 1970s expansion in training facilities. However, the assumptions sustaining these positive results were seen to require further consideration, especially as earnings differentials did not appear to have been improving since 1965 if externalities were not included in training evaluation. Given this, the conclusion was that further work might warrant a 'go-slow' approach to training with greater attention to selective investment in profitable trades.

In response to the circulation of the Phase II results, economists and administrators at the Treasury urged that more work be done on the indirect effects of training, as this seemed to be an important, or potentially important, area of impact upon the economy. However, TOPS officials were generally sceptical about the value of the evaluation project for their operations. Their central argument was that cost–benefit result from 1972–3 when the labour market was generally buoyant had little, if any, relevance for decisions concerning training in 1976–7 given the depressed state of the labour market in these latter years. In addition, TOPS officials emphasized that Skillcentres constituted only one part of their operations and that, therefore, the training study did not throw any light on aggregate training targets or on questions such as the trade-off between clerical and non-clerical training that were at that time at the centre of the debate about resource allocation within TOPS.

Despite the attitude of the TOPS officials, development of the probabilistic model proceeded apace, as did the investigation of replacement and displacement. Early in 1978, for example, the TSA group produced a paper that compared the Phase II figures for earnings in the absence of training, obtained using a control group, with figures for non-trainee earnings obtained using a Markov chain simulation. This analysis suffered from many of the weaknesses inherent to the early papers on Markov chain simulation (especially the tendency to confuse extrapolations with actual data about earnings). At the same time, it indicated the compelling attraction of the contractor's original search for a regularized and inexpensive way of assessing costs and benefits from training.

Conclusions

During the course of the late 1950s and early 1960s official perspectives regarding vocational training (and other aspects of labour policy) altered quite markedly, largely as a result of the poor performance of the British economy at a time when many European countries were experiencing long periods of sustained growth. The view of training that emphasized its contribution to social welfare and the reduction of unemployment was surrendered in favour of a much more instrumental interpretation, one that gave great weight to the connection between training and productivity and, therefore, to the efficient use of human resources. As indicated in the earlier sections of this chapter, the economics profession benefited from this reinterpretation of training and the focus upon active programmes of manpower development that followed from it. However, British economists only entered the field in full force after they had mastered the tenets of the theory of human capital, and in most instances, this did not occur until the early 1970s.

The training study examined in this chapter was both the first concerted attempt to evaluate British institutional training in economic terms and a methodological experiment designed to determine whether or not the cost–benefit approach to the assessment of Skillcentre profitability, suitably adapted, was a credible means of monitoring the economic worth over the long term of at least one type of publicly sponsored training. As such, it embodied many of the simplifications characteristic of rational approaches to analysis. The training process is portrayed as a black box through which identifiable but essentially characterless individuals flow. Actors are reduced to their actions – whether they enter training or not, whether they receive a diploma or not, whether they enter work or not. This is especially evident in the discussion of displacement and replacement effects. Just as importantly, human thought processes are simplified. The assumption is that trainees assimilate the investment good (training) in a way that is non-problematic. There is no concern with how men augment their capabilities through training, only with the translation of training into labour market effects.

Yet despite its radical simplicity, the cost–benefit approach to training evaluation commanded a reasonable degree of credibility within official circles. There was an acceptance of the either/or junctures circumscribing the training process because these invoked the market. Moreover, training was viewed as an essentially unproblematic, static transformation process. Where there was concern, it focused on the need to demonstrate profitability, the need to relate training to as many economic objectives as feasible and the desirability of real-time training evaluation. The last demanded the simplification of the 'do-nothing' scenario.

Confronted with these imperatives, the contractor and, by extension, his official sponsors reacted in ways that indicate a strong adherence to the rational ideal. Given that the measurement of the direct benefits of training presented a variety of difficulties, the early papers in the training study focused on indirect effects and on time horizons – both of which could be expressed arithmetically. Moreover, several years later even the problem of direct benefit measurement yielded to a fully arithmetic treatment. Dissatisfied with control group methodology as a means of approximating the 'do-nothing' situation, the contractor decided to employ probabilistic modelling to simulate the labour market experience of non-trainees. This resulted in the full abstraction of the presentation of the 'do-nothing' situation from its former grounding in the behaviour of near-trainees, despite the fact that there were no particular reasons for confidence in the transition probabilities, or, indeed, in the probabilistic model upon which the calculation of average earnings for non-trainees had come to be centred. It was enough that the calculation of earnings was relatively simple and apparently determinate.

These efforts to calculate the economic impact of training displayed commitments to the rational ideal that went beyond a focus on numbers. For example, little empirical justification was provided for the analytical devices employed. This is especially marked in the case of the choice of time horizon for the evaluation of GTC training, the choice of transition probabilities for the simulation model, and the choice of replacement and displacement fractions for the assessment of indirect benefits. Instead of empirical validation, there are appeals to the reader's good sense, to sensitivity testing and, in the case of the time horizon for evaluation, to extrapolation. The important point in this connection is that each of these tactics is consistent with the casual knowledge syndrome or the anti-empiricism syndrome described in Chapter 1. The results achieved through these tactics were significant too. Specifically, they served to highlight sets of *numbers* (e.g. the transition probabilities, the replacement and displacement fractions) at the expense of the structure of the variables these numbers supposedly represented. Beyond this, they enouraged the conflation of analysis and evaluation in the assessment of training.

Did this approach succeed in persuading officials that the economic worth of vocational training could be evaluated in the ways outlined above? In one very important respect, the answer is yes. Officials may have had doubts about certain aspects of the evaluative methodology (e.g. the general suitability of the transition probabilities), but they were apparently convinced of the value of its logic. Indeed, the training project clearly illustrates that economists can exercise considerable influence within the administrative environment solely by stressing that they, as interpreters of the fundamental tenets of economic theory, are capable of making sense of the policy problems at hand. Certainly, the major thrust of the training evaluation project was in this direction. Especially from the Phase I Report onwards, there was more interest in establishing a credible methodology for assessing profitability over the long term than in reviewing the significance (or lack of it) of specific results. This had considerable appeal for officials. The arithmetic approach to training evaluation meant that monitoring could be apparently determinate, and the various numbers employed lent something resembling concreteness to the exercise. The Markov chain model promised to eliminate the substantial costs and aggravation associated with the use of control group methodology. Finally, the new methodology had the advantages of allowing administrators to take a very liberal view of what vocational training achieves. The Phase I approach was essentially agnostic with regard to the nature of the training process, and certain administrators were critical of this. But, as economists in TSA later noted, it also enabled administrators to appeal to one or several of a variety of macroeconomic objectives in justifying training programmes. This flexibility can be useful in the administrative environment.

6

Microeconomics and health: screening for spina bifida

Economic analysis and health

It is only in the last fifteen to twenty years that health care delivery has become a significant field of study for British economists, and even more recently that cost–benefit analysis has been used in any systematic way.[1] Until the mid-1960s most of the economic reasoning that was applied to the care supplied by the National Health Service (NHS) tended to be naive by economic standards. Costings were often elaborate, but little or no consideration was given to the alternative ends to which scarce resources might be allocated or to alternative means of delivering specified services. From the standpoint of the economics profession, traditional clinical medicine of the 1950s was dominated by an unreasoned emphasis upon the continuous elaboration of established practice through yearly increases in funding across all fronts.[2]

Economic analysis might well have continued to have had a limited role in the health field. Even in recent years discriminating economists have admitted that the tools of economics may be very blunt in the evaluation of health care delivery. This arises from a recognition that many of the categories of the multipolar model of the market have limited plausibility in the health field. First, and foremost, the development of a Neoclassical demand function for health care in the British context is fraught with difficulties. The NHS guarantees that for the vast majority of Britons there is no market for health care. Thus, demand for care cannot be assessed as the amount that individuals are willing and able to pay at some prevailing price, for prices in this sense are generally not part of the institutional arrangements for the delivery of health care that apply in the UK.[3] It follows, moreover, that economists cannot readily identify the mechanism whereby individual demands for health care are constrained so that an optimal solution to the problem of the allocation of limited resources is possible.

In addition, the profession has been obliged to recognize that the provision of health care is an area in which the egalitarianism and individualism of the multipolar model have limited relevance. In contrast to the Neoclassical model, in which both the formulation of wants and their curtailment are processes inherent to individuals, no description of the provision of health care can neglect to mention that the amount of care an individual receives depends upon the nature of the relationship that has evolved between the individual and his medical adviser.[4] Medicine operates with the concept of need, rather than demand because medical professionals not only give care but also arbitrate as to the degree of care that individuals receive (this is known as the 'agency relationship'). Even superficially, medicine presents a much more structured problem than the amorphous, multipolar model is able to accommodate. There is, thus, no escape from the 'morass of needology' that encompasses medicine.[5]

The difficulties the profession encounters in the health field are not confined to the problem of demand. In Chapter 1, it was noted that economic rationality subordinates problems associated with knowledge and technology so that the allocation problem can be addressed. This type of subordination is only plausible, however, in special circumstances. The cost–benefit studies analysed in Chapter 5 were made possible because the training process was regarded as transparent and unchanging. In the COBA case the impact of the road-building technologies in use was sufficiently removed and sufficiently long-term that it never posed a direct challenge to the adequacy of those technologies or to the evaluative strategies in which they were assumed. In medicine, however, these conditions never fully apply, and are only approximated in very limited circumstances. In general, medical technologies are in a state of flux, and medical practitioners are endlessly engaged in assessing the degree to which certain types of treatment are justified given the 'state of the art' at a specific point in time, the severity of the diseases and cases under consideration, and the wishes of the patients concerned. Furthermore, the issue of technological adequacy is not easily avoided or postponed. Since mortality and morbidity are at stake, professional ethics require doctors and other health professionals to be scrupulous in ensuring that medical treatment is genuinely conducive to improved health or, in the case of preventive programmes, that tests and advice are neutral. For this reason health economists are seldom able to subsume problems of knowledge and technology to the same degree as economists in other areas of study.

Another feature of the ends–means grammar that is implausible in a medical context is the emphasis it assigns to discretely distinct choices in the allocation of given means to given ends. This emphasis is epitomized by the terms 'alternative' and 'trade-off', which are consistently at the centre of an economist's vocabulary when he is arguing for the application of economic reasoning in a new area.[6]

Chapter 4 contains evidence to the effect that the economist's commitment to choice diminishes as his methods and worldview become institutionalized and his authority increases concomitantly. Health economics is an area in which this process has apparently not proceeded very far. Instead, health economists adhere closely to the doctrine of choice, for the obstacles to the 'formalization of choice' (in the manner characteristic of the COBA system, for example) are formidable.

Economists operate with a specialized concept of choice in which the social actor faces an array of distinct options, and by experimenting with various substitutions at the margin, attempts to maximize his satisfaction given the circumstances of his particular equilibrium. This understanding may appear to have a certain plausibility when options are separable as in the case of the highway schemes described in Chapter 4. However, these circumstances are exceptional, rather than routine, in the public policy field. The exercise of choice, either for the individual or for the polity, is usually concerned with options that are at least as temporally, spatially and structurally differentiated as the options that confront a chess player in the middle stages of a chess game's development.[7] Yet in addressing the problem of choice economics is equipped with a logical structure that is more primitive than the flow-charts and logical trees of elementary decision theory.

This approach to choice is a liability in the health field. Health care goods are rarely infinitely divisible and subject to indifferent substitution. Rather these goods, and the technologies in which they figure, are frequently structured such that ends and means (or both) are integrated and often hierarchically ordered. Acceptable clinical outcomes for many diagnostic systems, for example, are premised upon the adequacy of each component in an ordered and mutually dependent set of procedures. Contrary to the thrust of the ends–means grammar, the development of a satisfactory good at a crucial stage in such a system may well be a precondition for the definition, much less the exploitation, of the technology in question. In addition, the successful treatment of many conditions is based upon the ordering and reconciliation of outcomes (as in the treatment of a heart patient who develops diabetes). Under both sets of circumstances the economic conception of choice is inapplicable because ends and means are not discretely distinct and, therefore, amenable to being manipulated and juxtaposed under the influence of a decision rule so that the most advantageous combinations fall out. Furthermore, in many aspects of medicine the distinction between ends and means cannot be readily sustained, even as a heuristic. Some forms of treatment yield results that cannot be reproduced by alternative methods.

Others alter the system to which they are directed in irreversible ways. In these instances, means are to varying degrees assimilated to ends, and it proves fruitless to attempt to allocate ends and means to separate arrays in the tradition of economic analysis.

Despite these limitations, the economics profession has made headway in the health field to the extent that a recognizable speciality, health economics, has emerged. Partly this was in response to the tremendous impetus provided by the previously mentioned human capital research programme. A much more important contributor, however, was the issue of cost.

Health care costs and preventive strategies

During the 1960s in almost all industrialized countries health expenditure became the centre of a debate concerning the most appropriate ways in which to deliver health services given the relationships between various institutional arrangements, cost and standards of care prevailing at the time. In the United States and Canada the debate involved the consideration of a number of suggestions for institutional change, including national health insurance, a proposal that was adopted in Canada but not in the United States. In Britain, the institutional pattern for health care delivery was established in the immediate post-war period with the creation of the NHS, and this pattern was not challenged to any great degree in the 1960s. Yet in Britain, as elsewhere, political parties debated the merits of the level and rate of growth of health expenditures as a percentage of Gross National Product (GNP). Although Britain ranked low among industrialized nations both in the share of GNP devoted to health and in the growth of that share over the 1960s,[8] the series of economic crises that plagued Britain during the decade and the concomitant belief of a sizeable fraction of the public that Britain was spending too much in the public sector served to sharpen the debate over costs in the health sphere.

The issue of costs facilitated the entry of economists into the health field in Britain and other countries. The profession argued that health expenditure could be more easily controlled if greater attention were given to efficiency in the delivery of health care, although the detailed interpretation of this concept has remained in dispute among health economists.[9] Moreover, it soon became clear that the efficiency ideal could serve a variety of ends. Certain health economists found support for their work within universities and research institutes, others within government. Still others found sponsorship from private manufacturing groups with a stake in the health sector and an interest in ensuring that economic analysis bolstered their reputation as economizers of resources and, at the same time, left the market for health care products intact. One organization that epitomized this latter type of sponsorship was the Office of Health Economics created by the pharmaceutical manufacturers in 1962 'because of their concern at that time over the widespread misunderstandings about expenditure on health'.[10]

While, as one might expect, the foregoing groups of economists have not always agreed about appropriate methodologies and correct policy stances, they have all been engaged in a similar learning process in the health field, the more so because their work has largely been addressed to the same audience, essentially medical professionals and the administrators of the Department of Health and Social Security (DHSS). In particular, all these groups have learned that economic analysis, if it is to be heeded, must not overtly contradict either the professional ideals or the ethical standards espoused by the British medical profession. For example, as noted in Chapter 4, British economists concerned with road accidents have employed lost output as a measure of the cost of mortality, a method that is apparently legitimate in America where it has been used to support heart and cancer campaigns. The Office of Health Economics used the lost output measure in its early reports, but later decided to exclude calculations of this type from its work because 'the real effect of changes in mortality come in their long-term effect on the demographic structure of the community and these may not always be beneficial'.[11] Government health economists also generally have not employed forgone production or forgone earnings measures, even when these measures might fall on the benefit side of a normative economic analysis.[12] Their experience has been that too often the use of these measures has thrown economic analysis into disrepute because the DHSS's medical advisers, doctors outside the Department and health care pressure groups have interpreted them as an unacceptable attempt to place a value on human life. The primary concern seems to be with mortality, as opposed to morbidity, for there are a limited number of areas (rehabilitation problems, hypertension) in which the consideration of earnings, understood as the ability to support oneself or one's family members, is apparently acceptable.

Moreover, the lost output instance is not the only case in which economists have modified their practices in recognition of the type of social authority that is dominant in the health field. Many of the variables that characterize conventional economic analysis have a reduced importance in studies of health care schemes. The following senior health economist's comments are typical of this orientation. At the end of an article in which he advocated the construction of 'painfulness – degree of restriction of activity' indifference curves to assess 'humanitarian benefits' from health care he wrote:

I am fortified in this view by the dangers I see in the opposite course (which is that economists concentrate entirely on the estimation of costs and 'economic benefits'), because this, unfortunately, taints us with the stigma of a 'commercial' or 'GNP'-oriented approach to health care systems, and while I should be the last to deny the GNP considerations are relevant, I should not wish anyone to think that I believed them to be predominant. It seems, therefore, to be extremely important that we demonstrate our practical concern for health service effectiveness in broader terms than these, and the plan of work set out in this paper is designed to do precisely that.[13]

One indication that the profession is sensitive to accusations of 'commercialism' is the tendency to avoid quantifying externalities. Glass has observed that many health economists have framed their studies in a cost-effectiveness format because of the difficulties of quantifying benefits in both a socially acceptable and commensurable manner.[14] Economists who choose this option have the advantage that their data, which usually take the form of 'administrative' costs, are uncontroversial. However, they are limited in the number of analyses they can perform because situations in which a variety of means can be used to achieve one fixed end are comparatively rare in medicine.

Not only have health economists altered the types of measures and procedures used in their work, they have also reached tacit understandings with the medical community concerning the subject matter of their studies. In general, the profession has tended to avoid the field of curative medicine. It has concentrated, instead, upon preventive medicine, and upon screening in particular. One commentator has remarked that 'the development of screening programmes and presymptomatic treatment was probably more responsible than any other single factor in the introduction of rational economic principles into the assessment of medical care'.[15] As Roberts has noted, it is the series of papers initiated by Reynolds concerning the economic merits of road accident *prevention* (measured in terms of hospital costs and productivity) that is considered to mark the inception of health economics in Britain.[16] Since Reynold's 1956 paper in the area there have been numerous studies focused on prevention with subjects such as polio, tuberculosis, bacteruria, hypertension, smoking, various types of cancer and, more recently, prenatal diagnosis.

Some indication of the reasons for this emphasis upon preventive medicine in the selection of topics for study may be gleaned from a number of papers published in the 1970s that reviewed the course of research in health economics. Roberts and Williams, for example, observed that economic studies in the field of curative medicine have tended to focus upon one of two kinds of issues: alternative types of care or alternative location of care.[17] In both cases, however, economists have found that the number of subjects that they are able to address with some degree of credibility is very limited because of the difficulties associated with the quantification of benefits cited earlier. Generally, they have confined themselves to simple, well-defined problems in which the points at issue centre upon alternative methods of delivering relatively fixed benefits. By way of illustration, there are few instances in which health economists have addressed the issue of 'different subjects for treatment, either within or between conditions'.[18] In contrast, the issue of benefits is not so central to the field of preventive medicine in large part because the ethical codes which circumscribe preventive practice ensure that benefits are unambiguous before medical intervention is contemplated, with the result that the economics profession has been able to identify topics for study in which ends and means are either separable, at least superficially so, or relatively fixed. Just as importantly, the cost issue, which first precipitated the entry of the economics profession into the health field, has acquired a new dimension in prevention. When everyone in society comes to be regarded as a 'potential presymptomatic victim of every disease',[19] programme design demands a cost control element, and there is, therefore, a greater likelihood that economists will be consulted.

Upon entry into the realm of presymptomatic medicine economists elaborated their criteria for selecting topics for investigation still further. In examining the role that economics should play in the evaluation of a particular kind of preventive medicine, screening, for example, J.D. Pole commented:

> It seems reasonable to assume that the introduction or otherwise of screening is more subject to administrative control than are many other types of medical expenditure. The ethical problem is also less obtrusive than elsewhere, as the potential beneficiaries are, of course, unidentifiable before screening takes place. Thus screening is favourably placed for an economic evaluation, although the usefulness of such an appraisal must be the less because there are other fields of medicine to which economic criteria cannot be effectively applied for ethical or administrative reasons.[20]

Two principles of selection are implicit in Pole's discussion of screening:

(1) economists are well advised to choose topics that may be construed in a programme sense, in other words, those that are amenable to administrative rationalization, and
(2) in choosing subject areas economists should avoid topics in which the ethical considerations of the adviser–patient relationship are salient. According to this view, economists will succeed when the subject area is one in which administrative and financial considerations are prominent and ethical and medical considerations are less salient than usual.

Thus, health economists not only favour topics in preventive over curative medicine, but also differentiate topics within the presymptomatic field. This arises in large part from the divisions within preventive practice between primary and secondary prevention.[21] Primary prevention consists in using information available about the incidence of a disease as a basis for attempting to avert or minimize the effects of the condition in question. Secondary prevention, alternatively, is the process of searching for disease at the presymptomatic stage in the population at large or in certain 'high-risk' groups. Thus, an anti-smoking programme designed to curtail the incidence of lung cancer and other diseases related to smoking would fall into the primary prevention category. Secondary prevention for the most part is synonymous with screening individuals to detect health problems.

The two types of prevention present quite different analytical problems. Government reports have drawn attention to the administrative and ethical difficulties of operating programmes in the main areas of primary prevention (smoking diseases, coronary heart disease, alcoholism, dental health, family planning, etc.).[22] In the anti-smoking campaign, for example, administrative objectives have proliferated as each foray by government has been countered by the tobacco interests (through advertising and the introduction of substitutes and additives) and as the many dimensions of the smoking problem have been elucidated. The fight against coronary heart disease, to cite another area, has been complicated because the 'fat–sugar' controversy has given rise to ethical and administrative ambiguities. Government has become engaged in attempts to cover all clinical risks, while administrators and medical practitioners have debated the ethics of recommending specific courses of action given that the aetiology of coronary heart disease is not fully understood.

In comparison, screening remains a relatively rigorous field of medical practice dominated by a strict ethical code. A screening project is not contemplated until the epidemiology of the disease in question is well understood, adequate screening and diagnostic tests are available and, more importantly, patients identified as a result of screening can be given treatment that will improve their condition over what it would have been if screening had not taken place.[23] For these reasons screening is characterized by finite objectives and a relatively clear division of labour between medical personnel and administrators. The logic of screening allows economists to distance themselves from ethical controversy while stressing the possibilities for rationalization inherent in this kind of preventive practice. They have chosen their areas of study accordingly.[24]

The distinctions economists draw between different screening evaluations constitute a final illustration of the pervasive influence of the foregoing selection principles at all levels of economic analysis in the health field. Economists have evaluated a wide variety of screening projects directed at conditions ranging from tuberculosis through different kinds of cancer to genetic disorders of the newborn. The varying clinical and social characteristics of the diseases in question mean that each type of evaluation has a distinct configuration. Some topics are judged to be more amenable to economic analysis than others. For a period in the 1970s this was judged to be the case with prenatal screening, a new speciality in obstetrics that promised reductions in the incidence of congenital disorders.

Prenatal screening is founded upon a series of rapid advances that have taken place in techniques to detect and diagnose 'abnormal conditions of the foetus with the object, where these are serious enough, of considering abortion'.[25] These technical advances have been especially marked for chromosomal abnormalities such as Down's syndrome (mongolism) and malformations of the central nervous system, particularly spina bifida. This kind of screening differs from the more familiar population screening in that no treatment in the conventional sense can be offered once a disease is detected. Doctors can only suggest the termination of an affected pregnancy, although there is always the hope that eventually some *in utero* treatment will become available. From the economic standpoint, prenatal screening is especially amenable to analysis because the effectiveness of treatment is not an issue in the way that it is, for example, in breast cancer or cervical cancer screening.[26] Benefits do not flow to a constituency of suffering individuals, but rather to the parents of a prospectively affected child and to the state in the form of avoided expenditure. In the case of the parents, the benefits are often taken as intangible, but in the case of the state the economist confronts a manageable problem, that of aggregating the costs of caring for a cohort of affected newborns. Thus, the displacement of benefits characteristic of prenatal screening simplifies the evaluation problem. The ends in prenatal screening have appeared to be relatively clearly delineated, and, as a result, economists have felt able to concentrate upon the rational deployment of means within the administrative context of the NHS. Some of the limits of this strategy will be explored later in this chapter, but for the moment it is sufficient to note that economists have favoured the evaluation of screening projects in which the ethical dimension may be sidestepped and the administrative dimension accentuated. In short, economic analysis is viable in the case of prenatal screening because debate need not be excessively preoccupied with the ethical and medical concerns at the clinical level.

To a certain extent economists have compromised their own cognitive standards in submitting to the authority of the medical profession on a number of procedural questions. However, more importantly, health economists have found ways of avoiding the control of the medical profession, especially by selecting topics in the health field that are conducive to the maximal exercise of their own worldview. In favouring topics in preventive medicine over those in curative medicine, in secondary prevention over those in primary prevention and in prenatal screening over those in other types of screening, economists have gravitated towards those areas of study in which a certain distance is easily maintained between the analyst and his work, on the one hand, and the impact (usually construed in ethical terms) of the medical technology under discussion, on the other.

This evolution supports the contention that economists, governed as they are by a rational ideal, give precedence to those topics that are conducive to the subordination of problems of technology and knowledge in favour of problems of administration and allocation. Moreover, the coupling of administrative considerations with ethical considerations in the discussion of the merits of selecting one topic over another at various levels of analysis supports the hypothesis that administrative rationalization is the organizational correlate of the tendency among economists to search out situations in which the ends–means grammar may be plausibly applied. Thus, the evidence indicates that economists adhere fairly rigidly to the rational ideal even in fields in which they are especially vulnerable.

It should be noted, however, that the search for ways to apply economic reasoning in the health field has not been without its contradictions. In attempting to convince other health professionals of the merits of their perspective, health economists have repeatedly emphasized that their expertise lies in assessing alternatives. Earlier in this chapter, this process was referred to as the espousal of the 'doctrine of choice'. However, as they have gained experience in health economics, economists have become more and more discriminating in their selection of topics and, hence, in the range of alternative scenarios that they feel confident in analysing. The result has been that, while the doctrine of choice is perpetuated, the analytical significance of the term 'alternative' in health economics has actually become less and less.

Screening for congenital malformation

The remainder of this chapter is concerned with a specific application of economic analysis to health care, namely the use of cost–benefit analysis in several attempts to evaluate a proposal for a national screening programme designed to detect spina bifida and other neural tube defects in the unborn. A review of the economic analysis that has been performed in this area presupposes, however, a brief description of the experimental and clinical background to the proposal for a national spina bifida screening programme.

Especially since the early 1930s safety during delivery and adequacy of prenatal and postnatal care have been central concerns of the British

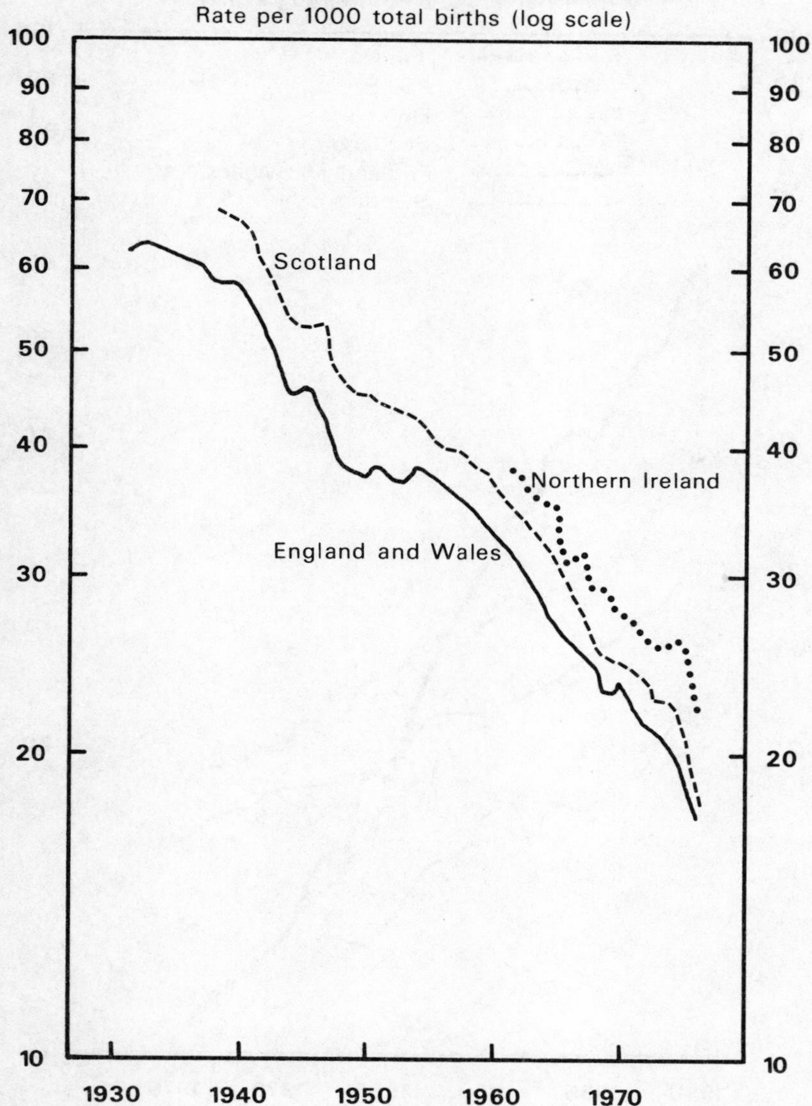

Figure 6.1 Perinatal mortality, 1931–76. Source: Department of Health and Social Security, *Prevention and Health, Reducing the Risk: Safer Pregnancy and Childbirth* (London, HMSO, 1977), p. 11.

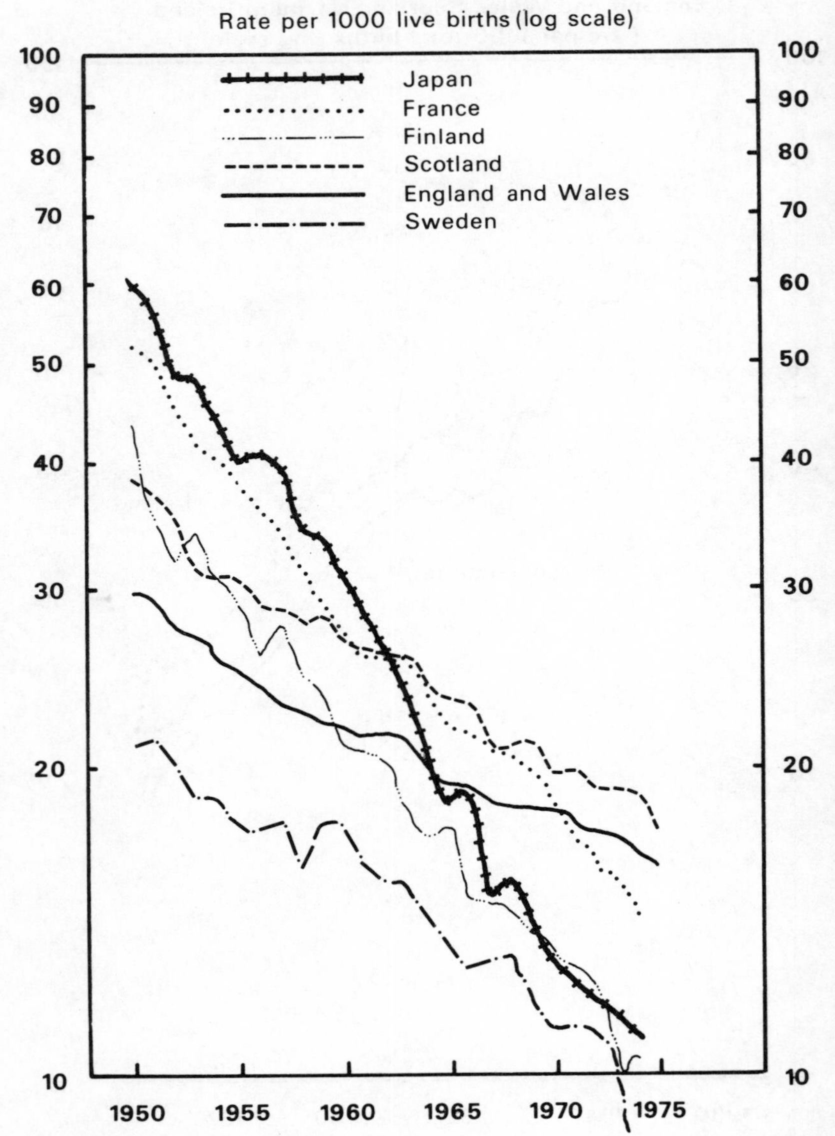

Figure 6.2 Infant mortality in selected countries, 1950–75. Source: Department of Health and Social Security, *Prevention and Health, Reducing the Risk: Safer Pregnancy and Childbirth*, p. 13.

medical profession. The national drive of that period against high maternal mortality levels led to approved professional accreditation and training (College of Obstetricians and Gynaecologists founded in 1929, the Central Midwives Board created under the Midwives Act of 1936), higher levels of hospitalization during delivery, and the widespread use of a number of technical advances in the treatment of haemorrhage following delivery and the control of childhood fever. These developments were complemented by the increasing attention given to maternal nutrition during and after the Second World War, the introduction in 1952 of systematic confidential enquiries into all maternal deaths in England and Wales, and, more recently, the provision of comprehensive information and advice about family planning.[27] The results have been dramatic. In 1975 the number of maternal deaths was between 1 and 2 per 10,000 births in England and Wales compared with 40 to 50 per 10,000 births four decades before.[28] There have also been large declines in perinatal and infant mortality since the 1930s although in the last decade Britain fell behind a number of other industrialized nations in these areas (see Figures 6.1 and 6.2).

The advances made in the fields of obstetrics and pediatrics during the last decades have generally been in the control of infection, the improvement of delivery technique and the regularization of pre- and postnatal care. Not only have these advances been instrumental in reducing maternal and infant mortality rates, they have also contributed to reducing the incidence of certain types of handicap in the newborn.

Thus, immunization for rubella has reduced the incidence of the severe multiple handicap that the presence of a rubella infection early in pregnancy can cause. Improved standards of care during pregnancy and at birth have reduced the risks of handicap associated with fetal oxygen shortage and low birth weight, and the regularization of prenatal care has made more women aware of the risks to the fetus associated with drugs, smoking and excessive alcohol.[29]

However, the risks involved in pregnancy have by no means been eliminated. As deaths and instances of handicap due to infection and poor care have fallen, medical attention has shifted to the consideration of those conditions that have not yielded to improvements in hygiene or medical supervision. Among these are a variety of malformations that present at birth. Unfortunately, significant advances in this area were slow to emerge, despite a major research effort. The thalidomide tragedy served to alert the public and government to the existence of pharmaceutical teratogens, and rubella was identified as an infection with frequent teratogenic effects. Even with these advances, however, infant mortality due to malformations had not decreased by the mid-1970s.[30]

The lack of progress in the field of congential malformations stemmed in part from the fact that the area is characterized, not by one problem, but by many. The term 'malformation' is convenient at the clinical level because it allows the obstetrician to group many of the abnormalities he encounters into one category on the basis of gross symptoms. However, it is not an especially useful research term. In particular it obscures the numerous classification problems that characterize the study of congenital defects. The aetiology of most malformations is complex. For heuristic purposes they may be classified in the following manner: (1) malformations arising from chromosomal abnormalities, (2) malformations produced by environmental factors, in some instances identified as specific teratogens and, (3) malformations arising from a variety of genetic, environmental and social agents interacting in a complex causal mechanism.[31] Down's syndrome is an example of the first type of malformation. By the mid-1970s, a wide variety of agents had been considered as possible initiators of the second type of malformation although the number for which the evidence appeared convincing was limited (e.g. alcohol, anticonvulsants, warfarin, the operating room environment).[32] Spina bifida and other neural tube defects are examples of the third type of malformation. Unfortunately, while this classification may be used as a rough guide in an introductory discussion of congential defects, it highlights, rather than resolves, the many aetiological and epidemiological quandaries that characterize research in this field. The limitations of our understanding in this regard have become especially apparent as researchers and practitioners have sought means to curtail the incidence of malformation.

A number of approaches to reducing the frequency of malformation have been contemplated. One method would be to identify those parents at risk of having an affected child, and then persuade them to avoid conception. However, this course of action presupposes a much more detailed understanding of the origins and incidence of malformation than presently exists in most cases. Epidemiologists have devoted much attention in recent years to the effect of variables such as maternal age, birth order, season of birth, and social class upon the frequency with which malformations occur, but their studies have not yielded many examples of clear associations upon which genetic counselling measures may be founded, with the notable exception of the association between maternal age and Down's syndrome. In some cases high-risk groups have been identified, particularly on the basis that a malformation has already occurred in a previous pregnancy. However, it has been found that the additional risk implied by the existence of a previous affected pregnancy has not been sufficient to dissuade parents in these groups from having another child.[33]

Another approach to the curtailment of the incidence of malformation consists in the selective treatment of defects after birth. Without intervention, in the mid-1970s about 27 in 1000 total births were characterized by some type of malformation, although many of these were minor. Of these 27 affected births, between 1 in 6 and 1 in 10 posed serious problems. In some of these cases of serious disability (e.g. spina bifida cases) life could have been prolonged by medical intervention. However, major problems emerged regarding the morality of lengthening the lives of the severely handicapped.

A further approach to the prevention of malformation consists in attempting to monitor prenatal development so that the risks of producing a malformed baby are reduced. There are two dimensions to this last approach. First, physicians can attempt to ensure that mothers are aware of and avoid all known teratogens (immunization for rubella is a case in point). However, as explained earlier, many malformations are not associated with a specific teratogen, and even if it were possible to ensure that all pregnant women avoided all known teratogens the effect on the frequency of malformation would be small. It is for this reason that the second dimension of this approach to prevention has been emphasized in recent years. This is the attempt to identify malformed embryos or fetuses before birth so that abortions or induction of labour may be offered.

Chemical, chromosomal and physical methods exist whereby a number of malformations in the fetus may be identified with a very high degree of accuracy, but there have been difficulties associated with the application of these methods.[34] Physical methods (sonar scanning, fetoscopy, radiology) have two primary limitations; on their own they may not be sufficient to establish a certain diagnosis and two of the methods (fetoscopy and radiology) have presented hazards both to the mother and to the fetus. Therefore, more and more attention has been devoted over the last fifteen years to chemical and chromosomal methods of detection. Both of these methods depend upon the use of amniocentesis so that material from the uterus can be obtained for analysis. Amniocentesis is a much safer procedure than either fetoscopy or radiology, and the chemical and chromosomal tests that have been developed for use on the uterine material obtained from amniocentesis are very accurate. Nevertheless, in the mid-1970s amniocentesis was estimated to carry about a 1 per cent risk of precipitating an abortion.[35] Moreover, like sonar scanning (ultrasound), amniocentesis is a technique that must be performed by skilled personnel. Also, like ultrasound, assessment is predicated upon the availability of sophisticated and costly equipment. For these two reasons both diagnostic techniques are expensive and, thus, impractical as screening vehicles for a nationwide programme. Yet if the incidence of malformation was to be reduced significantly through prenatal screening techniques either all pregnancies had to come under scrutiny or there had to be at least sufficient epidemiological grounds for the identification of high-risk groups for testing. As noted previously, the latter course is feasible for Down's syndrome (if only for one epidemiological dimension), but is not effective for other conditions. It is for this reason that the discovery in the early 1970s of a method for detecting neural tube defects that did not require material from the uterus was so significant.

Common congential malformations may be grouped according to the bodily system involved. One such group is composed of the neural tube defects (NTDs) including anencephalus and spina bifida cystica.[36] The defects in question are lesions that result in various types of damage to the central nervous system. Anencephalus is a condition in which the brain fails to develop normally, and is almost always fatal at birth or within a few days of birth (only a very few cases of survival to one year have been reported). Spina bifida cystica is a condition characterized by a wide range of disability. The lesions may be either open, if there is exposed neural tissue or a lesion covered by a thin transparent membrane, or closed, if the lesion is covered by skin or thick opaque membrane.[37] Those babies with closed lesions have a better survival rate than those with open lesions, but clinically open lesions are much more common. In the mid-1970s, closed lesions accounted for only about 14 per cent of all NTDs compatible with survival;[38] a fifth of all spina bifida babies (open and closed lesions) were stillborn, and the survival rate for the remainder depended upon the surgical policy that was followed. Those with closed lesions usually survived with little handicap. As for the majority with open lesions, such information as was available in 1976 concerning survival rates under the selective surgical policy generally employed in Britain suggested that about 40 per cent of those babies born with open lesions survived until their fifth year in states ranging from virtually no disability to severe handicap.[39] A mildly disabled spina bifida child is of normal or above normal intelligence but has difficulty walking. A severely or very severely disabled child requires a wheelchair or swivel walker, suffers from incontinence and is generally of below normal intelligence. There are many stages of disability between the mild and the severe.

In their 1976 review of the statistics available concerning amencephalus, spina bifida and congenital hydrocephalus Rogers and Weatherall gave the incidence of notified anencephalus in England and Wales from 1964 to 1972 as 1.81 per 1000 total births and the incidence of notified spina bifida for the same period as 1.74 per 1000 total births.[40] These are, of course, averages. According to the breakdowns presented by the same authors the frequency of both malformations fluctuated over time (see Figure 6.3 for spina bifida), and varied by region. The incidence of anencephalus and

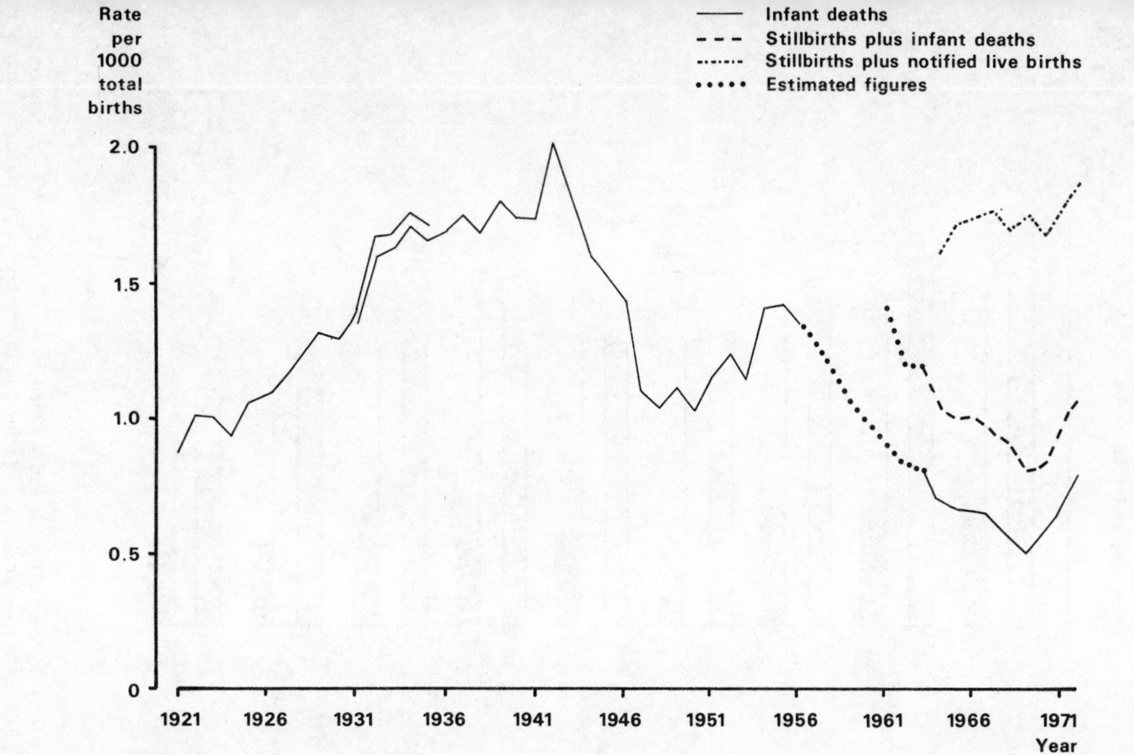

Figure 6.3 Incidence of spina bifida, England and Wales. Source: Dr S.C. Rodgers and Dr J.A.C. Weatherall, *Anencephalus, Spina Bifida and Congenital Hydrocephalus: England and Wales, 1964–72*, Office of Population Censuses and Surveys, Studies on Medical and Population Subjects, No. 32 (London, HMSO, 1976), p. 7.

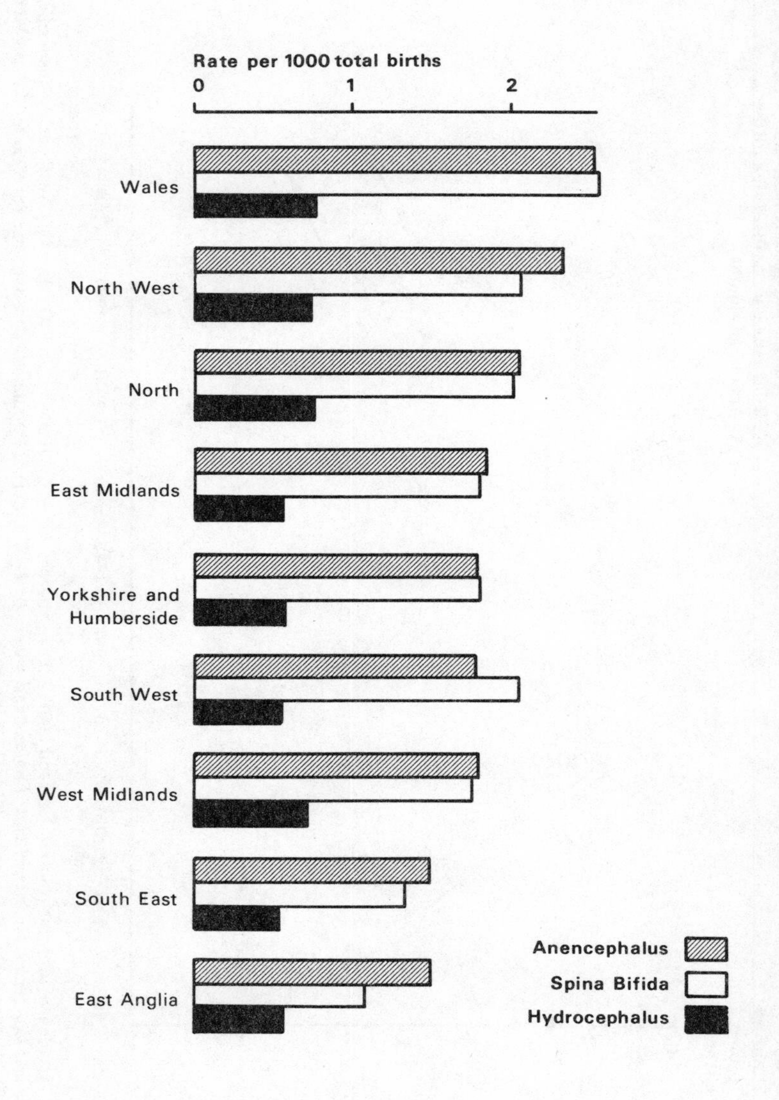

Figure 6.4 Combined stillbirth and notified live birth rate, 1964–72. Source: Dr S.C. Rodgers and Dr J.A.C. Weatherall, *Anencephalus, Spina Bifida and Congenital Hydrocephalus: England and Wales, 1964–72*, p. 23.

spina bifida was highest in Wales, followed by the North West and the North (see Figure 6.4). Outside England and Wales, parts of Scotland and Northern Ireland were recognized to have acute problems. For example, in Belfast the level of incidence for both anencephalus and spina bifida was frequently recorded as about 4 per 1000 total births.[41] These levels of incidence placed anencephalus and spina bifida among the most common of the serious malformations and other (e.g. genetic) disorders that presented at birth. The regional and temporal variability of the incidence of neural tube defects was cited as evidence by researchers that the aetiology of NTDs is not simple.

It is against this complex clinical and epidemiological background that the discovery of a means to diagnose neural tube defects without resort to amniocentesis appears so important. But before discussing this development, it is appropriate to review the more conventional advances in detection based on material from the uterus that preceded it.

In 1972 Brock and his associates at the University of Edinburgh demonstrated that neural tube defects with open lesions could be detected in the unborn by monitoring the concentration of alphafetoprotein (AFP) in the amniotic fluid during early pregnancy. The group at Edinburgh had reasoned that as there was evidence that fetal blood or blood components leak into the amniotic fluid through the open lesions characteristic of most NTD cases it might be possible to use a feto-specific protein as a marker for the presence of lesions.[42] Subsequent trials confirmed that AFP is indeed present in elevated concentrations in the amniotic fluid surrounding a fetus with an open NTD. Moreover, the trials indicated AFP could form the basis of a highly specific test for open NTDs because of the low frequency of 'false positives' in the trials. However, such tests were and are only judged viable for women at risk (i.e. those who have already had a child with an NTD), and even if all women at risk were tested only some 10 per cent of NTD cases would come under scrutiny.

Then in 1973 Brock and his colleagues showed that AFP marking could be carried a stage further. They found elevated levels of the feto-specific protein in the blood serum of mothers with affected pregnancies, and later found strong evidence to the effect that radioimmunoassays for AFP in serum at sixteen weeks of pregnancy could be used to detect open NTDs. Those connected with this early work realized that, unlike the test on amniotic fluid, the serum test is not sufficiently sensitive, or specific, to be used for diagnostic purposes. However, the 1973–4 findings suggested that the serum test might be an effective screening vehicle. In other words, it might be a means of selecting those mothers from a population of pregnant women who would be well advised to submit to amniocentesis and the amniotic fluid test.[43] In 1974 a UK Collaborative Study involving nineteen centres was launched under the auspices of the Institute for

Research into Mental and Multiple Handicap and funded by the Wellcome Trust to consider the clinical merits of this hypothesis.[44]

The UK Collaborative Study reported in 1977, but in the meantime interest developed in the possibility of a large-scale, perhaps nationwide, screening programme for neural tube defects within DHSS. About halfway through the Collaborative Study, the group steering the project invited DHSS to send an observer to their proceedings. In this way neural tube defect screening acquired administrative status as one of the many projects that DHSS monitors in the anticipation that a number of them will merit consideration at the central policy level and possibly eventual implementation. While the Joint Standing Sub-Committee on Screening in Medical Care (formerly under the chairmanship of Professor T. McKeown, Professor of Social Medicine at the University of Birmingham) kept a watching brief on progress in the field of NTD detection, the Department's administrators, sensing that NTD screening promised to be a viable clinical option, initiated studies of their own into the administrative aspects of this type of screening.[45]

Prevention, economy and economic evaluation

Administrative interest in NTD screening within DHSS arose from concern with a number of public issues that began to coalesce in the mid-1970s. In response to the economic restraint that prevailed after 1973, Ministers began to urge the importance of finding ways of economizing in the health care field. In general, government policy tended to discourage initiatives with resource implications unless corresponding benefits could be demonstrated.[46] In a similar vein, Members of Parliament voiced concern with the high and increasing cost of the NHS that 'absorbed 5.65 per cent of Gross Domestic Product in 1975, as opposed to 3.71 per cent in 1959'.[47] The House of Commons Expenditure Committee wondered whether NHS moneys were being allocated in the most effective manner 'in terms of the health benefits conferred'.[48] What is significant for the present discussion is that this concern with effective resource allocation took on a particular complexion. Economy within the NHS came to be identified at least in part with the advocacy of preventive medicine. One manifestation of this was that under the chairmanship of Mrs Renée Short MP, the Social Services and Employment Sub-Committee of the House of Commons Expenditure Committee (the Short Committee) launched an investigation of preventive health services in November 1975, in the belief that prevention might constitute one means of curtailing health care expenditure.[49] The Committee's choice of topic reinforced and publicized a new emphasis upon prevention and economy within DHSS. Although in the course of its proceedings, DHSS officials stressed that preventive medicine was not necessarily less costly, the association between prevention and economy seemed sufficiently substantive to many administrators that they tended to give increased priority to projects of a preventive character that promised government savings.

The administrative and parliamentary advocacy of economy through preventive medicine was further sustained and strengthened because prevention is a medical priority that has been sponsored by a wide variety of groups within the medical community at both the national and international levels. The Short Committee's hearings revealed that the NHS reorganization had not led to an increased emphasis on preventive services as had originally been intended. However, they also demonstrated the existence of a sizeable constituency of medical professionals in areas like health education and the speciality of community medicine for whom prevention is a crucial component of good medical practice. Granted, these professionals, and the groups to which they are affiliated are not especially prestigious within the medical community;[50] nevertheless, in most cases, they are important to the operation of the NHS, and their activities have acquired added stature as interest has increased in recent years outside the medical profession in the proposition that 'it is the way in which western man now lives his life that is the principal factor in the causation of the diseases which afflict him'.[51]

The hearings also revealed that the specialists in community medicine and health education have allies among those who have perceived the numerous research opportunities that follow when a disease is thought of as a potentiality rather than an actuality. Thus, university and medical institute researchers and administrators have joined professionals in community medicine, health education and other areas in urging the importance of prevention. The research dimension has, moreover, constituted a means of linking prevention with prestige medicine. Whether the object of investigation is the aetiology of coronary heart disease or asymptomatic bacteriuria, the merits of the preventive approach must be sustained. Finally, a number of the governing bodies of the medical profession (e.g. the British Medical Association) have accepted that prevention, rather than cure, appeals to consumers' groups concerned with health care and to a public that is better informed about the origins of disease and available methods of curtailing its incidence. In consequence, these bodies have concluded that preventive medicine is too important to be left to the discretion of DHSS alone.

Thus, the 1970s saw the development of a loose compact involving politicians, administrators, certain categories of clinicians and educators, and medical researchers. It centred upon a complex of commitments perhaps best summarized as follows: prevention = good medicine = sensible administration = less costly health care. The last commitment, moreover, provided an entrée for a further set of specialists, namely the economics profession. The emphasis in the 1970s upon prevention and economy, and the relationship between them, parallels the tendency for economists to stress prevention, and within prevention, topics amenable to administrative rationalization in selecting subjects for analysis. Of course, it has not been possible within DHSS to look at prevention simply in cost-benefit terms. The primary justification for a project has always been the reduction of human suffering. Nevertheless, in the wake of the 1973 recession, the ends–means grammar became an important element in the procedures DHSS administrators used to select health projects for consideration by senior officials and Ministers.

Thus, while medical considerations were paramount, economic expertise assumed an increased importance as DHSS administrators launched a number of initiatives in the field of preventive medicine. One of these was concerned with neural tube defects.[52]

By 1976 it had become apparent to DHSS administrators that the UK Collaborative Study results were likely to confirm the clinical feasibility of a screening programme for neural tube defects. These administrators, therefore, began to look more closely at a number of other aspects of NTD screening in anticipation that a Health Circular might eventually be sent to the Regional Authorities recommending the implementation of this type of screening. For example, DHSS officials began negotiations with the Welsh Office concerning the possibility of a jointly funded feasibility study in Cardiff to examine the many specific aspects of introducing an NTD screening programme into routine prenatal care. They also stepped up their monitoring of a number of pilot screening programmes that had been in operation in various parts of the country since 1975. In addition, DHSS staff decided to launch an in-house examination of the economic aspects of NTD screening. An economist from the Department's Economic Advisers' Office (EAO) was called upon to prepare an evaluation of the costs and benefits that would be associated with the introduction of a national programme. The intention of this follow-up research was to have evidence available as to the administrative, technical, psycho-social and economic elements of NTD screening in the event that Ministers wished to proceed to the stage of advising Regional Authorities concerning the benefits of this type of prenatal diagnostic technique.

Economic evaluation of NTD screening

The remainder of this chapter focuses on the specifics of the economic evaluation of NTD screening. It is appropriate, therefore, to present a brief sketch of the organizational context in which this evaluation was conducted. Although the tenets of allocative theory are now commonplace in many areas of health care policy, in the mid-1970s the number of economists within DHSS remained small, and their organizational arrangements fluid. The alliance between administrators and economists in the field of preventive medicine was of recent origin. Moreover, it focused upon only one of the many spheres of activity with which DHSS deals. For these reasons it had not had a noticeable impact upon organizational structures.

Pole has observed that there were two principal causes that led DHSS to employ economists in the study of health and health services.[53] In the first place, a number of senior personnel became concerned with the cost implications of certain forthcoming health care innovations (e.g. mass screening programmes). In addition, the Department wished to enhance its planning capabilities through the introduction of programme budgeting. The organization of the Economic Advisers' Office reflected this. In 1976–7 the EAO, located within the Administration Group at DHSS Headquarters, consisted of a Chief Economic Adviser, a Senior Economic Adviser, and about six Economic Advisers together with a complement of supporting staff at the Economic and Senior Economic Assistant levels. A number of these economists were contributing to planning within the Department generally and to the development of a programme budget in particular. Others were engaged in evaluating medical developments and other policy issues using cost–benefit and cost-effectiveness analysis. In addition, economists in the Office were undertaking projects in the field of social security, especially in the consideration of living standards and income redistribution. Beyond this, certain economists were examining the impact of the Department's revenue and expenditure patterns upon a number of macroeconomic variables, and there was 'a substantial programme of sponsored research in the field of health economics'[54] in which the Department's economists collaborated.

Like economists in other departments, DHSS economists were not involved in line management. Instead, they were required to give advice on policy to the parallel administrative divisions and medical 'commands' of the Department whenever such advice was requested.[55] Again, as in other Departments, DHSS economists were to be found working in areas in which there was some potential for the regularization of tasks (e.g. planning, allocation), but they have not been as successful in this regard as some other government economists. This was especially true of work on the health side, and a number of reasons for this may be gleaned from an examination of the manner in which cost-effectiveness and cost–benefit projects in the medical field were selected and performed.

Typically, the administrative divisions and medical authorities proposed the subject matter for economic evaluations on a 'we need to know' basis.

Creative administration frequently required that departmental analysis keep pace with diverse and often rapid developments at the clinical level. The result was that economists were required to produce original studies in short periods of time (six months was average), often in circumstances in which adequate data was scarce. Moreover, the character of medicine and medical technology is such that in each project ends and means were usually integrated and ordered in distinct patterns (or configurations). Thus, it was rare that analytical frameworks or measures used in one project could be applied without modification to the next. Hence, the economists' efforts tended to be fragmented and without a clear focus.[56] Nevertheless, the emphasis assigned to preventive medicine meant that the subjects proposed to the Economic Advisers' Office for economic analysis became more frequently amenable to economic evaluation. This was especially true of the proposal for a national NTD screening programme.

When the possibility of an NTD screening service was first broached in economic terms within DHSS a number of precedents had already been established in the economic analysis of prenatal screening programmes. The most important of these are worth reviewing.

In 1973 a paper by Stein *et al.* considered the feasibility of introducing a prenatal screening programme for Down's syndrome in New York City.[57] For some years it had been possible to detect this condition in the fetus by amniocentesis and karyotyping. As noted earlier, the British medical community has not been able to condone amniocentesis as a screening technique, but this type of procedure has been advocated in a number of places in the literature. What is singular about the 1973 study is that, along with other issues, the authors examined the efficacy of Down's syndrome screening from an economic standpoint. While not strictly an economic analysis, the paper weighed the cost of screening against the burden of caring for affected children and found:

> The cost of screening mothers over thirty, at the current rates charged in New York City, is certainly less than that of caring for cases of Down's syndrome among them. We are less certain about the balance of costs at current rates, of screening the whole pregnant population. But is a detailed estimate of money costs required? The lifelong care of severely retarded persons is so burdensome in almost every human dimension that no preventive programme is likely to outweigh the burden.[58]

Given the rising prevalence of Down's syndrome and the high specificity of karyotyping as a diagnostic technique, the judgement was that there were no economic grounds to prevent the eventual introduction of universal screening for the condition. Instead, the paper considered that the major obstacle to screening lay in restrictive legal and social policies with regard to abortion generally. However, it went on to note that in New York State, Britain, Sweden, and Japan, and other jurisdictions where there are no bars to legal abortion, prenatal screening for Down's syndrome might be adopted in stages with the ultimate objective of universal screening. The reasoning was that if screening were introduced gradually, beginning with those most at risk, manpower shortages could be avoided and any risks associated with the programme could be monitored, and, if possible, minimized.

The evaluation by Stein *et al.* of Down's syndrome screening introduced economic arguments into the discussion of prenatal disease detection, although not in such a way as to encourage detailed economic analysis in the field. Nevertheless, it was a beginning, and the correspondence that ensued from their paper, a Technical Report from the World Health Organization and contemporaneous work by Milunsky, confirmed that medical practitioners were willing to tolerate a certain level of economic debate in this area.[59] Moreover, the 1973 study had dealt explicitly with the ethical aspects of prenatal screening, and had concluded that in a legal and social climate that permitted elective abortion it did not present contentious ethical problems. This expression of medical opinion proved a useful bridgehead between ethics and economics to those economists who subsequently entered the field. Economic analyses of prenatal screening published after 1973 generally took the position that the ethics of abortion, therapeutic or otherwise, is beyond the economics profession's sphere of competence, while at the same time contending that medical precedents in the field of ethics lent plausibility to the application of economic analysis in this area.

In Britain, too, economic evaluation of proposals for Down's syndrome screening paved the way for similar work on NTD screening. A 1975 paper on Down's syndrome screening, prepared by the analyst who later undertook the first government-sponsored evaluation of NTD screening, established a number of precedents in this field.[60] In particular, it pointed to the lack of any detailed economic, and specifically quantitative, analysis to sustain the conclusions of Stein *et al.* about the feasibility of a screening programme for Down's syndrome. On the basis that resources devoted to screening for Down's syndrome might be deployed in other ways, the 1975 paper recommended that screening of this type be treated like any other investment and evaluated using the 'well-tested techniques' of allocative theory.[61]

In order to realize this project the ends and means associated with the investment, as well as the concomitant gainers and losers of Paretian theory, had to be identified. This was accomplished in a singular manner. The 1975 study argued that benefits accrue to the parents of an affected fetus in the form of avoided expenditure and to the state in the form of avoided outlays for the institutional care of affected children. Alternatively, losses are incurred by the state in the form of the costs of the screening programme. This was a limited interpretation of costs and benefits in the first instance. On the benefit side, the analysis of the expenditure avoided by the parents was cursory, consisting only of an estimate of the expenditure avoided through not having an additional child whether with Down's syndrome or not, and the anguish avoided by the parents was not pursued in any depth. On the cost side, no account was taken of the lives that are curtailed as a result of screening or of the effects of losing a child upon the parents (e.g. emotional and psychological distress, effects on future reproductive patterns).

As noted earlier, medical opinion has generally precluded the consideration of expenditure forgone as a result of mortality (in later studies of this kind only social security payments for the maintenance of affected children have been taken into account). Moreoever, the reluctance to attribute 'losses' to the unborn may explain the analyst's wish to avoid the abortion issue. It is more difficult, however, to account for the neglect in the 1975 paper of the effects of losing a child upon the parents as against the anguish avoided through not bearing an affected child. However, some understanding of the reasoning involved may be gained from the following passage:

> As for the parents of Mongoloid children, there would appear to be conflicting views on the extent to which they find the burden of caring for their children intolerable. But even if it were true that the burden is an intolerable one from the parents' point of view this is not altogether germane. Since the 'community' is to provide the resources for a screening program, the question to be decided is whether 'the community' regards the burden borne by the affected parents as intolerable. This is clearly a rather different question from that of whether the parents themselves find it intolerable.[62]

The paper presented the argument that because only approximately 10 per cent of children with Down's syndrome were institutionalized in Britain in 1975, either the parents do not find the burden of care intolerable or the community does not judge that the burden justifies the allocation of more resources to institutional care. Thus, the specific effects of a screening programme upon individuals were not central to this evaluation as they have been at least nominally central to cost–benefit studies discussed in previous chapters. Rather, the concept of community was emphasized without being explicated in terms of the conventional gainers and losers of welfare theory, and the analysis was, therefore, less a cost–benefit study and more a review of the implications of Down's syndrome screening for public expenditure.[63]

This emphasis on public sector resource costs (and benefits in the form of avoided costs) is reflected in the paper's focus on the administrative and financial implications of screening. The costs of a screening programme were identified as the hospital resources required for amniocentesis, plus the laboratory resources for karyotyping. In order to arrive at a total figure that reflected the specific epidemiological and clinical features of Down's syndrome, it reviewed the incidence of the disease by age group, the likelihood that prospective mothers would report to a medical agency in time for effective treatment, and the probable current and capital expenditure required to provide safe amniocentesis and subsequent karyotyping. The benefits from screening were seen as stemming from savings to the state as a result of forgone institutional care, training and family costs. These were calculated using information that had recently been collected concerning the average lifetime experience of children with Down's syndrome.

Based on the foregoing assumptions, the 1975 study found that screening was economically justified for women over 40, but not for women of 40 and under. This was in marked contrast to the study by Stein *et al.*, which had called for universal screening. In the opinion of one commentator, the 1975 paper had shown that economic analysis could exclude as well as justify a contemplated project.[64] Nevertheless, the evaluation was questioned on a number of counts, even by those sympathetic to the methodology. The results are, of course, premised upon a discounting procedure, and the study followed standard practice in using the Treasury's 10 per cent figure. Discounting has a dramatic effect upon the estimation of benefits in this instance because most of the institutional savings associated with Down's syndrome screening do not occur until fifteen or more years after the birth of an affected child. The foregoing commentator felt that applying a conventional discounting procedure to screening was fraught with danger presumably because discounting presupposes an overly simple relationship between time and benefit.[65] Suffice it to say here that a proposal for Down's syndrome screening would suffer by comparison with a screening proposal involving a condition requiring more immediate treatment if the 1975 procedure were to be universally applied. Another criticism of this approach centred upon its refusal to assess, even if only qualitatively, the less tangible externalities associated with screening.[66]

The 1975 paper on Down's syndrome established some of the procedures that were to apply in the government evaluation of NTD screening, notably the emphasis on public sector resource costs and the reluctance to associate the impact of screening with individuals. In addition, its conclusions regarding the economic feasibility of Down's syndrome screening were to receive broad confirmation in a 1976 cost–benefit analysis of Down's syndrome screening undertaken by S. Hagard and F.A. Carter (a doctor and an operations research specialist, respectively).[67] But while the results of the two evaluations were similar (largely as a result of the dramatic effects of discounting), the

Hagard and Carter study demonstrated that the 1975 approach to screening evaluation was by no means definitive. In particular, the 1976 paper considered a number of variables which the 1975 study had excluded from its brief, such as the effects of bearing a child with Down's syndrome upon the mother's future employment prospects. The Hagard and Carter study also introduced the concept of 'replacement' into its evaluation. The argument was that the benefit derived from preventing the birth of an affected child should be measured in relation to the secondary impact of screening, in other words, whether or not the parents have another child after the first has been aborted as a result of the proposed preventive programme. If the parents have another child (replacement), the argument went, the benefit from screening is the difference between the cost of caring for a handicapped child and the cost of caring for a normal child. It can be objected that this procedure is illegitimate because the foregoing measures are associated with an event (the birth of another child) that, in the absence of evidence to the contrary, must be assumed to be unconnected with the programme under evaluation. Nevertheless, however questionable the replacement concept was, it did constitute an attempt to anchor the economic analysis of Down's syndrome screening in individual measures, something the 1975 paper did not do.

In 1976 Hagard and Carter, in this instance aided by R.G. Milne, an economist, also published a detailed cost–benefit study of the feasibility of an NTD screening service based on Brock's blood serum test.[68] The object was to construct and test a cost–benefit index for NTD screening using statitics from the West of Scotland. However, this time, possibly as a result of the influence of Milne, the 'replacement' concept was dropped. NTD screening constituted a much more complex proposition than screening for Down's syndrome epidemiologically, clinically and in terms of the natural history of the conditions that present at birth. The study sought to accommodate this complexity. In particular, it considered the sensitivity and specificity of both the screening and diagnostic tests for neural tube defects upon the cost–benefit index. It also considered antenatal attendance, attitudes on the part of mothers towards amniocentesis and the availability of ultrasonography for 'checking dates' as variables affecting the coverage and specificity of screening.

The study also reviewed the relationship between regional location and incidence, arguing that if a national screening programme were not possible, it might be feasible to introduce screening into those areas (Western Scotland and Belfast were cited) where the incidence of malformation is high. It concluded that there was a strong economic case for introducing a screening programme in the West of Scotland. More generally, the study emphasized that the cost–benefit index it contained is a function of the sensitivity of the screening test and the incidence of malformation. If the sensitivity of the screening test were low (below 40–50 per cent), screening might only be justified in areas where the incidence of malformation is high (above 2.5 per thousand total births for spina bifida).

This, then, was the state of the art in the economic evaluation of prenatal screening when DHSS officials requested an analysis of NTD screening from the Economic Advisers' Office.[69] The analyst assigned to the study was impressed by both the comprehensiveness and detail of the work of Hagard *et al.*, but their approach was not adopted unconditionally. In the first place a number of departmental policy positions had to be taken into account. For example, administrators within DHSS were only interested in the viability of a national screening programme for NTDs because it was judged that a regional approach would be politically untenable. More importantly, the DHSS evaluation, like the 1975 paper on Down's syndrome, avoided the consideration of any effects that were not the immediate concern of the public sector. Thus, the 'spina bifida' evaluation was limited to a review of the economic consequences of spina bifida screening for the government purse, and all measures of costs and benefits to the individual were excluded (including, for instance, the costs that Hagard *et al.* had imputed to patients and their spouses for travelling and time off work incurred as a result of screening).

This interpretation of the brief simplified the task substantially. Indeed, the study, when complete, resembled the 1975 Down's syndrome study in its almost exclusive emphasis upon the administrative and financial features of screening. On the cost side, it focused upon the incidence of malformation nationally, the expected participation rates for the programme (by gestational age and social class) and the characteristics both of the serum test and of amniocentesis, including the issue of whether or not ultrasound should be provided in certain cases to ascertain gestational age more accurately. On the benefit side, the study reviewed the incidence of NTD malformations, and estimated the survival rates and levels of disability for those babies with NTDs born alive in the future. The costs to the public sector of maintaining these children were then calculated. These included the use of hospital resources, allowances for appliances to aid mobility, education and social security payments. The paper concluded that if a 75 per cent screening test sensitivity is assumed 'the public sector costs avoided by preventing the birth of an affected cohort exceed the public sector costs of the screening programme within one year in all cases'. Alternatively, if a 45 per cent sensitivity is assumed, it was estimated that the programme would pay for itself within, at most, four years.[70]

This emphasis on the administrative and financial implications of NTD screening conformed with the EAO's perspective on economic evaluation. The important features of an analysis were generally considered to be the generation of accurate programme costings and the investigation of alternatives that would enhance the policy objectives and the economic status of the project.

In the case of the spina bifida study, the importance of the departmental evaluation lay in the discussion of alternatives given prevailing medical opinion and the work that had already been performed in the field. These referred to public sector costs. For example, the Office's work introduced some flexibility into the discussion of participation rates for screening. In discussing the characteristics of the screening test the DHSS evaluation observed that, if no publicity were employed, participation rates would depend upon the choice of cut-off date (i.e. the date beyond which an abortion for therapeutic reasons becomes impossible given existing estimates of risks to the mother). Like Hagard *et al.*, the DHSS study pursued the implications of choosing a fairly late cut-off date. The suggestion was that a screening test might be undertaken as late as the 20th week of pregnancy.[71] Unlike Hagard *et al.*, however, the DHSS paper also pursued the effect of this recommendation upon participation rates (assuming no publicity). Using data for hospital attendance in a number of urban centres, it estimated that about two-thirds of those women who proceed to term would report for examination by 16 weeks, a further 10 per cent by 18 weeks, and another 5 per cent by 20 weeks. On this basis, it recommended that a screening test could be conducted at any time between 16 and 20 weeks, arguing that even in the absence of publicity the figures justified weighing the advantages of discovering a greater number of cases against the disadvantages of late abortion. In this instance, the trade-off concept was employed to broaden the temporal spectrum under consideration, and, thus, the discussion of policy options.

The DHSS evaluation broadened options in a second sense. Hagard *et al.* had envisaged five or six regional laboratory centres to handle the analysis of the blood samples obtained during screening. However, DHSS estimated that the cost-effectiveness of the programme could be enhanced if only one or two centres were established. The anticipation was that certain economies of scale would result if the number of centres were reduced, including the use of a fully automated, as opposed to a semi-automated, assay process. Yet while the one- or two-centre proposal seemed the less costly the fully automated technique was relatively untested in 1976.

Finally, and again on the cost side, the DHSS evaluation included a discussion of the clinical options available during screening and subsequent diagnosis. In particular, it noted that the AFP test depends crucially upon the correct estimation of gestational age. Levels of AFP rise rapidly to about 30 weeks, and then begin to decline. Therefore, an AFP level that would be abnormal at 16 weeks gestation might be normal at 20 weeks.[72] According to the hospital statistics that were consulted, as many as 40 per cent of the women who attend prenatal clinics are unsure of their dates. Consequently, it was suggested that all women who are uncertain in this respect should be given ultrasound scans in order to confirm the gestational age of the fetus. The DHSS study noted, however, that ultrasound is both expensive and time consuming. Moreover, according to its estimates, ultrasound would only yield more accurate assessments of dates than conventional methods in 11 per cent of cases. For these reasons, it concluded that the extensive use of ultrasound would be unwarranted, especially as false negatives would be impossible for those women who would be later than estimated and false positives would be given ultrasound in any case before amniocentesis.

In contrast to the discussion of costs, the discussion of benefits contains no trade-off analysis. The study estimated benefits according to the results of recent work on the survival rates and levels of disability in children with NTDs.[73] Benefits included the costs avoided for in-patient episodes (including those for corrective surgery), out-patient visits, mobility appliances, and education and social security payments for the disabled. Again, all avoided costs are for the public sector. The impact of discounting upon the estimation of benefits was not as dramatic as in the case of Down's syndrome because most of the costs that the state would incur for the maintenance of spina bifida children fall within the first ten years of life. On the basis of the foregoing assumptions, the DHSS evaluation found NTD screening to be economic in the sense that benefits greatly exceeded the costs. Benefits were found to increase with increased sensitivity in the spina bifida screening test and with later cut-off dates.

Thus, the EAO's evaluation of NTD screening suggested that a national programme would be justified on economic grounds. However, it is important to stress once again the characteristics of the analysis that underlay this conclusion. The evaluation focused exclusively upon the economic consequences of NTD screening for the public sector. While it gave extensive consideration to alternative means of implementing a national screening programme, it contained no such analysis with respect to benefits. Even the consideration of means remained restricted. For example, the evaluation dwelt upon the administrative and economic implications of choosing one laboratory facility over another, but failed to review the clinical options associated with screening (such as more or less counselling and at which stage in the screening process).

Economics, ethics and medical practice

When the Economic Advisers' Office reported to DHSS administrators and to the Joint Standing Sub-Committee on Screening in Medical Care, preliminary results from the UK Collaborative Study were reaching the Department. The Economic Advisers' Office study had concluded that a national programme would be economically viable with test sensitivities of 45 per cent and over. The first results from the UK Collaborative Study indicated high sensitivity levels for both anencephalus and spina bifida. (The published report later stated that 'at 16–18 weeks of pregnancy 88% of cases of anencephaly, 79% of cases of open spina bifida and 3% of unaffected singleton pregnancies' had AFP levels equal to or greater than the cut-off level which was set at 2.5 times the median for unaffected singleton pregnancies.)[74] Furthermore, the combined results of the economic and clinical studies were having a dramatic effect on administrative thinking. Health and finances were the most important considerations governing choice of programmes. To paraphrase one administrator, NTD screening was given enormous priority relative to other types of antenatal screening (and other types of screening generally) because in this instance the unique features of the screening process permitted a high degree of sensitivity and specificity without enormous expense per case detected.[75]

With the knowledge that the UK Collaborative Study was yielding favourable results, that the economic analysis was positive, and that the Cardiff study was proceeding, DHSS administrators decided to take the first steps in implementing a national screening programme on the assumption that such a screening service was desirable and would be undertaken by the Regional Health Authorities. They promoted the project to a wide number of groups within the medical fraternity, and Ministers were reminded regularly. In the interests of effective presentation, neural tube defect screening became 'spina bifida screening' on the assumption that the project would have more appeal to the public at large and to the medical profession if the more technical term were avoided.

The DHSS administrators found during their campaign that there was substantial support for NTD screening among the Regional Health Authorities. Indeed, the pressure for this type of screening had not been in one direction only. Certain regional administrations had been involved in pushing NTD screening for some time. Thus, from the administrative perspective, there seemed to be every justification for proceeding with a Health Circular advising the Regional Health Authorities of the existence of the serum test and recommending the establishment of routine NTD screening services. The Health Circular, as finally drafted, recommended a different organizational framework for screening from that originally proposed in the DHSS economic evaluation. The reorganized National Health Service was intended to function in accordance with the principles of maximum delegation downwards and maximum accountability upwards. Thus, any attempt by DHSS to recommend centralized screening facilities would be likely to have floundered as a result of objections from Regional Health Authorities jealous of their powers. For this reason, DHSS administrators decided that the centres for analysis of serum samples would be based in the regions, with one, or at most two, per region. The Department did not abandon its commitment to institute a national programme by accepting this change in organizational format. If one or two regions were slow in implementing NTD screening, DHSS officials indicated that the Department might be willing to provide the necessary funds. This reformulation of the project did, however, require some reworking of the economics, although the basic structure of the earlier evaluation was retained. In the updated analysis (75–80% sensitivity and a 78% uptake) savings exceeded costs in the second year and all subsequent years.[76]

In August 1977 DHSS distributed a draft Health Circular concerning spina bifida screening to the regions for comment. By January 1978 it was apparent that, while the Regional Health Authorities generally approved of the draft scheme, there was opposition to a national programme from those specialists who would, of necessity, be most closely connected with its implementation. Specifically, the Royal College of Obstetricians and Gynaecologists (RCOG) issued a warning to the Department to make haste slowly in the area of NTD screening.[77] The honorary secretary of the RCOG, Raymond Booth, explained his organization's concern on two grounds: first, the costliness of the scheme given the other priorities the government had set especially in the light of a recent 10 per cent cut in spending on maternal services; and second, possible medical hazards arising from the shortage of properly trained staff and sophisticated medical equipment in many areas of the country. With respect to the latter point, the RCOG noted that there had been cases in which healthy fetuses had been aborted as a result of false positives in both the screening and diagnostic tests. In addition, the RCOG voiced concern about the dangers of spontaneous abortion as a result of amniocentesis.[78]

The objections of the RCOG to a national screening programme for neural tube defects deserve further scrutiny. There is no doubt that the serum test devised and perfected by Brock and his colleagues does yield a certain percentage of false positives (in the first report of the UK Collaborative Study these amounted to about 3 per cent of unaffected singleton pregnancies). However, experience indicated that a proportion of these could be eliminated by retesting.[79] More importantly, the serum test is never used for diagnostic purposes, and false positives with ultrasonography and amniocentesis are rare. Moreover, amniocentesis was only being proposed for those pregnant women (2–3%) who because they have elevated AFP values have a risk of at least 1 in 10 of carrying a fetus with NTD.[80] Medical precedent in many areas (e.g. women over 40 years of age for Down's syndrome, women who have previously had a child affected by Down's syndrome or a neural tube defect) indicates that this level of risk justifies the provision of prenatal screening facilities. Finally, screening programmes for neural tube defects had been launched in many UK centres particularly in Scotland, and especially in the wake of the UK Collaborative Study, with encouraging results.[81]

The RCOG was more persuasive on the issue of resource costs for the programme and the need for skilled personnel. Screening is expensive and time consuming. Many hospitals and medical centres were not in a position to provide the equipment and skilled staff required for procedures such as ultrasonography. In addition, the savings the DHSS Circular projected over the short term presupposed discretionary sums in the budgets of the Regional Health Authorities, sums that did not appear to be available in 1978 without pressure on other hard-pressed services. None the less, in December 1977, Mr Roland Moyle, Minister of State for Health, stated that finances for screening were not a problem. This indicates that at that time the government was prepared to find and allocate the necessary resources for the programme given official estimates of the savings to the public purse that would follow NTD detection.[82]

Despite this, the Royal College retained its scepticism as to the importance the DHSS had assigned to NTD screening in its draft Health Circular. This placed a major obstacle in the path of further development, and by early 1978 the Department had acknowledged this by postponing the implementation of routine national screening indefinitely. Moreover, the government did so despite the protests of some two hundred Members of Parliament from all parties who stressed the medical benefits associated with NTD screening and objected to what they regarded as the overly cautious position of the RCOG.[83]

What is significant about this episode for present purposes is that the analysis that DHSS undertook before the introduction of the draft Health Circular apparently did not prepare Ministers or officials for the subsequent response. Administrators and economists focused upon the sensitivity and specificity of the screening test, the humanitarian benefits of NTD screening and the administrative and economic implications of a national screening programme. In general, officials assumed that, as the various dimensions of the diagnostic technology for NTD detection became more clearly established, the humanitarian benefits of a national screening programme would become very obvious and ethical questions would tend to be less salient. Under these circumstances, the administrative and economic aspects of a national screening programme could be pursued in depth.

In contrast, the response to the draft Health Circular, and the debate over the last several years about spina bifida in *The Lancet*, indicate that many members of the medical profession were not prepared to accept the Department's judgements regarding the relative ethical neutrality of NTD screening.[84] The nature and tenor of the clinical objections that the RCOG advanced suggest its executive was primarily concerned with the ethical or moral aspects of prenatal screening. DHSS officials clearly failed to anticipate the full range of the medical profession's concerns in this sphere.

These observations suggest that the opposition to the draft Circular might have been less surprising had the preceding analysis adopted a broader perspective. The debate in the medical journals about spina bifida screening has been diffuse and, therefore, difficult to interpret with any great degree of confidence. But it does indicate that explanations for the medical profession's opposition to NTD screening lie in the intellectual commitments and social relations characteristic of those medical specialities that would be most affected by the implementation of a national screening programme.

In a 1976 paper Macintyre contended that work within the speciality of obstetrics and gynaecology is conditioned by two potentially contradictory themes – the promotion and prevention of childbirth.[85] Under normal circumstances clinicians engaged in this speciality succeed in minimizing conflicts arising from the contradictory aspects of these themes by a number of organizational strategies and by an interactional style that appeals to certain reasonable characterizations of the normal social world. Thus, typically, obstetrician–gynaecologists separate women who want children from those who have doubts by dealing with them in two separate locations: the prenatal clinic and the gynaecological out-patient clinic, respectively. Obstetrician–gynaecologists also rely upon certain widely held views of normalcy in advising women about promoting or preventing childbirth. By way of illustration, women are expected to want some children, but not too many, and not when they are too young, too old or unmarried. Thus, clinicians generally assign women to certain categories by age, marital status, parity, and advise them about the prevention and promotion of childbirth accordingly.

Yet if NTD screening were to become a routine part of prenatal care both strategies for conflict minimization would be jeopardized. The pro-birth, pro-life atmosphere of the antenatal clinic might well be threatened by the assumption implicit in screening that all is not necessarily normal. A concern with this type of threat to the childbirth promotion aspect of obstetrics–gynaecology may explain the preoccupation with what has been called 'fetal wastage' in the debate about spina bifida screening.[86] This term may have been invoked against NTD screening because some, perhaps many, doctors doubt whether systematic intervention to detect NTDs is justified if there is *any* risk that a healthy fetus may be aborted and the speciality's pro-birth stance thereby brought into question. NTD screening also threatens the obstetrician–gynaecologist's role in recommending either for the promotion or prevention of childbirth. What typifications of the normal social world can a clinician appeal to in advising a woman who has submitted to spina bifida screening and obtained a 'positive' diagnosis? Ethics concerning abortion, even in the case of abnormality, remain unsettled, and in the absence of clear social standards to invoke, the clinician may find it difficult to sustain his authority in the course of consultations with patients. It is perhaps for this reason that a number of medical commentators have recommended very strongly that much more detailed attention be given to issues such as counselling and the development of ethical codes in the area before a national screening programme is implemented.[87]

Before we leave this subject, there is another and complementary hypothesis that may account for some of the reluctance to implement spina bifida screening that many members of the medical profession have displayed. Just as NTD screening may threaten intellectual commitments and social relations within obstetrics–gynaecology, it may also jeopardize the stability of the relations between specialities. In all fields of medicine the medical profession interprets prevailing social standards with respect to life and death, illness and health. In some areas this task is more onerous than in others. Thus, in the absence of NTD screening, pediatricians have the difficult responsibility of deciding in consultation with parents which infants with neural tube defects should receive surgery and which should not receive sustained medical support. If universal screening for neural tube defects were introduced, the burden of decision would largely be lifted from pediatricians and parents and placed with obstetricians and prospective parents. However, unlike pediatricians who can claim to maintain and improve life through selective surgery, obstetricians have no treatment to offer except termination of the pregnancy when an affected fetus is discovered. Also, pediatricians have to date decided upon appropriate treatment for infants with defects in the relative privacy of consultations with parents and colleagues as and when a malformation presented, but obstetricians would be expected to make their recommendations as part of a universal programme with a high public profile. Thus, a national programme of the kind outlined by DHSS would result in a major transfer of responsibility from pediatrics to obstetrics–gynaecology in circumstances not especially favourable to the latter speciality. Obstetrician–gynaecologists seem to have accepted that, if properly implemented, NTD screening is ethically sound, but the consequences of universal, routine NTD screening for their speciality are potentially very great, especially as abortion continues to be a controversial issue in Britain. Their acceptance of responsibility in this domain may be premised upon the gradual introduction of NTD screening and a less public, more selective approach to prenatal, preventive medicine generally.

Conclusions

Despite the pioneering work described in this chapter and a number of favourable clinical developments since, the early 1980s saw no national screening programme for spina bifida. The Second Report of the UK Collaborative Study appeared in September 1979.[88] It found that 98 per cent of both anencephaly and open spina bifida cases could be detected through the amniotic fluid AFP test. It also confirmed low false positive rates for this test (0.27% for clear samples). Furthermore, evidence was accumulating at this time to the effect that a test for raised levels of acetylcholinesterase (AchE) in amniotic fluid offered the prospect of acting as an adjunct to, or indeed improving upon, the AFP amniotic fluid tests.[89] However, neither of these developments precipitated the introduction of a national screening programme.

The reasons are varied. In 1978 a Medical Research Council report on amniocentesis concluded that this procedure contributed to a 1.0–1.5 per cent rate of fetal loss and a possible 1.0–1.5 per cent increase in certain types of major infant morbidity.[90] These results were said to cast doubt on the viability of a national screening programme, even though earlier American and Canadian studies[91] had found no significant risk from amniocentesis and the British study's risk estimates were not greatly different from those that had informed the discussion of NTD screening all along. Then in 1979 the Conservative Government of Mrs Margaret Thatcher took office. With the notable exception of Sir George Young, the Parliamentary Secretary for Health, the Conservatives have displayed ambivalence about prevention, primarily because it appears too interventionist. Early on in the administration, a working group of the Standing Medical Advisory Committee on screening for neural tube defects reported on prospects in this area.[92] The Working Group focused on issues associated with the implementation of a screening programme (for example, in recommending that women should be fully counselled *before* blood is taken). Its failure to endorse national screening was taken by DHSS to mean that rapid progress towards a national screening programme would be unwise, and this message was conveyed in a DHSS

Health Notice accompanying the Working Group's report.[93]. More recently, the cautious approach to the development of a national screening programme has received reinforcement from reports citing a declining incidence of NTDs[94] and research results which suggest that NTDs can be prevented by antenatal vitamin supplementation.[95]

What this brief history illustrates is that from its inception the national screening programme concept has met with resistance from a sceptical medical profession, latterly supported by Conservative politicians. In most respects, this represents an unsurprising extension of the early developments described in this chapter. Despite the medical and economic evidence in favour of a national screening programme, the RCOG's original admonition still has force. There are, therefore, two questions at issue in regard to the economic contribution to the debate over NTD screening. What has been the nature of the balance of influence in this area? Why has the appeal of the economic, the cost-effective, as represented by the national screening programme concept, been so limited?

In developing a response to the first question, it is important to note that the evidence assembled in this chapter suggests health economics as practised within DHSS is conditioned by competition for intellectual and social authority between departmental economists and the medical professionals who contribute to health care policy both inside and outside the Department. This is not to say that competitition between these two groups is either unremitting or uniform in its focus. Depending upon the issue at stake, compromises, even coalitions, have evolved in which each group (or fraction thereof) has agreed upon a division of labour in the pursuit of policy objectives in which they have a mutual interest. The compact involving administrators, economists, certain types of clinicians, medical researchers, and politicians centred upon preventive medicine is a case in point. Nevertheless, the relatively low status of the clinicians involved in this compact and the objections that the prestigious RCOG raised in connection with the DHSS plans for NTD screening also suggest that the compromises that are sometimes achieved are often tenuous. Put in another way, these compromises cannot be explained adequately without reference to the competition that has been partially restrained in order to achieve some measure of cooperation.

One of the more obvious features of health economics has been the protracted competition between economists and members of the medical profession concerning the nature of adequate measures and procedures in the evaluation of health care. Since entering the medical field, economists have stressed the distinctiveness of their contribution to the analysis of health and health services (especially the doctrine of choice), yet they immediately encountered opposition to their approach from medical professionals who were concerned that economic analysis misrepresented many of the issues central to medical care.

Significantly, however, economists have not tended to respond in kind. Certain members of the profession, particularly academics removed from the policy context, have been very blunt in criticizing the medical profession's role in formulating health care policy, but, in general, health economists, and especially DHSS economists, no matter how sympathetic they may be to such criticisms, have refrained from expressing open disapproval of medical practice (except under limited or special circumstances). Instead, as outlined in this chapter, they have reached tacit understandings with the medical profession concerning what is, and what is not, appropriate in the application of economic methodology to health care. In the same vein, economists have come to accept that the economic arguments surrounding a health project may not be advanced very explicitly because the primary justification for a project must centre upon its contribution to the reduction of human suffering.

This reticence on the part of health economists suggests that they recognize they are unable to challenge the medical ethos successfully. Microeconomic analysis, founded as it is upon the tempered self-interest of Walrasian mechanics, cannot command the same degree of social authority as arguments that invoke humanitarianism and the special relationship between doctor and patient at the foundation of the doctrine of clinical freedom. In the words of one economist, decision-makers in health have tended 'to scorn the "man as machine" type of valuation'.[96] Moreover, the reluctance of health economists to offer an intellectual challenge to the medical profession has social parallels. DHSS economists lack control over the purposes and direction of many of their tasks, and hence, have encountered limitations in their ability to impose a fully rationalistic approach upon much of the work process in public sector health care evaluation. In this instance, the methods by which work is assigned in the economic field, the manner in which studies are conducted, and the organizational arrangements of the EAO have in large measure reflected the perspective and priorities of the medical profession.

The dominance of the medical profession within the health sphere has, however, not resulted in the full subordination of the economics profession. Rather, in establishing themselves in the health care field economists have adopted a number of strategies that serve both to enhance the applicability of their techniques and to reduce the likelihood of confrontations with the medical fraternity. A number of these have been discussed in some depth within the body of this chapter. Suffice it to say at this point that these strategies embrace selection principles that have allowed health economists, in part at least, to avoid the control of the medical profession by focusing their attention upon subject areas in which administrative and financial considerations are prominent and medical and ethical considerations are less salient than usual. In particular, the application of economic analysis to neural tube defect screening is the product of a series of selection processes in which economists gravitated to those topics that promised to be conducive to the subordination of problems of technology and knowledge to those of administration and allocation.

In this context, it is significant that economists in the area of prenatal screening endorsed the observation of Stein *et al.* that the consequences of prenatal screening do not differ substantially from elective abortion, without, however, countenancing much else in their approach. This particular precedent was important because it allowed the difficult ethical questions surrounding screening to be set aside. In the process, ends and means could apparently be resolved more clearly. If abortion is no longer an issue, then the point at which the fetus is aborted can serve to separate benefits from costs in a rigorous, arithmetic manner. All of the cost–benefit analysis that followed hinged upon the rigidity of this distinction. Thus, by selecting their medical precedents carefully, the economists in question succeeded in justifying the use of an ends–means dichotomy in the analysis of prenatal screening and, simultaneously, avoided making statements concerning the ethics of screening that might have brought them into direct confrontation with doctors.

The inclination to avoid measures of cost and benefit associated with individuals may also be symptomatic of an ongoing effort to avoid confrontations with the medical profession. Medical practitioners base their claims to professional authority upon the unique and novel features of every professional–patient relationship. An economist is, therefore, wise to focus his attention upon the aggregate aspects of health care so that he does not risk infringing professional discretion at the level of professional–patient contact. Admittedly, as mentioned earlier in the chapter, this approach departs from many of the conventions of microeconomic analysis. In particular, welfare theory does not provide a justification for restricting analysis to public sector expenditure patterns, or for combining measures based upon public sector administrative costs with a few selected measures based upon the consideration of the impact of a programme upon individuals (as, for example, in the 1975 Down's syndrome study). In the case of the DHSS analysis of NTD screening, work was focused at a level where the analyst was least likely to encounter resistance from the medical profession. Thus, the laboratory costs involved in NTD screening were discussed at some length, but the topic of counselling, and any costs associated with it, was neglected.

Finally, the differences that exist in the NTD screening study between the treatment of costs and the treatment of benefits indicate yet again the degree to which economic analysis within DHSS is conditioned by competition between the professions. As economists divorced themselves from the ethical questions surrounding prenatal screening, they emphasized the administrative and financial aspects of proposed programmes. However, ends and means, benefits and costs, were not always dealt with equally. The DHSS evaluation of NTD screening stressed the alternatives that administrators have available to them in establishing and costing a routine screening service, but alternatives were not introduced into the discussion of benefits. The study's conservatism in this regard is in keeping with earlier observations that economists, especially those in DHSS, are loath to risk charges of 'commercialism' from the medical profession and others by applying their methods too explicitly in areas in which disability and mortality are central issues. Economists recognize that the propensity of health professionals to accept the validity of methods and measures associated with market valuations (however conceptualized) is very limited.

Yet the economics profession has not succeeded in abating all the potential contradictions of their stance within the health care field. The contradiction associated with the doctrine of choice has already been reviewed, but there are other contradictory aspects to the profession's pursuit of plausibility in the health field. A few examples will suffice to illustrate this.

In their discussion of NTD screening Hagard *et al.* at one point speculated that the cost of prenatal detection might be regarded as payment for a scruple; abortion is legal, but euthanasia is not, and all of the proposals for a screening programme follow from this difference.[97] Neither Hagard *et al.* nor the DHSS analysts pursued this type of reasoning very far; to have done so would have been to question the rigid dichotomy between cost and benefit upon which their analyses were founded. Nevertheless, the observation of Hagard *et al.* does display a nascent recognition that the logic of their evaluation of NTD screening might conceal a number of fundamental problems. In the first place, even within the confines of the economic perspective, the rigid distinction that they, and later DHSS analysts, posited between cost and benefit is contradictory. The contention was that benefit in the case of NTD screening is, at least in large measure, the cost *avoided* for the treatment of affected infants brought to term. The result in each case was a comparison of the costs of one procedure (prenatal screening) with the costs of another (remedial care). Yet there is no sense in which this comparison elucidates the changes in social well-being yielded by either procedure. Thus, it is difficult to construe these studies as cost–benefit analyses although they, and similar evaluations, have been described as such by many commentators.[98] Moreover, they do not fall within the category of cost-effectiveness analyses for there is no obvious sense in which prenatal screening and remedial care yield consequences that are the same.

Considerations of this kind do not seem to have impinged directly upon the economists involved in evaluating NTD screening, but they may be central to their failure to anticipate the controversy that followed upon the publication of the DHSS draft Health Circular. In economic analysis attention is focused upon the identification of benefits and costs in an arithmetic manner, and economists apparently favour problems that can be plausibly presented in this way. However, in this case the ends–means dichotomy seems to have obscured rather than clarified the full range of the medical profession's concerns in the area of NTD screening. Although, as indicated earlier, the exact significance of the various components of the controversy following the distribution of the draft Health Circular is difficult to specify, it is relatively clear that many medical practitioners were unwilling to accept either the legitimacy or the ethical neutrality of the distinctions at the centre of the administrative/economic presentation of NTD screening. Indeed, if the 1978 debate in *The Lancet* is any indication, for those professionals most directly concerned with NTD screening the abortion issue is fundamental in defining the nature of the care they provide. According to this view the abortion of an affected fetus is not an arithmetic barrier, but an act that precipitates radical changes in the *quality* of care and, therefore, has vast implications for medical ethics. Furthermore, if the hypotheses advanced earlier in an attempt to explain the nature of the objections the Circular provoked have any validity, it may be that a national NTD screening programme would threaten many of the intellectual commitments and social relations at the centre of at least one, and perhaps two, medical specialities. Suffice it to say that no appeal by economists to the doctrine of choice will restore the rigidity of the distinction between costs and benefits inherent to the economic evaluations of NTD screening if there is little congruity between economic logic and medical interpretation in this area.

The evidence contained in this chapter suggests that in recent years economists have had some limited success in the health care field. By confining their attention to selected areas of medicine, they have gained a measure of credibility as the 'economizers' of health resources, particularly as the preventive approach has increased in popularity among administrators and some clinicians. However, as the contradictions cited in the previous paragraphs indicate, health and health care are subjects that continue in large degree to elude the economist.

7

Microeconomics and governing

As the rapid melding of microeconomics and policy indicates, the cost–benefit calculus draws upon a variety of thought patterns that are deeply ingrained in liberal, Anglo-Saxon social and political culture. The utilitarians rejected the strictures involved in the feudal concept of moral obligation in favour of a vision of the individual as a moral and social actor. In contrast to his medieval forebears, modern man was to be free, was to resist coercion and was to pursue a diversity of ends in search of individual happiness. Social institutions were to be reorganized to facilitate these individual aspirations, and the collective good was redefined as the aggregate of individual well-being – the 'Greatest Happiness of the Greatest Number'. Man was seen as a creature of desire, with unlimited and essentially random wants. Nature had, however, also endowed man with reason, and the task of social and political philosophy became to distinguish between desires according to their ends. In this undertaking juxtaposed opposites based on moral or psychological preference assumed an early importance, and liberal thought is replete with distinctions between good and evil, pride and humility, pleasure and pain, and so forth.[1] Thus, a strong normative element was introduced into liberal philosophy. Happiness became not what man wants, but what he ought to want.[2] From the stern judgements of the Puritans about proper action to the modern preoccupation with reform, liberal thought has embodied a call to do what is demonstrably right. To do less is to fall into error, to be misinformed or, perhaps worst, to subscribe to neutralism.

Cost–benefit analysis, with its emphasis on one-to-one dichotomies and its rational norm of efficiency, draws deeply on the liberal tradition, particularly so in that it embodies a process of self-conscious deliberation about alternatively courses of action. Fundamentally, CBA is about the calculation of consequences and the desire to be 'right' in whatever choices are taken. From this follow the efforts at measurement and the elaboration of systems for the ordering and juxtaposition of ends and means, where everything is in its place and some security about the rightness of choice in an uncertain world can thereby be achieved. This is a compelling vision because it focuses on the practical and the doable, with the result that it has a strong attraction for the politician and the administrator, each of whom is endowed with a mandate to evaluate proposals for social improvement. Moreover, in a changing world, the ethical and technological aspects of the ends–means grammar provide a framework for coming to terms with altered circumstances and a vehicle for projecting today's insights forward into an unknown future. Some of the specifics of how this is achieved are worth reviewing in some detail, drawing where appropriate on the content of the case studies.

An all-encompassing discipline

One of the most striking features of the case studies in this book, and of the history of applied welfare economics generally, is the all-inclusive view economists have adopted of both the boundaries and the nature of economics. Taking the issue of disciplinary boundaries first, it is significant that in the fields of transport, labour and health, public sector economists have been able to construe a multitude of problems as economic problems. This has been true even in cases, such as the decision about whether or not to condone the therapeutic abortion of fetuses with neural tube defects, in which it is highly debatable whether the action in question is wholly, primarily or even partially economic in any conventional (i.e. Neoclassical or neo-Paretian) sense. When, however, economics is defined as the study of behaviour that seeks the optimum use of scarce means, all purposive activity becomes potentially economic. In practice, if a problem involves exchange or, more broadly, choice, it becomes subject to economic analysis.

An important consequence of this viewpoint is the tendency for economists to claim that they are in possession of a general, rather than a particularistic, type of expertise. In this economists resemble administrators and lawyers, but differ from engineers, medical personnel and other professionals who derive their authority from their command over a specific type of subject matter and are said to have more circumscribed horizons.[3] At times, economists have been able to gain a significant measure of administrative authority and control over a policy area on the basis of their claims to general rather than particular knowledge – the COBA system of inter-urban road assessment is a case in point. At other times, they have been less successful in this enterprise because of competing claims from other professionals – as in the prenatal screening case.

Another consequence of the inclusive view economists have taken of the boundaries of their discipline is the tendency for the divisions between public sector specialities to diminish as each area of public policy has yielded to economic analysis. This is perhaps most evident when some of the prominent attributes of human capital theory are considered. The theory establishes parallels between physical investment and investment in 'human resources' – thereby facilitating the extrapolation of the logic of physical investment appraisal into social policy. Beyond this, it provides a unified framework for the economic treatment of various areas of social policy, most notably education, training, health and social services. Finally, human capital theory has broadened the brief of the economics profession to encompass subject matter that was formerly judged beyond the profession's competence, yielding, for example, an economics of marriage and an economics of fertility.[4] Transport, labour and health economics remain distinguishable because, to the uninitiated, they treat different subject matters. However, in the wake of the development of the human capital research programme, economists have applied an identical evaluative logic to the problems of each speciality. It is in this sense that the divisions between them have become less meaningful.

We may now turn to consider the all-inclusive view that economists have adopted of the nature of economics. For example, Neo-Paretian theory and cost–benefit analysis are replete with theoretical problems, and yet, most economists working in the public sector operate as if they were not. Moreover, the economics profession has displayed considerable persistence in applying neo-Paretian categories whatever the specific circumstances of each application. In the case of inter-urban road evaluation, the shape of the demand curve for trips is seldom known. Despite this, the COBA system was based on a simplified version of consumer surplus theory. In a similar vein, Neoclassical and neo-Paretian categories seem to have a limited applicability to health owing to the agency relationship between doctor and patient, the non-market character of the delivery of health care in Britain and the integration of ends in health, which stands in marked contrast to the diversity of ends characteristic of economic theory. Nevertheless, much effort has been expended in recent decades towards searching curative and, more importantly, preventive practice for those scenarios that might plausibly be said to yield to Neoclassical analysis, albeit with somewhat limited results, as we have seen.

The case studies display a further facet of this all-inclusive view of the nature of economics. Specifically, a concern with validity and even, at times, plausibility has been lacking in policy analysis and evaluation. This is perhaps most evident in the evaluation of training, in which the leading participants established a logical scaffold for the valuation of the economic worth of Skillcentre courses without devoting much attention to the adequacy of their creation. But a lack of concern with the validity of economic knowledge and economic practice is also apparent in COBA. The highway economists involved in inter-urban road assessment largely confined their evaluation of the adequacy of the COBA system to sensitivity testing – a technique that can reveal how evaluative outcomes change with alterations in the values assigned to certain input variables, but conveys little about the validity of these values or the method in which they are employed.

Moreover, in the absence of a consistent theoretical framework for applied welfare economics and a tradition of testing the adequacy of economic knowledge,[5] public sector economists have frequently resorted to *ad hoc* or casual knowledge[6] in the development of their evaluations, and in so doing have often broadened the scope of their work. In the evaluation of training, the emphasis on extended time horizons, transition probabilities and indirect effects such as replacement and displacement did not give the analysis a secure empirical foundation. It did, however, increase the scope of the analysis and, thereby made a positive outcome possible. This facilitated the elaboration of an administrative system for training assessment. Similarly, those involved in the design of COBA borrowed widely and eclectically from engineering and operations research in an effort, first, to reproduce the physical aspects of road assessment within the COBA framework and, latterly, to ensure adequate results (e.g. the MAX DELAY cut-off). When various engineering and statistical components of the system proved questionable, the priority placed on adequate outcomes and system stability meant that initial assumptions tended not to be re-examined.

It would be a mistake, however, to describe the *ad hoc* aspects of the analyses reviewed in the case studies as lacking in design. For instance, that which was *ad hoc* in the case studies was very frequently arithmetic.[7] In the training evaluation, analysis of skill-sharing in the work place, though introduced at one point in the development of the study, was not pursued in any depth. Instead, work rapidly focused on the elaboration of replacement and displacement ratios and the calculation of the implications of these ratios for Skillcentre profitability.

In addition, seemingly *ad hoc* choices concerning how to cast a particular analysis reflect what is appropriate within the intellectual and the ethical framework of Neoclassical theorizing. For example, the training evaluation assumed that trainees engage in training exclusively because they anticipate higher earnings after training than they otherwise would have had without the training experience. Given that there are many motives that could have been attributed to the trainee, this initial assumption deserves attention. It would seem to rest upon an appeal to what is fitting within the rationality-centred context of microeconomics. A trainee might be motivated to train by a desire to learn more about his chosen trade or to enhance his future job security, but, were this so, he could not easily be said to be oriented to the type of public, or objective, standard (i.e. labour market equilibrium) that is so central to Neoclassical theory and cost–benefit analysis. Alternatively, the trainee who engages in training to improve his earnings can be easily said to be so oriented, and there is, therefore, a sense in which his action can be posited to be appropriate, or right. One choice gives the economist access to training construed as an economic problem, while the other is less likely to do so.

Impact on the policy process

Making sense of the contribution of economists to the policy process is frequently a difficult task in that the categories economists apply in the public sector lack precision by comparison with strict Neoclassical or Paretian standards. Further, the methodological frameworks employed to evaluate policy are sufficiently open as to admit a variety of interpretations both on the part of the economics profession and on the part of outside observers. Nevertheless, as this book has sought to demonstrate, there appears to be a broad pattern to the way microeconomic expertise, and particularly CBA, is deployed in government.

One prominent aspect of this pattern is the divorce of economic expertise from much of the purpose or sense of the policy context.[8] Economists work with discretely distinct theoretical categories – ends and means, benefits and costs – which, when they are used in the public sector, are removed from the search for optimality at the centre of Neoclassical economics, much less more policy-specific purposes such as the search for appropriate materials, technologies or strategies to undertake public functions like building roads or improving the health of newborns. Cost–benefit practitioners typically fill the open categories of their methodology with material that seems to reflect the particular forms, the particular purposes characteristic of the situation that is under evaluation. Yet the logic they attempt to apply ultimately does not admit consideration of form, scale, history or purpose, and, therefore, forces those who use it back upon an arithmetic, and often physical interpretation of the problem at hand.

This is perhaps most evident in the case of the evaluation of inter-urban roads. The interpretation of travel over a road network that yields most easily to economic assessment bars the consideration of the purpose of travel from its brief. Indeed, COBA can almost be construed as a method for comparing and contrasting the physical properties (length, junctions, etc.) of road networks in isolation from the concerns of road users. The training study goes further in illustrating the tendency to interpret problems in ways that subordinate form and purpose and emphasize the physical (in the guise of the mechanical or the probabilistic). The black-box view of training and the use of probabilistic modelling to approximate the 'do-nothing' situation do not convey a developed understanding of human behaviour, but in reducing the latter to the arithmetic make the economic assessment of training possible. The same phenomenon is also evident in health economics. The evaluation of prenatal screening assumed that the act of abortion could be taken as a radical disjuncture permitting the discrete separation of benefits and costs, so much so that the issue of whether or not the outcomes associated with screening and remedial care are the 'same' was bypassed. Later, however, it became apparent that other professionals concerned with prenatal screening did not see abortion in this light.

This relative neglect of form and purpose has a variety of implications for policy development. At the most extreme, it can lead to a type of mindlessness in policy evaluation, formulation and implementation arising from a total failure to assess the nature of ends in relationship to the nature of means and the appropriateness of various types of ends–means couplings. Anatol Rapoport and others have observed, for example, that the discussion of what is rational in the field of thermonuclear strategy can become a 'ghastly farce' when the contemplation of alternative strategic scenarios clouds the awful nature of the ends and means at stake in thermonuclear conflict.[9] In the case of the policy issues dealt with in this book, the divorce of economic expertise from the purpose or sense of policy is not so complete as in the thermonuclear example, but in these areas, too, policy development has been affected. COBA encouraged the construction of road projects of indeterminate conformation, size and even number because it embodied no view of the purpose of travel and, concomitantly, no precise view of the shape or scale a road project should assume. The training evaluation discouraged those involved in planning for vocational training from regarding trainees in their full human dimensions and from investigating the ways in which training transforms both people and the work process. Economists and administrators associated with the thrust for economy through prevention did not appreciate the depth of the screening problem (professional, ethical, etc.) in their efforts to encapsulate the screening process in an arithmetic format.

A general agnosticism with respect to form and purpose has a further effect upon policy development. Put briefly, it can result in the elevation of certain subject areas to policy prominence and the lowering in status of others. Broadly speaking, the application of economic expertise tends to highlight policy directed towards physical investment at the expense of social policy because the problems of the former area are more tractable using the tools available to the economist. This effect is, however, best represented in the case studies by the contribution economic evaluation has made to highlighting preventive medicine by comparison with curative medicine, secondary with primary prevention, and genetic screening by comparison with other types of screening. The character of preventive medicine is such that the purpose, efficacy and ethical character of medical intervention do not confront the analyst as directly as they do in curative practice. The same is true of primary prevention with relation to secondary prevention and genetic screening with relation to other types of screening. Since economics is unable to deal with the qualitative dimensions of medical and ethical issues, the economics profession devotes more effort, and, therefore, lends greater prominence to the three former areas of medical concern than to the latter three. Some might argue that this relative emphasis is progressive, but such a judgement would be based on criteria other than those the profession applies in the health care field. In the economic context, preventive medicine is simply more amenable to analysis than curative medicine.

Another aspect of the separation between economic expertise and the sense of the policy context is the tendency economists have displayed to seek hegemony in the policy areas they enter. Economic expertise does not derive from a special knowledge of the particular forms or particular purposes characteristic of individual policy areas. Rather, their contribution to policy debate and development consists in efforts to sift, to order, to organize and, eventually, to control the contributions of others. We have seen in the case studies how reliant public sector economists are upon the expertise of other professionals for the 'stuff' of their analyses. Yet once established in a policy area, they typically assume influence, authority and eventually precedence on the basis of their command of the calculation of consequences. Thus, from the economic standpoint, engineering expertise, while admittedly indispensable to the full anslysis of subjects such as road provision, remains a limited rationality – one that must be subjected to, if not displaced by, economic expertise.[10] Similarly, economists have often shown impatience with the patient-centred, and, from their perspective, idiosyncratic prescriptions of the medical profession regarding health care. According to this view, the precedent-centred and essentially gradualist approach of the medical profession to the development and delivery of health services should be interpreted through analysis benefiting from the universal insights into the problem of how best to deploy scarce resources. The engineers have, with time, yielded influence, at least in so far as the road programme has been concerned. The medical profession has, on the other hand, been slow to surrender its authority. Its position may, however, become progressively more vulnerable, especially if it fails to develop internal mechanisms for resolving the cost problem and improving standards of health care delivery.

The instrument whereby the economics profession can achieve a measure of authority within a policy area is the component-centred, hierarchical administrative system of the kind operated by the COBA designers and managers. This, as we have seen, performs many more functions than the monetization and aggregation of the variables central to the economic evaluation of investment projects. To begin with, the economic scaffolding constrains all parties to the system to a single view of the policy problem at hand. In addition, largely as a result of its arithmetic character, a COBA-type administrative format can serve to quell conflicts between competing expert or professional groups within a policy area, to systematize the treatment of specific policy problems and to give the impression that government can be locally, if not universally, efficient. These are advantages that few members of the bureaucracy, especially senior officials, are likely to treat lightly.

In the process, however, important administrative distinctions, such as that between policy formulation and implementation, are progressively conflated. Moreover, the introduction of such a system in one area means that it becomes more difficult to compare and contrast policy development across policy areas. This is manifest, for example, in the Leitch Committee's observation that the evaluation of road and rail were isolated specialities within DOT and in its own failure to penetrate and analyse the various components of COBA so that the system made sense on any but its own terms.[11] With time, it becomes more and more difficult for the participant to escape the totality of the system, or for the critic to highlight its weaknesses.

Rationalizing welfare economics

What, finally, has been the total phenomenon we have been witnessing in the extensive application of the welfare-based cost–benefit analysis within the public domain? In each of its tenets and in its mode of application CBA reflects what has been called the mystery of welfare economics.[12] The market model, with its emphasis on multipolarity, does not provide an account of how the power to make and enforce laws is conferred on particular individuals, in short of how governments are created and maintained.[13] Yet cost–benefit analysis, as indicated by its modern revival in the US water works programme, is intimately associated with governance and the public sector, especially so in that it offers one of the few methodologically developed vehicles for coming to terms with public benefit. Similarly, the market model cannot sustain interpersonal comparisons of utility, thereby confounding attempts to aggregate utility. In contrast, cost–benefit analysis countenances just such comparisons, and derives its economic and administrative significance from the aggregation of individual utilities to yield a measure of the collective good. In the process, government and public administration become less identified with interference in the private sector and more with the planning and management of collective enterprise. Just as importantly in the British case, while the multipolarity and unrestricted wants of the market model appear most apt as a description of a rapidly expanding high growth capitalist society,[14] cost–benefit analysis acquired prominence in an era of low growth, cost consciousness and finite horizons when the institutional dimensions of policy-making were becoming more defined and the justice of market precepts less accepted.

These contrasts point to an as yet unresolved tension at the centre of CBA between the private and the public, the multipolar and the structured, an infinity of wants and the reality of finite resources. Moreover, they are becoming more acute. Accelerating Soviet–American tension has caused the aptness of mechanistic analogies, such as those associated with the nuclear defence doctrine of mutual deterrence, to be questioned. Moreover, infinite wants and infinite appropriation seem increasingly out of keeping with the growing recognition that our environment is both finite and fragile. In the public sector, the tension is perhaps most evident in the stark juxtaposition of gainers and losers that CBA affords, a juxtaposition that for many is becoming increasingly untenable. Whether the issue is physical infrastructure, the environment, social services or peace, acceptance of loss is out of favour, despite the many calls to sacrifice embodied in the new conservatism. Much of this stems from the recognition that within the Neoclassical framework there is no obligation for the gainers to compensate the losers and that losses aggregate to certain social groups, thereby aggravating hardship and inequity. At a deeper level, however, resistance to loss follows from a suspicion that the aggregation of utilities in the evaluation of policy arises from an incomplete conception of public action, in particular one that neglects man's role as a doer and an exerter. This is perhaps most evident in the health care case study which, because it is concerned with reproduction, brings some of the differences between man as consumer and man as doer most clearly to the fore.

The economics of health care is, as we have seen, an uneasy discipline for a variety of reasons, not the least of which is that health care does not readily fit the pattern of a consumer good. Modern industrial societies invest in health care provision for the most part because they wish to improve the duration and quality of life, not to maximize the satisfactions of their population. Added difficulties arise when the issue at stake is the health of children, as was the case with the evaluation of the spina bifida screening proposal. Given its orientation to the future, children and young people have long been the validating class of liberal philosophy, so much so that the discussion of social need most frequently begins with family welfare, education and other children's needs.[15] In these circumstances, bearing and rearing children are not likely to be seen primarily as sacrifices, or the costs associated with these activities primarily as losses, even when the situation is as difficult as it was in the case of the spina bifida evaluation.

With this shift in perspective on the nature of loss and cost, moreover, other aspects of the economic assessment of prenatal screening take on a new light. What appears to have been of primary significance in the spina bifida screening case was less the burden of caring for spina bifida children and more than a new effort was being made to reduce the incidence of malformation and in the process a new activity was emerging (serum screening), which in turn generated new aspirations (a national screening service) and new wants. What was apparently needed, therefore, was an analysis that focused on changes in efforts and the emergence of new activities and on the way in which wants come to be adjusted or defined by activities. Health care in this context is no longer a consumer good, but a vehicle for allowing the population to develop its human capacities to the fullest. In Parsons's words, 'What is the aim of life, what is life itself, cannot well be interpreted as a cost which must be incurred in the attainment of ends outside itself.'[16]

Thus, just as a consideration of the various dimensions of the cost concept have broadened the scope of economics to encompass the investment sector and the public sector, so a re-examination of the loss–cost nexus affords a more vivid and complete account of the motives underlying change and the 'economics' of the emergence of new activities. In this context, cost is less associated with use and therefore loss, and more with the overcoming of obstacles and therefore effort. With this changed understanding of cost, moreover, a variety of new issues surface. Effort, by definition, is towards some historically defined end, with the result that activities assume social and temporal dimensions. A focus on effort and activity stimulates an interest in supply factors, an emphasis that is Classical, rather than Neoclassical. Wants adjusted to activities (effective demand) are no longer either random or infinite. Moreover, where ends vary with the elaboration of the process whereby they are attained, the rationality standard, both in its technical and ethical aspects, ceases to apply.[17]

It is this dimension of the cost–benefit format, furthermore, that would appear to account for the ongoing attraction that CBA and welfare economics generally holds for economists. So often it is from members of the economics profession that we have had the clearest expositions of the inadequacies of welfare economics, both pure and applied. Little, for example, laid bare the many problems of welfare theory in 1950.[18] Mishan crusaded for many years to rid the cost–benefit field of feeble thinking. Significantly, however, even those members of the profession who have been most severe in their criticisms of welfare economics have stopped short of abandoning or belittling the welfare edifice. Much of this adherence to welfare theory may be explained by noting that welfare economics is close to the centre of Neoclassical economics, which is, in turn, vital to the self-image, particularly the professional self-image of the economist.[19] Hicks, however, has suggested a more direct explanation.[20] He has voiced a fundamental optimism about welfare economics. He has, of course, played a role in elucidating its many contradictions. But he also came to regard welfare economics as an important means of escape from the confines of the Neoclassical worldview. Specifically, for Hicks, the use of Classical concepts and modes of reasoning in welfare economics is less the last stage in a degenerative progression away from strict Neoclassicism and more a first step towards a general realization among economists that real human beings are more than 'preference machines'.[21] For this reason he has described the whole of welfare economics as a 'critique' of orthodox theorizing.

Against the potentiality for liberation from the Neoclassical framework must, however, be weighed the actuality of the record of the application of welfare concepts in the public sector. As we have seen, the Neoclassical worldview has many defensive attributes. The monolithic character of rationality protects all branches of Neoclassical theorizing from criticism by invoking a single all-encompassing paradigm both for the social sciences and for public policy. The rational emphasis on scalarity both feeds and aggravates a government preoccupation with numbers, with statistics, and with quantity over quality in the definition of policy. The ethical imperative associated with rationality teaches that what is, is right, and serves to isolate and limit dissent from established wisdom. Moreover, these features of the Neoclassical enterprise are as compelling for economists as for other groups in society.[22] If this complex of commitments is to be breached, it would appear that greater attention must be given to those dimensions of CBA that separate it from the Neoclassical vision and lead back to the Classical insights associated with efforts to identify and assess the Social Product. The alternative is to yield to a type of moral and social aimlessness where calculation looms large for its own sake and the only imperative is a hollow efficiency.

Notes

Notes for Chapter 1

1 D. Winch, *Economics and Policy: A Historical Survey* (London, Collins/ Fontana, 1972), pp. 265–321.

2 Ibid., pp. 322–49; E.J. Mishan, *The Costs of Economic Growth* (Harmondsworth, Middx, Penguin, 1969); E.J. Mishan, *The Economic Growth Debate* (London, George Allen and Unwin, 1977).

3 A.E. Booth and A.W. Coats, 'The market for economists in Britain, 1945–75: a preliminary survey', *Economic Journal*, **88**, 351 (1978). These figures do not include agricultural economists, who were graded separately from other economists until 1975.

4 Some indication of the importance CBA has assumed in the political sphere can be gleaned from P. Self, *Econocrats and the Policy Process: The Politics and Philosophy of Cost–Benefit Analysis* (London, Macmillan, 1975).

5 For the popularity of multipolar models, see G.J. Stigler, 'Perfect competition' in his *Essays in the History of Economics* (Chicago, University of Chicago Press, 1965), especially pp. 266–7.

6 Sources for this and subsequent analysis include J.A. Schumpeter, *History of Economic Analysis* (New York, Oxford University Press, 1954); G. Routh, *The Origin of Economic Ideas* (London, Macmillan, 1975); G.L.S. Shackle, *Epistemics and Economics: A Critique of Economic Doctrines* (Cambridge, Cambridge University Press, 1972); J.A. Kregel, *The Reconstruction of Political Economy: An Introduction to Post-Keynesian Economics* (London, Macmillan, 1975); T.W. Hutchison, *A Review of Economic Doctrines, 1870–1929* (Oxford, Clarendon Press, 1953) and, by the same author, *On Revolutions and Progress in Economic Knowledge* (Cambridge, Cambridge University Press, 1978); T.C. Koopmans, *Three Essays on the State of Economic Science* (New York, McGraw-Hill, 1957); F.H. Knight, *On the History and Method of Economics* (Chicago, University of Chicago Press, 1956).

7 P.D. McClelland, *Causal Explanation and Model Building in History, Economics and the New Economic History* (London, Cornell University Press, 1975), especially Chapter III, 'Causal explanation and model building in economics'; the quotations are from p. 118.

8 L. Nizard, 'Planning as the regulatory reproduction of the status quo' in J. Hayward and M. Watson (eds), *Planning, Politics and Public Policy: The British, French and Italian Experience* (London, Cambridge University Press, 1975), p. 433.

9 G.L.S. Shackle, *Epistemics and Economics*, p. 139. See also G. Routh, *The Origin of Economic Ideas*, Chapter 4.

10 N. Georgescu-Roegen, *The Entropy Law and the Economic Process* (Cambridge, Mass., Harvard University Press, 1971), p. 41.

11 G.L.S. Shackle, *Epistemics and Economics*, pp. 10–12, 55–7. There have been changes in business cycle theory that have tended to de-emphasize clock time. See N. Georgescu-Roegen, *The Entropy Law and the Economic Process*, pp. 139–40.

12 T.W. Hutchison, *A Review of Economic Doctrines, 1870–1929*, Part I, Chapters 1, 9, 13 and 14; L. Walras, *Elements of Pure Economics*, W. Jaffé, translator (Homewood Ill., Richard D. Irwin, 1954), especially Lessons 1 to 4; J.A. Schumpeter, *History of Economic Analysis*, Part IV, Chapter 7.

13 N. Georgescu-Roegen, *The Entropy Law and the Economic Process*, p. 14.

14 Ibid., p. 45; G.L.S. Shackle, *Epistemics and Economics*, Book I, Chapters 1 and 5; R. Harré, *Matter and Method* (London, Macmillan, 1964) and by the same author *The Principles of Scientific Thinking* (London, Macmillan, 1970).

15 N. Georgescu-Roegen, *The Entropy Law and the Economic Process*, pp. 318–19. Also M. Hollis and E.J. Nell, *Rational Economic Man* (Cambridge, Cambridge University Press, 1975), particularly Chapters 1, 2 and 8. Note especially the Appendix to Chapter 1.

16 G.L.S. Shackle, *Epistemics and Economics*, p. 104; G. Routh, *The Origin of Economic Ideas*, Chapter 4.

17 N. Georgescu-Roegen, *The Entropy Law and the Economic Process*, p. 343. This tendency is, of course, present in Classical writings, although it is more marked in Neoclassical presentations. See, for example, T.W. Hutchison, *On Revolutions and Progress in Economic Knowledge*, p. 145.

18 G.L.S. Shackle, *Epistemics and Economics*, Book I, Chapters 6 and 7, Book II, Chapters 8–12.

19 Ibid., pp. 131–3.

20 See, for example, Simon's definition of substantive rationality in H.A. Simon, 'From substantive to procedural rationality' in S.J. Latsis (ed.), *Method and Appraisal in Economics* (Cambridge, Cambridge University Press, 1976).

21 R.B. Ekelund and R.F. Hebert, *A History of Economic Theory and Method* (New York, McGraw-Hill, 1975), p. 326.

22 G.L.S. Shackle, *Epistemics and Economics*, p. 131.

23 R.B. Ekelund and R.F. Hebert, *A History of Economic Theory and Method*, Chapter 12; Sir John Hicks, '"Revolutions" in economics' in S.J. Latsis (ed.), *Method and Appraisal in Economics*; M. Morishima, *Walras' Economics* (Cambridge, Cambridge University Press, 1977).

24 M. Blaug, *Economic Theory in Retrospect* (Cambridge, Cambridge University Press, 1978), p. 4.

25 See, for example, A. Coddington's comments about General Equilibrium Theory in 'The rationale of general equilibrium theory', *Economic Inquiry*, XIII, 4 (1975), 541.

26 M. Blaug, *Economic Theory in Retrospect*, Chapter 9.

27 T.W. Hutchison, *A Review of Economic Doctrines 1870–1929*, pp. 28–31.

28 Ibid., pp. 47–8, 148, 200–1, 210–15, 224–30.

29 T. Parsons, *The Structure of Social Action* (New York, The Free Press, 1968), Volume I, p. 64.

30 Ibid., pp. 67–8.

31 R. Whitley, 'Changes in the social and intellectual organisation of the sciences: professionalisation and the arithmetic ideal' in E. Mendelsohn, P. Weingart and R. Whitley (eds), *Sociology of the Sciences, A Yearbook, The Social Production of Scientific Knowledge*, Vol. 1 (Dordrecht, D. Reidel, 1977), p. 147.

32 T. Parsons, *The Structure of Social Action*, Vol. I, pp. 56–7.

33 P.D. McClelland, *Causal Explanation and Model Building in History, Economics and the New Economic History*, p. 125. See also T.C. Koopmans, *Three Essays on the State of Economic Science*, pp. 142–9; M. Blaug, *Economic Theory in Retrospect*, Chapter 16; J. Robinson, 'What are the questions?', *Journal of Economic Literature*, **15**, 4 (1977); T.W. Hutchison, 'History and philosophy of science and economics', in S.J. Latsis (ed.), *Method and Appraisal in Economics*, p. 202.

34 L.A. Boland, 'Conventionalism and economic theory', *Philosophy of Science*, **37**, 2 (1970), 239.

35 F. Suppe, 'Historical background to the received view' in F. Suppe (ed.), *The Structure of Scientific Theories* (Urbana, University of Illinois Press, 1974), particularly pp. 8–9.

36 G.J. Stigler, 'The development of utility theory' in G.J. Stigler, *Essays in the History of Economics*, p. 152.

37 Ibid.

38 M. Blaug, *Economic Theory in Retrospect*, p. 369.

39 G.J. Stigler, 'The development of utility theory', pp. 152–3; for a brief review of a number of the problems of 'knowledge' that microeconomics excludes from its brief, see A. Coddington, 'Creaking semaphore and beyond: a consideration of Shackle's "Epistemics and Economics"', *British Journal of Philosophy of Science*, **26**, 2 (1975).

40 See H.A. Simon, *Administrative Behavior* (New York, Macmillan, 1957), Chapters IV and V.

41 In recent decades virtually all specialities of economics have become increasingly mathematical in their orientation, some more so than others. This has not meant, however, that the profession has been especially adventurous in applying mathematics to economics. Koopmans noted in the 1950s that economics teaching had generally failed to introduce economics students to branches of mathematics such as topology or symbolic logic despite what he perceived to be the increasing importance of fundamental mathematics within economics. T.C. Koopmans, *Three Essays on the State of Economic Science*, pp. 172–8. This type of conservatism may have an inhibiting effect on the discipline. Blin, for example, has argued that economists have not taken full advantage of the 'rich' algebras presently available in approaching the aggregation problem. J.M. Blin, *Patterns and Configurations in Economic Science* (Dordrecht, D. Reidel, 1973).

42 P.D. McClelland, *Causal Explanation and Model Building in History, Economics and the New Economic History*, p. 107.

43 D. Winch, *Economics and Policy: A Historical Survey*, pp. 334–5 for his comments concerning Keynes's affiliation to standard Marshallian microeconomics. Also, see the first pages of R. Bartlett, *Economic Foundations of Political Power* (New York, The Free Press, 1973).

44 It should be noted in this connection that the authority of rationality is very significant even within those specialities, such as economic history, that are on the periphery of the economics discipline. See D.C. North, 'The place of economic history in the discipline of economics', *Economic Inquiry*, XIV, 4 (1976).

45 Note L. Walras, *Elements of Pure Economics*, pp. 71–2. Microeconomics was not always so anti-empirical. Cournot, Dupuit, Jevons and Marshall are examples of economists who gave attention to the empirical and the practical in the development of economics, but as Neoclassical theory became entrenched these concerns waned.

46 In the academic environment more weight is given to distinctions based upon the proximity of a speciality to the rationalistic, hence, theoretical core of the discipline. Thus, in general, within this context the analytical economist is more prestigious than the applied economist, and, for example, the pricing expert is more prestigious than the specialist in labour economics.

47 This is not to say that distinctions on the basis of speciality affiliations have never been made. Agricultural economists were denied entry to the Government Economic Service in 1965 because it was considered that they were not engaged in legitimate economic analysis. However, in general, the Service has tended to be egalitarian, and with time even the agricultural economists were incorporated. A.W. Coats, 'The development of the agricultural economics profession in England', *Journal of Agricultural Economics*, **27**, 3 (1976).

48 Interview, senior civil servants, Civil Service Department, London, 2 November 1976. See also G.J.A. Stern, 'SOSIPing, or Sophistical Obfuscation of Self Interest and Prejudice', *Operations Research Quarterly*, **27**, 4 (1976); J. Lesourne, 'Operational research in government and planning', *Omega*, **2**, 3 (1974).

49 R. Whitley, 'Changes in the social and intellectual organisation of the sciences: professionalisation and the arithmetic ideal', p. 151. Whitley has observed that arithmetic sciences deal with a small number of classes containing very large numbers of individuals. A corollary of this is that disciplines like economics that attempt to subsume configurational subject areas in an arithmetic way permit the proliferation of analytical categories in order to take in as many qualities as possible while at the same time treating these numerous qualities, not as a foundation for the definition of many classes, but as individuals in the arithmetic sense.

50 Monolithic rationality of this type has not been without its critics even within the policy sciences community; see, for example, R.E. Floden and S.S. Weiner, 'Rationality to ritual: the multiple roles of evaluation in governmental processes', *Policy Sciences*, **9**, 1 (1978), especially the remarks under 'Some implications' which refer to the disciplinary basis of this type of rationality.

51 J.R. Ravetz, *Scientific Knowledge and its Social Problems* (Harmondsworth, Middx, Penguin, 1973), p. 343.

52 A. Wildavsky, 'Evaluation as an organisational problem', London, Centre for Environmental Studies, University Working Paper No. 13, January 1972, p. 23, where he has noted that in certain systems (i.e. rational systems) objectives 'may have little to do with the ostensible purposes with which the program began, but a great deal to do with the ease of computation'.

Notes for Chapter 2

1 R.J. Hammond, *Benefit–Cost Analysis and Water-Pollution Control* (Stanford, Calif., Stanford University Press, 1960), p. 3. Some of the better known British surveys of cost–benefit analysis that discuss the methodology's development are: A.R. Prest and R. Turvey, 'Cost–benefit analysis: a survey', *Economic Journal*, LXXV, 300 (1965); T. Newton, *Cost–Benefit Analysis in Administration* (London, George Allen and Unwin, 1972), Parts I and V; J.N. Wolfe (ed.), *Cost Benefit and Cost Effectiveness, Studies and Analysis* (London, George Allen and Unwin, 1973), especially the introduction.

2 J. Dupuit, 'On the measurement of the utility of public works', R.H. Barback, translator, in *International Economic Papers*, Vol. II, 1952. See also R.B.

Ekelund and R.F. Hebert, *A History of Economic Theory and Method*, Part Four, Chapter 9.

3 V. Pareto, *Manuel d'économie politique*, translator A. Bonnet (Paris, R. Pichon and R. Durand Auzias, 1963); also R.W. Reder, *Studies in the Theory of Welfare Economics* (New York, AMS Press, 1968), Chapters I–VIII; J. Quirk and R. Saposnik, *Introduction to General Equilibrium Theory and Welfare Economics* (New York, McGraw-Hill, 1968) especially Chapter 4; M. Blaug, *Economic Theory in Retrospect*, Chapter 13.

4 V. Pareto, *Manuel d'économie politique*, Chapter VI, paras. 32–8; J. Quirk and R. Saposnik, *Introduction to General Equilibrium Theory and Welfare Economics*, pp. 124–47.

5 V. Pareto, *The Mind and Society: A Treatise on General Sociology* (New York, Dover, 1963), Vol. 4, Chapter XII, paras. 2126–30 and especially para. 2130. Also V.J. Tarascio, *Pareto's Methodological Approach to Economics* (Chapel Hill, University of North Carolina Press, 1968), pp. 77–84.

6 R.G. Lipsey and R.K. Lancaster, 'The General Theory of Second Best', *Review of Economic Studies*, **24**, 1 (1956). For a brief, but succinct, review of the 'devastating' impact of the General Theory of Second Best upon welfare economics, see D.M. Winch, *Analytical Welfare Economics* (Harmondsworth, Middx, Penguin, 1971), pp. 110–16. The General Theory of Second Best is not the only development in pure welfare economics to have had major implications for applied practice. See W.J. Baumol, 'Informed judgement, rigorous theory and public policy', *Southern Economic Journal*, **32** (1965).

7 C.M. Price, *Welfare Economics in Theory and Practice* (London, Macmillan, 1977), p. 23. E. Barone, 'The Ministry of Production in the collectivist state', in A. Nove and D.M. Nuti (eds), *Penguin Modern Economics Readings: Socialist Economics* (Harmondsworth, Middx, Penguin, 1972). N. Kaldor, *Essays on Value and Distribution* (London, Duckworth, 1960), Part III, Chapter 7; J.R. Hicks, 'The foundations of welfare economics', *Economic Journal*, XLIX (1939). T. Scitovsky, *Papers on Welfare and Growth* (Stanford, Stanford University Press, 1964) especially Chapter 7. See also Chapter 10 of this volume, 'The state of welfare economics' for a review of the history of welfare economics in the first half of this century. For a discussion of welfare theory generally, see K.E. Boulding, 'Welfare economics', in V.F. Haley (ed.), *A Survey of Contemporary Economics*, Vol. II (Homewood, Ill., Richard D. Irwin, for the American Economic Association, 1952); E.J. Mishan, 'A survey of welfare economics, 1939–59' in *Surveys of Economic Theory: Money, Interest and Welfare*, Vol. I (London, Macmillan, for the American Economic Association and the Royal Economic Society, 1968).

8 W.J. Baumol, *Economic Theory and Operations Analysis* (Englewood Cliffs, N.J., Prentice-Hall, 1977), Chapter 21, Section 14.

9 A. Marshall, *Principles of Economics* (London, Macmillan, 1890), Book III, Chapter IV.

10 J.R. Hicks, 'The four consumer's surpluses', *Review of Economic Studies*, XI, 1 (1943); D.M. Winch, 'Consumer's surplus and the compensation principle', *American Economic Review*, LV, 3 (1965). Also E.J. Mishan, *Cost–Benefit Analysis: An Informal Introduction* (London, George Allen and Unwin, 1975), Part II and Part VII, Note B. For an exposition of consumer's surplus typical of those found in many practitioner-oriented explanations of the basis of CBA methodology see the Introduction to R. Layard (ed.), *Cost–Benefit Analysis* (Harmondsworth, Middx, Penguin, 1972).

11 M. Blaug, *Economic Theory in Retrospect*, pp. 377 and 422.

12 G.L.S. Shackle, *Epistemics and Economics*, p. 261. Samuelson has

questioned whether the consumer's surplus concept is plausible even under these circumstances. P.A. Samuelson, *Foundations of Economic Analysis* (New York, Atheneum, 1967), Chapter VIII, especially pp. 208–10.

13 M. Blaug, *Economic Theory in Retrospect*, p. 421.

14 G.L.S. Shackle, *Epistemics and Economics*, pp. 109–10.

15 Marshall was aware of these obstacles to aggregation, but his successors have often been inclined to set them aside. See H. Myint, *Theories of Welfare Economics* (New York, A.M. Kelley, 1965) Chapter IX, and especially pp. 145–7.

16 C.M. Price, *Welfare Economics in Theory and Practice*, p. 29.

17 V. Pareto, *The Mind and Society: A Treatise on General Sociology*, Vol. 4, Chapter VII, paras. 2126–30.

18 As will become evident later in this chapter, the collectivity is a virtual, rather than an actual, 'agent of choice'.

19 T. Parsons, *The Structure of Social Action*, Vol. I, pp. 228–41 and especially p. 231 for the quotation.

20 See, for example, T. Newton, *Cost Benefit Analysis in Administration*, Chapter I; E.J. Mishan, *Cost–Benefit Analysis: An Informal Introduction*, Part I; A.R. Prest and R. Turvey, 'The main questions' in R. Layard (ed.), *Cost–Benefit Analysis*.

21 This type of usage of CBA is perhaps most evident in the military field. See C.J. Hitch and R.N. McKean, *Economics of Defense in the Nuclear Age* (Cambridge, Harvard University Press, 1960), Part II.

22 H.G. Walsh and A. Williams, 'Current issues in cost–benefit analysis', CAS Occasional Paper No. 11 (London, HMSO, 1969); A. Peacock, 'Cost–benefit analysis and the political control of public investment' in J.N. Wolfe (ed.), *Cost Benefit and Cost Effectiveness, Studies and Analysis*.

23 B. Stafford, 'The policy techniques of welfare economics in the context of theories of governing' in A.J. Culyer (ed.), *Economic Policies and Social Goals* (London, Martin Robertson, 1974), p. 26. Note also A. Williams, 'Cost–benefit analysis: bastard science? and/or insidious poison in the body politick?' in J.N. Wolfe (ed.), *Cost Benefit and Cost Effectiveness, Studies and Analysis*.

24 E.J. Mishan, *Cost–Benefit Analysis: An Informal Introduction*, Chapter 11.

25 See R.A. Dahl and C.E. Lindblom, *Politics, Economics and Welfare* (Chicago, University of Chicago Press, 1976), Part I, Chapter 1, Section II C.3; Part I, Chapter 2, Section II B; Part III, Chapter 5.

26 See J.M. Buchanan, *Cost and Choice: An Inquiry in Economic Theory* (Chicago, Markham, 1969), Chapters 1–3 in which the development of the opportunity cost concept is reviewed in some detail; the quotation is from p. 46. See also, H. Myint, *Theories of Welfare Economics*, Chapters I to V; G.F. Thirlby, 'Economists' cost rules and Equilibrium Theory', *Economica*, XXVII, 106 (1960); M.S. Feldstein, 'Opportunity cost calculations in cost–benefit analysis', *Public Finance*, **19** (1964); S.A. Marglin, 'The opportunity costs of public investment' in R. Layard (ed.), *Cost–Benefit Analysis*; A.A. Alchian, 'Cost' in D.L. Sills (ed.), *International Encyclopedia of the Social Sciences*, Vol. 3 (United States, Crowell Collier and Macmillan, 1968); R.W. Judy, 'Costs: theoretical and methodological issues' in G.G. Somers and W.D. Wood (eds), *Cost–Benefit Analysis of Manpower Policies* (Kingston, Ontario, Industrial Relations Centre, Queen's University, 1969).

27 J.R. Hicks, 'The scope and status of welfare economics', *Oxford Economic Papers*, **27**, 3 (1975), 313.

28 Ibid., p. 314.

29 E.J. Mishan, *Cost–Benefit Analysis: An Informal Introduction*, p. 112; W.J.

Baumol, *Welfare Economics and the Theory of the State* (London, G. Bell and Sons, 1965), pp. 24–36 and Part I; J.M. Buchanan, *The Demand and Supply of Public Goods* (Chicago, Rand McNally, 1968); J.E. Meade, *The Theory of Economic Externalities* (Leiden, A.W. Sijthoff, 1973); E.J. Mishan, *The Costs of Economic Growth* (London, Staples Press, 1976).

30 Although there are certain instances in which externalities are considered to be 'internalized' into the pricing mechanism – i.e. through the transformation of an individual by-product into a joint product.

31 E.J. Mishan, *Cost–Benefit Analysis: An Informal Introduction*, Chapter 18.

32 Ibid., p. 115.

33 T. Newton, *Cost–Benefit Analysis in Administration*, p. 23.

34 A.C. Pigou, *The Economics of Welfare* (London, Macmillan, 1962), Chapter 1 and especially p. 11 from which the quotation is taken.

35 This was a development that derived from Pigou's 'Classicism'.

36 R.N. McKean, 'The use of shadow prices' in R. Layard (ed.), *Cost–Benefit Analysis*; R. Millward, *Public Expenditure Economics* (London, McGraw-Hill, 1971), pp. 305–10; E.J. Mishan, *Cost–Benefit Analysis: An Informal Introduction*, Chapters 13 and 14.

37 R. Sugden, 'On the political economy of social discount rates' in A.J. Culyer (ed.), *Economic Policies and Social Goals*; W.J. Baumol, 'On the social rate of discount', *American Economic Review*, **58**, 4 (1968); M.S. Feldstein, 'The social time preference discount rate in cost–benefit analysis', *Economic Journal*, **74**, 294 (1964); S.A. Marglin, 'The social rate of discount and the optimal rate of investment', *Quarterly Journal of Economics*, **77**, 306 (1963); K.J. Arrow, 'The social discount rate' in G.G. Somers and W.D. Wood (eds), *Cost–Benefit Analysis of Manpower Policies*.

38 *Nationalised Industries: A Review of Economic and Financial Objectives*, Cmnd. 3437 (1967); interview, civil servant, H.M. Treasury, London, 16 September 1976; interview, senior civil servants, H.M. Treasury, London, 9 November 1976; J.S. Fleming *et al.*, 'Trends in company profitability', *Bank of England Quarterly Bulletin*, **16**, 1 (1976); M.F.G. Scott and M. Dowley, 'The test rate of discount and changes in base-level income in the United Kingdom', *Economic Journal*, **87** (1977).

39 E.J. Mishan, *Cost–Benefit Analysis: An Informal Introduction*, Chapter 12.

40 See the Introduction of R. Layard (ed.), *Cost–Benefit Analysis*; E.J. Mishan, *Cost–Benefit Analysis: An Informal Introduction*, Chapter 44.

41 Reviews of investment criteria relevant to CBA are contained in A.J. Merrett and A. Sykes, *The Finance and Analysis of Capital Projects* (London, Longmans, 1963), Part I, Chapters 2 and 5; O. Eckstein, 'A survey of the theory of public expenditure criteria' in R.W. Houghton (ed.), *Public Finance* (Harmondsworth, Middx, Penguin, 1970); P.D. Henderson, 'Investment criteria for public enterprises' in R. Turvey (ed.), *Public Enterprise* (Harmondsworth, Middx, Penguin, 1968); R. Rees, 'The economics of investment analysis', CAS Occasional Paper No. 17 (London, HMSO, 1973). For an overview of the way in which the cost–benefit methodology has been applied in the public sector in Britain, see the references contained in Note 1 of this chapter (with the exception of Hammond); R. Millward, *Public Expenditure Economics*, Chapter 9 entitled 'Problems in cost/benefit estimation'; M.S. Feldstein, 'Cost–benefit analysis and investment in the public sector', *Cost–Benefit Analysis and Public Expenditure* (London, Institute of Economic Affairs, 1966); D.W. Pearce, *Cost–Benefit Analysis* (London, Macmillan, 1971).

42 B. Stafford, 'The policy techniques of welfare economics in the context of theories of governing' in A.J. Culyer (ed.), *Economic Policies and Social Goals*, pp. 23–4.

43 E.J. Mishan, *Cost–Benefit Analysis: An Informal Introduction*, Part VII contains a detailed review of the Paretian foundations of CBA.

44 C. Nash, D. Pearce and J. Stanley, 'An evaluation of cost–benefit analysis criteria', *Scottish Journal of Political Economy*, XXII, 2 (1975). See also, R.W. Boadway, 'The welfare foundations of cost-benefit analysis', *Economic Journal*, LXXXIV (1974); R. Boadway, 'Integrating equity and efficiency in applied welfare economics', *Quarterly Journal of Economics*, XC, 4 (1976); B.A. Weisbrod, 'Deriving an implicit set of governmental weights for income classes' in R. Layard (ed.), *Cost–Benefit Analysis*; A.J. Culyer, 'The quality of life and the limits of cost–benefit analysis' in L. Wingo and A. Evans (eds), *Public Economics and the Quality of Life* (Baltimore, Johns Hopkins University Press, 1977).

45 See the discussion of N. Lichfield's work and accompanying references in T. Newton, *Cost–Benefit Analysis in Administration*, Chapter 9.

46 K.E. Boulding, 'Welfare economics', pp. 4–5. In this, Boulding is simply reiterating Ricardo's view of welfare.

47 The first view is historically associated with L.C. Robbins, *An Essay on the Nature and Significance of Economic Science* (London, Macmillan, 1932). Note also G.C. Archibald, 'Welfare economics, ethics and essentialism', *Economica*, XXVI, 104 (1959). The contrary view (i.e. that which stresses the ethical character of welfare theory) is associated with the work of writers like Little, de Van Graaff, and, more recently, Nath. See I.M.D. Little, *A Critique of Welfare Economics* (London, Oxford University Press, 1973); J. de Van Graaf, *Theoretical Welfare Economics* (Cambridge, Cambridge University Press, 1957); S.K. Nath, *A Reappraisal of Welfare Economics* (London, Routledge and Kegan Paul, 1969).

48 M. Blaug, 'Kuhn versus Lakatos *or* paradigms versus research programmes in the history of economics' in S.J. Latsis (ed.), *Method and Appraisal in Economics*, p. 175. Treatments of some of the more detailed aspects of cost–benefit methodology, including a number of the topics covered in this chapter, are contained in J.S. Fleming, 'What discount rate for public expenditure'; A. Williams, 'Income distribution and public expenditure decisions'; and E.J. Mishan, 'Welfare economics and public expenditure' all in M. Posner (ed.), *Public Expenditure: Allocation Between Competing Ends* (Cambridge, Cambridge University Press, 1977). See also A. Bergson, 'A note on consumer's surplus', *Journal of Economic Literature*, XIII, 1 (1975); E.J. Mishan, 'The use of compensating and equivalent variations in cost–benefit analysis', *Economica*, **43**, 170 (1976); R.D. Willig, 'Consumer's surplus without apology', *American Economic Review*, **66**, 4 (1976).

Notes for Chapter 3

1 Note M. Posner (ed.), *Public Enterprise: Allocation Between Competing Ends*; M. Sharp, *The State, the Enterprise and the Individual* (London, Weidenfeld and Nicholson, 1973); C.M. Price, *Welfare Economics in Theory and Practice*; B. Smith, *Policy Making in British Government: An Analysis of Power and Rationality* (London, Martin Robertson, 1976), especially Chapter 9.

2 For a review of the development and operation of PESC and PAR see H. Heclo and A. Wildavsky, *The Private Government of Public Money: Community and Policy inside British Politics* (London, Macmillan, 1974). Note also HM Treasury, *Public Expenditure White Papers: Handbook on Methodology* (London,

HMSO, 1972); M. Spiers, *Techniques and Public Administration* (London, Fontana/Collins, 1975) and A. Wildavsky, *Budgeting, A Comparative Theory of Budgetary Processes* (Boston, Little, Brown, 1975), especially Chapters 18 and 19 in which PESC and programme budgeting are contrasted. Note as well W.Z. Hirsch, 'Program budgeting in the United Kingdom', *Public Administration Review*, **33**, 2 (1973) in which PESC, PAR and CPRS are reviewed. By the mid-1970s enthusiasm for PESC and PAR was waning, especially as concern with financial control deepened from 1975–6 onwards. See, in particular M. Wright, 'Public expenditure in Britain: the crisis of control', *Public Administration*, **55** (1977); Third Special Report of the Select Committee on Expenditure, *Cash Limit Control of Public Expenditure Programmes*, H.C. 204, Session 1975–76; M. Wright, 'From planning to control: PESC in the 1970s' in M. Wright (ed.), *Public Spending Decisions* (London, George Allen and Unwin, 1980); A. Gray and B. Jenkins, 'Policy analysis in British central government: the experience of PAR', *Public Administration*, **60**, 4 (1982). On the application of output or programme budgeting in British central government in the 1970s, see M. Spiers, *Techniques and Public Administration*; A. Williams, 'Output budgeting and the contribution of microeconomics to efficiency in government', CAS Occasional Paper No. 4 (London, HMSO, 1970); Department of Education and Science, 'Output budgeting for the Department of Education and Science', Education Planning Paper No. 1 (London, HMSO, 1970); G.J. Wasserman, 'Planning programming budgeting in the police service in England and Wales', *O & M Bulletin*, **25**, 4 (1970); J.G. Bagley, 'Planning programming budgeting in DES', *O & M Bulletin*, **27**, 2 (1972); R. Klein 'The politics of PPB', *Political Quarterly*, **43**, 3 (1972); C.K. Fry, 'Policy-planning units in British Central government departments', *Public Administration*, **50** (1972). For a discussion of the impact that output or programme budgeting has had upon public affairs, see H.R. van Gunsteren, *The Quest for Control* (London, Wiley, 1976). Note also H. Glennerster, *Social Budgets and Social Policy: British and American Experience* (London, George Allen and Unwin, 1975). A number of the methodological issues associated with the use of CBA in the public sector are reviewed in H.G. Walsh and A. Williams, 'Current issues in cost–benefit analysis', CAS Occasional Paper No. 11 (London, HMSO, 1969). The problem of how one compares results from cost–benefit studies with results from more conventional financial analyses is treated in A.J. Harrison and P.J. Mackie, 'The comparability of cost benefit and financial rates of return', Government Economic Service Occasional Paper No. 5 (London, HMSO, 1973).

3 For two quite different, and often opposing views, concerning the suitability of CBA for the analysis of aggregate expenditure, see R.N. McKean, 'Cost–benefit analysis and British defence expenditure', in A.T. Peacock and D.J. Robertson (eds), *Public Expenditure Appraisal and Control* (London, Oliver and Boyd, 1963) and B. Contini, 'A critical survey of the use of cost–benefit analysis in public finance' in A.T. Peacock and D. Biehl (eds), *Quantitiative Analysis in Public Finance* (London, Praeger, 1969). British Government practice has tended to confirm Contini's emphasis on the limitations of CBA with regard to variegated expenditure.

4 A.R. Prest and R. Turvey, 'Cost–benefit analysis: a survey', *Economic Journal*, LXXV (1965), 686.

5 For example, HM Treasury, *Dossier on Cost Benefit Analysis in the Public Sector during 1973*, Vol. VI, May 1974.

6 A.R. Prest and R. Turvey, 'Cost–benefit analysis: a survey', p. 731.

7 Ibid., p. 683.

8 *Control of Public Expenditure* (The Plowden Report), Cmnd. 1432 (1961).

See also the articles in *Public Administration*, **41** (1963) under the heading *The Plowden Report*; W.J.M. Mackenzie, 'The Plowden Report: a translation' in R. Rose (ed.), *Policy Making in Britain* (London, Macmillan, 1969).

9 C.D. Foster, *Politics, Finance and the Role of Economics: An Essay on the Control of Public Enterprise* (London, George Allen and Unwin, 1971), pp. 47–52. Note also M.V. Posner, 'Pricing and investment policies of nationalised industries' in A. Cairncross (ed.), *The Managed Economy* (London, Basil Blackwell, 1970).

10 *Nationalised Industries: A Review of Economic and Financial Objectives*, Cmnd. 3437 (1967).

11 Ibid., paras. 8–16.

12 As Foster noted, discounting is one of the most appropriate devices for a non-interventionist government to employ so as to appear to be exercising investment control while avoiding the details of the structural problems of investment. C.D. Foster, *Politics, Finance and the Role of Economics*, p. 47.

13 This was particularly important given that the bureaucracy had been under attack for a decade for its inefficiency. See J. Garrett, *The Management of Government* (London, George Allen and Unwin, 1972); M. Nicholson, *The System* (London, Hodder, 1967); H. Thomas (ed.), *Crisis in the Civil Service* (London, Anthony Blond, 1968); W.A. Robson, 'The Fulton Report on the civil service', *Political Quarterly*, **39**, 4 (1968).

14 In particular, it gave no guidance as to whom costs and benefits do, or ought to, accrue. The term 'social' could imply a concern with the public at large, with government, with representative interest groups, with the private sector, with the nationalized sector, or with combinations of some of the foregoing, but its meaning was not made clear.

15 First Report from the Select Committee on Nationalised Industries, *Capital Investment Procedures*, H.C. 65, Session 1973–74.

16 Ibid., pp. 242–7, 291–305.

17 Ibid., pp. 70–83.

18 Ibid., p. 72, para. 281.

19 Ibid., p. 72, para. 282.

20 First Report from the Select Committee on Nationalised Industries, *The Role of British Rail in Public Transport*, Volume I, H.C. 305-I, Session 1976–77. Note especially, Department of Transport, *Report of the Advisory Committee on Trunk Road Assessment*, Chairman: Sir George Leitch (London, HMSO, 1978), particularly Chapters 25–7.

21 For a brief review of some aspects of this process in the early 1970s, see D. Keeling, *Management in Government* (London, George Allen and Unwin, 1972), particularly Chapter 6.

22 This approach was employed in the Roskill Commission's work on the Third London Airport.

23 N. Georgescu-Roegen, *Energy and Economic Myths: Institutional and Analytical Essays* (New York, Pergamon Press, 1976), p. 33.

24 Ibid., p. 9.

25 H. Heclo and A. Wildavsky, *The Private Government of Public Money*, Chapter 6, especially pp. 280–4.

26 Lord Diamond, *Public Expenditure in Practice* (London, George Allen and Unwin, 1975), pp. 161–5.

27 Note W. Godley, 'The measurement and control of public expenditure', *Economic Policy Review*, **2** (March 1976).

28 C.D. Foster, *Politics, Finance and the Role of Economics*, pp. 57–67.

29 H. Heclo and A. Wildavsky, *The Private Government of Public Money*, Chapter 6.

30 D. Munby, 'The assessment of priorities in public expenditure', *Political Quarterly*, **39**, 4 (1968), particularly pp. 379–80.

31 A.T. Peacock, 'The fiscal economist and quantitative analysis', in A.T. Peacock and D. Biehl (eds), *Quantitative Analysis in Public Finance*, pp. 7–8.

32 The commitments and constraints of the Treasury *vis-à-vis* CBA are indicated in the First Report from the Select Committee on Procedure, *Scrutiny of Public Expenditure and Administration*, H.C. 410, Session 1968–69, pp. 1–14, 21; note also, HM Treasury, *Public Expenditure White Papers: Handbook on Methodology*.

33 Interview, civil servant, HM Treasury, London, 16 September 1976; interview, senior civil servant, HM Treasury, London, 9 November 1976; interview, senior civil servant, Department of the Environment, London, 27 October 1976.

34 For descriptions of the principal features of the GES, see R.G.S. Brown, *The Administrative Process in Britain* (London, Methuen, 1970), pp. 76–9; Sir Alec Cairncross, *Essays in Economic Management* (London, George Allen and Unwin, 1971), Chapters 10–11; A.E. Booth and A.W. Coats, 'The market for economists in Britain, 1945–75: a preliminary survey', pp. 442–5. Some insight into the personalities holding high office in the GES became available as a result of a variety of almost simultaneous changes in personnel in the Treasury and other parts of government during 1976–7. See P. Riddell, 'Liesner for top advisory post', *Financial Times*, 18 August 1976; M. Crawford, 'Let's play musical economists', *The Sunday Times*, 22 August 1976; 'Finding the top economist', *Financial Times*, 23 August 1976; F. Cairncross, 'Tonight a dinner is being held to mark one of the most extraordinary bouts of musical chairs that Whitehall has ever seen', *The Guardian*, 29 June 1977; P. Riddell, 'Treasury selects adviser after three-month search', *Financial Times*, 20 January 1978. For a historical perspective upon 'the age of the official economic adviser', see D. Winch, *Economics and Policy: A Historical Survey*, Chapter 14.

35 The relations between departmental economists and Treasury officials (particularly economists) sometimes proceeded beyond intellectual affinities to include a weak 'division of labour' in some areas. As one Treasury official noted, there is a sense in which weaknesses in the Treasury's capabilities in certain areas have been complemented by strengths in the same areas in the Departments and *vice versa*, see H.C. 65, Session 1973–74, pp. 257–9.

36 Interview, civil servant, Department of the Environment, London, 23 August 1976.

37 This is analogous to the line-staff division so frequently found in industry – the origins of which are discussed in A.W. Gouldner, *Patterns of Industrial Bureaucracy* (New York, The Free Press, 1954), especially pp. 224–8. In this connection note also P. Self, *Administrative Theories and Politics* (London, George Allen and Unwin, 1973), Chapter 4 and M.J. Hill, *The Sociology of Public Administration* (London, Weidenfeld and Nicolson, 1972), Chapter 8.

38 Interview, civil servant, Department of the Environment, 23 August 1976.

39 Interview, civil servant, Department of Health and Social Security, London, 15 September 1976. Note also Dr D. Owen, *In Sickness and in Health* (London, Quartet Books, 1976).

40 For summaries of Sir William Armstrong's stance on a variety of issues connected with the management of government, see Sir William Armstrong, 'Room at the top in ministries', *The Sunday Times*, 16 March 1969; M. Shanks,

'Inside Britain's biggest conglomerate', *The Times*, 23 May 1969; E. Jacobs, 'Cleaning up the corridors of power', *The Sunday Times*, 15 September 1968; P. Jay, 'New man at the helm in Whitehall', *The Times*, 1 May 1968.

41 *Report of the Committee on the Civil Service* (The Fulton Report), Cmnd. 3638 (1968); R. Williams, 'Administrative modernisation in British government', *International Social Science Journal*, XXI, 1 (1969); L.A. Gunn, 'Ministers and civil servants: changes in Whitehall', *Public Administration* (Sydney), XXVI, 1 (1967). Note also the articles in *Public Administration*, **47** (1969) under the heading, *The Fulton Report*.

42 R.G.S. Brown, *The Administrative Process in Britain*, p. 78.

43 T.H. Profitt, 'Great Britain' in F.F. Ridley (ed.), *Specialists and Generalists* (London, George Allen and Unwin, 1968).

44 T.W. Hutchison, *Economics and Economic Policy in Britain, 1946–1966* (London, George Allen and Unwin, 1968).

45 Ibid., 'Conclusions'.

46 Ibid., pp. 256–62, particularly p. 257.

47 Ibid., pp. 256–62.

48 Ibid., p. 274.

49 Ibid., pp. 272–3.

50 Ibid., p. 273.

51 A.K. Cairncross, 'On being an economic adviser', *Scottish Journal of Political Economy*, **2**, 3 (1955).

52 E. Devons, 'The role of the economist in public affairs' in E. Devons, *Essays in Economics* (London, George Allen and Unwin, 1961).

53 P.D. Henderson, 'The use of economists in British administration', *Oxford Economic Papers*, **13**, 1 (1961).

54 Ibid., p. 25.

55 Ibid., p. 10.

56 All of the following appeared in the *Bulletin of the Oxford University Institute of Statistics*, **22**, 4 (1960): D.L. Munby, 'The roads as economic assets'; M.E. Paul, 'Covering costs by receipts'; D.J. Reynolds, 'Some problems of planning the improvement of the road system'; D.W. Glassborow, 'The Road Research Laboratory's investment criteria examined'; E.K. Hawkins, 'Surplus criteria for investment'. T.M. Coburn, M.E. Beesley and D.J. Reynolds, *The London–Birmingham Motorway: Traffic and Economics*, Road Research Technical Paper No. 46 (London, HMSO, 1960).

57 M.S. Feldstein, 'Economic analysis, operational research and the National Health Service', *Oxford Economic Papers*, **15**, 1 (1963); M.S. Feldstein, 'Cost-benefit analysis and investment in the public sector', *Public Administration*, **42** (1964).

58 M.S. Feldstein, 'Economic analysis, operational research and the National Health Service', p. 19.

59 Ibid., pp. 20–1.

60 Ibid., pp. 22–31.

61 C.D. Foster and M.E. Beesley, 'Estimating the social benefit of constructing an underground railway in London', *Journal of the Royal Statistical Society*, Series A (General), **126**, Part I (1963); M.E. Beesley and C.D. Foster, 'The Victoria line: social benefit and finances', *Journal of the Royal Statistical Society*, Series A (General), **128**, Part I (1965).

62 Sir Alec Cairncross, 'Economists in government', *Lloyds Bank Review*, **95** (1970); M.J. Hill, *The Sociology of Public Administration*, pp. 158–60; S. Brittan, *Steering the Economy: The Role of the Treasury* (Harmondsworth, Middx,

Penguin, 1971), pp. 38–40; A.E. Booth and A.W. Coats, 'The market for economists in Britain', pp. 442–5. For a description of one individual's experience as an economic adviser in the years before the Second World War, see G.C. Allan, 'Advice from economists – forty-five years ago', *The Three Banks Review*, **106** (1975).

63 Sir Alec Cairncross, 'Economists in government', p. 3.

64 A.E. Booth and A.W. Coats, 'The market for economists in Britain', p. 444.

65 Sir Eric Roll, 'The machinery for economic planning: 1. The Department of Economic Affairs', *Public Administration*, **44** (1966), 3.

66 Note, for example, W. Beckerman (ed.), *The Labour Government's Economic Record, 1964–70* (London, Duckworth, 1972).

67 G. Hallett, 'The role of economists as government advisers', *Westminster Bank Review*, May 1967.

68 Ibid., p. 11.

69 Ibid., p. 20.

70 M.M. Postan, 'A plague of economists?', *Encounter*, XXX, 1 (1968), 47. See also H.G. Johnson, 'A catarrh of economists?', *Encounter*, XXX, 5 (1968), and M.M. Postan, 'The uses and abuses of economics', *Encounter*, XXXI, 3 (1968).

71 R. Opie, 'The making of economic policy' in H. Thomas (ed.), *Crisis in the Civil Service*, and R. Opie, 'The menace of the amateur economists', *The Sunday Times*, 25 February 1968.

72 Sir Eric Roll, 'Economists in government', *The Economist*, **226** (1968). Note also J.R. Sargent, 'Are American economists better?', *Oxford Economic Papers*, **15**, 1 (1963). For a discussion of the role of the government economist in the United States see H.S. Norton, *The World of the Economist* (Columbia, University of South Carolina Press, 1973), Chapter 4.

73 K.E. Couzens, 'The Management Accounting Unit', *O & M Bulletin*, **23** (1968), 20.

74 HM Treasury, *Glossary of Management Techniques* (London, HMSO, 1967).

75 H.G. Walsh and A. Williams, 'Current issues in cost–benefit analysis'.

76 Ibid., p. 3.

77 Ibid.

78 Sir Alec Cairncross, 'Economists in government', p. 14.

79 A. Williams, 'Cost–benefit analysis' in A. Cairncross (ed.), *The Managed Economy*, pp. 147–8.

80 A. Wildavsky, 'The political economy of efficiency: cost–benefit analysis, systems analysis and program budgeting', *Public Administration Review*, **26** (1966), 304–5.

81 Sir Alec Cairncross, 'Economists in government', p. 6, quoted from Lionel Robbins.

82 Economists have a term for this – cost-benefiteering. For a description of the type of intellectual status that economists were attempting to avoid, see Expenditure Committee (General Sub-Committee), *Developments in the Civil Service since the Fulton Report*, H.C. 29–iii, Session 1976–77, especially the Memorandum submitted on behalf of the Councils of the constituent members of the Consultative Committee of Accountancy Bodies, paras. 19–21.

83 A. Peacock, 'Giving economic advice in difficult times', *The Three Banks Review*, **113** (1977).

Notes for Chapter 4

1 Commission on the Third London Airport, *Papers and Proceedings* (London, HMSO, 1970), especially Vol. 7, parts 1 and 2; Commission on the Third London Airport, *Report* (London, HMSO, 1971); The British Channel Tunnel Co. Ltd., Société Française du Tunnel sous la Manche, *The Channel Tunnel: Economic and Financial Studies, A Report* (London, The British Channel Tunnel Co. Ltd., Société Française du Tunnel sous la Manche, 1973); *The Channel Tunnel: A United Kingdom Transport Cost Benefit Study*, a report by Coopers and Lybrand Associates Ltd. (London, HMSO, 1973); *The Channel Tunnel and Alternative Cross Channel Services*, a Report presented to the Secretary of State for the Environment by the Channel Tunnel Advisory Group (London, HMSO, 1975).

2 I.G. Heggie, 'Transport studies research in U.K. universities', *Transportation*, **6** (1977).

3 Ibid., p. 27.

4 Ibid., p. 30.

5 D.E. Regan, 'The expert and the administrator: recent changes at the Ministry of Transport', *Public Administration*, **44** (1966). In most of the civil Departments of Whitehall professional and non-professional staff have been organized into separate, although broadly parallel, hierarchies. Under this traditional arrangement administrators have had primary responsibility for the Departments' work programme, and professionals have acted as advisers to the administrative divisions and other bodies (e.g. local authorities). Thus, the integration of MOT engineers into the administrative hierarchy of the Ministry during the late 1950s and early 1960s constituted a major departure from established practice resulting in greater status for engineering professionals and a more equal division of responsibility for the development and implementation of work programmes.

6 J.-C. Thoenig and N. Despicht, 'Transport policy' in J. Hayward and M. Watson (eds), *Planning, Politics and Public Policy: The British, French and Italian Experience*, p. 406.

7 Ibid., p. 407; also I.C. Cheeseman, 'Transport technology – master or servant', *Chartered Institute of Transport Journal*, **35**, 2 (1973).

8 Traditionally, capital investment in roads and railways has fluctuated, often quite dramatically, as governments have sought means of curtailing public expenditure in periods of austerity and/or excessive inflation. In the 1970s transport investment, like other types of investment, remained subject to curtailment in the interest of macroeconomic objectives, but cuts were not as arbitrary as in the past. Indeed, with the advent of extensive programme management in the transport field, 'cuts' evolved into 'roll backs' and reductions in expenditure became circumscribed by rules concerning where they should fall so as to have least effect upon the structure and evolution of investment programmes. See, for example, Expenditure Committee (General Sub-Committee), Minutes of Evidence, *Control of Road Programme Expenditure*, H.C. 15, Session 1973–74, for a discussion of 'rules' governing the road programme.

9 T.M. Coburn, M.E. Beesley and D.J. Reynolds, *The London–Birmingham Motorway: Traffic and Economics*; C.D. Foster and M.E. Beesley, 'Estimating the social benefit of constructing an underground railway in London'; M.E. Beesley and C.D. Foster, 'The Victoria line: social benefit and finances'.

10 A.J. Harrison, *The Economics of Transport Appraisal* (London, Croom Helm, 1974), Chapter 1.

11 K.J. Button, 'Transport policy in the United Kingdom: 1968–1974', *The*

Three Banks Review, **103** (September 1974), 27.

12 D.L. Munby, 'Mrs Castle's transport policy', *Journal of Transport Economics and Policy*, **2**, 2 (1968).

13 W. Plowden, *The Motor Car and Politics in Britain* (Harmondsworth, Middx, Penguin, 1973), pp. 362, 383–4.

14 E.J. Judge and K.J. Button, 'Inter-urban roads in Great Britain: perspectives and prospects', *Transportation Planning and Technology*, **2** (1974), 185–90.

15 *Roads for the Future*, Cmnd. 4369 (1970).

16 The results they achieved were contained in the many volumes of *The Highways Manual*, a Department of Transport internal document that specifies the administrative procedures governing the planning and construction of trunk roads.

17 A. Peaker, 'Transport policy and regional development', *Banker's Magazine*, **212** (1971), 219.

18 E.J. Judge and K.J. Button, 'Inter-urban roads in Great Britain', p. 191.

19 E.J. Judge and K.M. Gwilliam, 'Economic impact of primary roads – what kind of evidence', *Regional Studies*, **10** (1976), 483. See also, K.M. Gwilliam, 'The indirect effects of highway investment', *Regional Studies*, **4** (1970); K.M. Gwilliam and E.J. Judge, 'Transport and regional development: some preliminary results from the M62 project', Working Paper No. 41, Institute for Transport Studies, Leeds University, 1974; A. Peaker, 'New primary roads and sub-regional growth: further results', *Regional Studies*, **10** (1976); and J.S. Dodgson, 'External effects and secondary benefits in road investment appraisal', *Journal of Transport Economics and Policy*, **7** (1973).

20 J.S. Dodgson, 'Motorway investment, industrial transport costs and sub-regional growth: a case study of the M62', *Regional Studies*, **8** (1974); E.J. Cleary and R.E. Thomas, *The Economic Consequences of the Severn Bridge and its Associated Motorways* (Bath, Bath University Press, 1973); A. Peaker, 'New primary roads and sub-regional economic growth'. See also, Department of Transport, *Report of the Advisory Committee on Trunk Road Assessment*, Sections 20.17–20.21 and Appendix G.

21 *Policy for Roads: England 1978*, Cmnd. 7132 (1978), p. 3; Expenditure Committee (Trade and Industry Sub-Committee), Minutes of Evidence, *Regional Development Incentives*, H.C. 85-I, Session 1973–74.

22 G. Mills, 'Economic appraisal and reappraisal of an inter-urban road in Great Britain', *Journal of Transport Economics and Policy*, **11**, 1 (1977), 3.

23 Walker's 1971 proposals for the road programme were somewhat less grandiose than those contained in Labour's *Roads for the Future*, especially with respect to moneys allocated to improving trunk roads. They also placed particular emphasis upon the environmental improvements that could be achieved by diverting traffic away from towns and villages. E.J. Judge and K.J. Button, 'Inter-urban roads in Great Britain', pp. 186–7, 189–91; Expenditure Committee (Public Expenditure (General) Sub-Committee), Minutes of Evidence, *Relationship of Expenditure to Needs*, H.C.281-ii, Session 1971–72.

24 Road programme priorities in the late 1970s are described in *Transport Policy: A Consultation Document*, Volume 1 (London, HMSO, 1976), Chapter 9; *Transport Policy*, Cmnd. 6836 (1977), Chapter 9; and Cmnd. 7132, pp. 14–17.

25 Cmnd. 7132, p. 16.

26 Cmnd. 6836, p. 55.

27 Published for the Department of Transport by HMSO in 1978.

28 G. Charlesworth and J.L. Paisley, 'The economic assessment of returns from road works', *Proceedings of the Institution of Civil Engineers*, **14** (1959).

29 T.M. Coburn, M.E. Beesley and D.J. Reynolds, *The London–Birmingham*

Motorway, and D.J. Reynolds, *The Assessment of Priority for Road Improvements*, Road Research Technical Paper No. 48 (London, HMSO, 1960).

30 Ministry of Transport (Highway Economics Unit), 'The economic appraisal of inter-urban road schemes', Technical Memorandum No. T.5/67, 1967; Department of the Environment (Highway Economics Unit), 'The economic appraisal of inter-urban road schemes', Technical Memorandum No. H.1/71, 1971. In addition, see R.F.F. Dawson, *The Economic Assessment of Road Improvement Schemes*, Road Research Technical Paper No. 75 (London, HMSO, 1968); this superseded Technical Paper No. 48.

31 Interview, senior civil servant, Department of Transport, London, 27 October 1976.

32 Interview, senior civil servant, Departments of the Environment and Transport, London, 15 February 1977.

33 Ibid. In this context, engineers in the field tended to regard all those engaged in preparing the COBA programme as economists although Law, for example, was an engineer.

34 Interview, senior civil servant, Departments of the Environment and Transport, London, 15 February 1977.

35 Department of the Environment, *Getting the Best Roads for our Money: The COBA Method of Appraisal* (London, HMSO, 1972).

36 G.A.C. Searle, 'COBA: a computer program for the economic assessment of road schemes', *Traffic Engineering and Control* (December 1972).

37 Department of the Environment, 'COBA – a method of economic appraisal of highway schemes', Technical Memorandum No. H.5/73, 1973 plus addenda; Department of the Environment, 'Standard forecasts of vehicles and traffic', Technical Memorandum H.3/75, 1975. Also, interview, senior civil servant, Department of Transport, London, 27 October 1976.

38 Interview, senior civil servant, Department of Transport, London, 27 October 1976; see also Cmnd. 7132, pp. 28–9 for a concise description of the evolution of a typical trunk road scheme.

39 Department of the Environment (Highways Economics and Modelling Analysis Division), *COBA: A Method of Economic Appraisal of Highway Schemes* (hereafter referred to as *The COBA Manual*). Like most procedural manuals, the COBA user manual has been updated and amplified at intervals. The references that follow refer to its composition in the late 1970s.

40 Interview, senior civil servant, Department of Transport, London, 27 October 1976.

41 *The COBA Manual*, Section 2.3.1.

42 Ibid., Section 2.2.2.

43 COBA was deemed not suitable for non-rural settings because improvements in built-up, congested areas might give rise to traffic redistribution or growth. The exception to this rule was the consideration of traffic flows through a small town when a bypass was contemplated, but in this situation, users assumed that if the town were below a certain size traffic redistribution and growth would not be substantial enough to affect the validity of the COBA analysis.

44 *The COBA Manual*, Section 1.1.10.

45 Technical Memorandum H.3/75; J.C. Tanner, *Forecasts of Vehicles and Traffic in Great Britain: 1974 Revision*, Transport and Road Research Laboratory Report 650 (LR 650), 1975.

46 One of the three forecasts, the central forecast, was regarded as the most probable.

47 Technical Memorandum H.3/75; Technical Memorandum H.5/73, addenda; COBA Advice Note No. 6, February 1973.
48 *The COBA Manual*, Section 2.4.2.
49 Ibid., Section 3.3.5.
50 R.F.F. Dawson and P. Vass, *Vehicle Operating Costs in 1973*, Transport and Road Research Laboratory Report 661, 1974.
51 *The COBA Manual*, Section 3.1.3.
52 Interview, senior civil servant, Department of Transport, London, 9 November 1976.
53 Interview, senior civil servant, Department of Transport, London, 27 October 1976.
54 *Report of the Advisory Committee on Trunk Road Assessment* (hereafter referred to as *The Leitch Committee Report*), Chapter 15.
55 *The COBA Manual*, Section 2.5.3; also Technical Memorandum H.5/73, addenda, COBA Advice Note No. 12, November 1975.
56 *The Leitch Committee Report*, Chapter 21, Section 21.41.
57 Technical Memorandum H.5/73, addenda, COBA Advice Note No. 1, July 1973.
58 Technical Memorandum H.5/73, addenda, COBA Advice Note No. 15, November 1976.
59 Ibid.
60 Interview, civil servant, Department of Transport, London, 29 November 1976.
61 Interview, civil servant, Department of Transport, London, 7 December 1976.
62 Interview, civil servant, Department of Transport, London, 29 November 1976.
63 Interview, civil servant, Departments of the Environment and Transport, Birmingham, 15 Febraury 1977. Also interview, senior civil servants, Departments of the Environment and Transport, Leamington Spa, 10 March 1977. Finally, *The Leitch Committee Report*, Chapter 1, Section 1.23.
64 Department of the Environment, Roads 502, Assessment of Schemes Valued Between £50,000 and £500,000.
65 Interview, senior civil servant, Department of Transport, London, 9 November 1976.
66 *The Leitch Committee Report*, Chapter 4, Section 4.12.
67 Interview, civil servants, Departments of the Environment and Transport, Birmingham, 15 February 1977.
68 Department of Transport, 'COBA: a practical exercise', and a sample COBA printout, 1976, unpublished; the foregoing is an update of the notes used in the original COBA training sessions in the field.
69 Even in 1973 many highway engineers were hardly enthusiastic about COBA. Note, for example, the tone of J.R. Whitehead and R. Sheath, 'Engineers' view of COBA', *Journal of the Institution of Highway Engineers* (December 1973).
70 See references in notes 14 and 15 of this chapter. Also, *Transport Policy: A Consultation Document*, Volume 1, Appendix, Table 5.
71 Cmnd. 6836, and Cmnd. 7132.
72 See, for example, The Report on The Independent Commission on Transport, *Changing Directions* (London, Coronet Books, 1974) especially Chapter 7, and Part VII of *The Leitch Committee Report*.
73 Interview, civil servant, Department of Transport, London, 7 December 1976.

74 M. Walker, '"Programme robust" – DOE', *New Civil Engineer*, 20 November 1975.

75 Indeed, note concerns about RCU personnel expansion in J. Bugler, 'The billion pound blunder?', *The Guardian*, 4 May 1977.

76 Interview, senior civil servants, Departments of the Environment and Transport, Leamington Spa, 10 March 1977.

77 Interview, civil servants, Department of Transport, Preston, 7 February 1977. Networks of 1000 links and above posed manual input problems; hence, programs that 'interfaced' between COBA and certain large network models were developed.

78 Interviews, civil servant, Department of Transport, London, 6 December 1976 and 17 January 1977.

79 Technical Memorandum H.5/73, addenda, COBA Advice Note No. 4, May 1974.

80 Interview, civil servants, Department of Transport, Preston, 28 March 1977. Interview, civil servant, Departments of the Environment and Transport, Nottingham, 23 March 1977.

81 Interview, civil servant, Department of Transport, London, 24 November 1976.

82 A.J. Harrison, *The Economics of Transport Appraisal*, p. 177; note also *The Leitch Committee Report*, p. 24, Sections 4.52 and 4.53; p. 106, Section 21.30.

83 Interview, civil servant, Department of Transport, London, 24 November 1976.

84 Interview, civil servants, Department of Transport, Leamington Spa, 28 April 1977.

85 Certainly *The Leitch Committee Report* did not achieve this. There were, however, a few cases in which COBA evaluations were effectively challenged at inquiries, although they remained isolated instances and were associated with particularly blatant 'abuses' of the methodology. See, for example, M. Sullivan, 'Battle of the printouts at Winchester', *New Scientist*, **72**, 1025 (1976).

86 Interview, civil servant, Department of Transport, London, 14 December 1976. Interview, civil servant, Department of Transport, London, 7 December 1976.

87 Interview, civil servant, Department of Transport, London, 14 December 1976.

88 Ibid.

89 Ibid., Interview, civil servants, Department of Transport, Preston, 28 March 1977.

90 Collation of interviews with EcHF staff.

91 Interview, civil servant, Departments of the Environment and Transport, Birmingham, 15 February 1977.

92 Note *The Leitch Committee Report*, p. 106, Section 21.32.

93 Interview, civil servant, Departments of the Environment and Transport, Birmingham, 15 February 1977.

94 Interview, civil servant, Department of Transport, London, 14 December 1976.

95 Interview, civil servant, Department of Transport, London, 7 December 1976. Interview, civil servant. Department of Transport, London, 29 November 1976.

96 Interview, civil servant, Department of Transport, London, 29 November 1976; also internal memos concerning particular road proposals evaluated using COBA, Department of Transport, 1976.

97 *The Leitch Committee Report*, p. 66, Section 14.13; p. 107, Section 21.35.

98 Ibid., p. 106, Section 21.32.

99 Ibid., Chapter 19; the Department's vehicle and traffic forecasts had been the subject of long-standing controversy. The Tanner forecasts were criticized by both road objectors and various professionals (see, for example, H. Ferguson, 'Traffic forecasts on the right road – DOE', *New Civil Engineer*, 16 October 1975; 'Traffic forecasts: more clouds over DOE's crystal ball', *New Civil Engineer*, 22 July 1976; 'Revised car model kept under wraps', *New Civil Engineer*, 21 October 1976). The Leitch Committee was expected to deal with the forecasting problem, and this was the subject that received most public attention when the Report was released (see, for example, I. Hargreaves, 'Government gives way on road forecasts', *Financial Times*, 11 January 1978; I. Hargreaves, 'Fuel for the anti-roads lobby', *Financial Times*, 11 January 1978). See also J. Hanlon, 'Expert rap for roadbuilders' knuckles', *New Scientist*, 12 January 1978.

100 *The Leitch Committee Report*, Chapter 21, Sections 21.4–21.22.

101 Collation of interviews with EcHF members; *The Leitch Committee Report*, Chapter 16. The Leitch Committee followed EcHF in basing much of its assessment of COBA upon sensitivity analysis; see Chapter 14 and Appendix D of its Report. Indeed, a variety of commentators noted that the composition of the Leitch Committee, like that of many ministerial advisory committees, was not conducive to a profound critique of the DOT's trunk road assessment practices. Note Department of Transport, 'Advisory committee on trunk road assessment announced', Press Notice No. 34, 3 February 1977 for the Committee's composition.

102 Department of Transport, Scottish Development Department, and Welsh Office, *Road Accidents: Great Britain* (London, HMSO, published annually).

103 D.J. Reynolds, 'The cost of road accidents', *Journal of the Royal Statistical Society*, Series A (General) **119**, 4 (1956); R.F.F. Dawson, *Cost of Road Accidents in Great Britain*, Road Research Laboratory Report LR79, Ministry of Transport, Crowthorne, 1964; R.F.F. Dawson, *Current Costs of Road Accidents in Great Britain*, Road Research Laboratory Report LR396, Department of the Environment, Crowthorne, 1971. Interview, civil servants, Department of Transport, London, 4 January 1977; internal memo on road accident costs, Road Safety General, Department of Transport, 1976.

104 *The Leitch Committee Report*, p. 104, Sections 21.17–21.20. M.W. Jones-Lee, *The Value of Life: An Economic Analysis* (London, Martin Robertson, 1976). Note also G.H. Mooney, *The Valuation of Human Life* (London, Macmillan, 1977), especially from Chapter 6 onwards.

105 Note *The Leitch Committee Report*, pp. 55–6, Section 12.14 and p. 110, Section 22.3.

106 Interview, civil servant, Department of Transport, London, 17 January 1977. For a general review of modelling practices in the transport field, see I.G. Heggie, *Transport Engineering Economics* (London, McGraw-Hill, 1972).

107 Interview, civil servant, Department of Transport, London, 30 November 1976; also note Dr V.E. Outram, 'Route choice', Mathematical Advisory Unit Note 256, Department of the Environment, 1976.

108 Interview, civil servant, Department of Transport, London, 14 December 1976.

109 *The Leitch Committee Report*, Chapters 20 and 22.

110 Ibid., p. 133, Section 28.5.

111 Cmnd. 7132, p. 11.

Notes for Chapter 5

1 This was virtually a universal phenomenon, although the reasons for it differed from country to country. For an account of the US case see D.A. Worchester, *Beyond Welfare and Full Employment* (Lexington, Mass., Lexington Books, D.C. Heath, 1972), Chapter 1.

2 A.P. Thirlwall, 'Government manpower policies in Great Britain: their rationale and benefits', *British Journal of Industrial Relations*, **10**, 1–3 (1972), 165–6.

3 M.R. Fisher, *The Economic Analysis of Labour* (New York, St Martin's Press, 1971), p. ix.

4 Ibid.

5 T.W. Schultz, *Investment in Human Capital* (New York, The Free Press, 1971); G.S. Becker, *Human Capital* (New York, National Bureau of Economic Research, 1975). The concept of human capital did not originate with Schultz and Becker. For a review of its history, see B.F. Kiker, 'The historical roots of the concept of human capital' in R.A. Wykstra (ed.), *Human Capital Formation and Manpower Develoiment* (New York, The Free Press, 1971). For surveys of the various uses to which human capital theory has been put, see the Wykstra book just cited and B.F. Kiker (ed.), *Investment in Human Capital* (Columbia, University of South Carolina Press, 1971).

6 M. Blaug, 'The empirical status of human capital theory: a slightly jaundiced survey', *Journal of Economic Literature*, **14**, 3 (1976), 827.

7 This is not to say that CBA in areas like education and health is necessarily synonymous with the calculation of rates of return on investment in human capital. The cost–benefit analyst's brief is potentially wider, encompassing, for example, the measurement of the consumption effects of education, health.

8 For example, if the theory is valid, the demand for professional education should fluctuate in accord with the average earnings of the professional classes.

9 M. Blaug, 'The empirical status of human capital theory: a slightly jaundiced survey', especially the Conclusion.

10 Blaug, for example, did not suggest that the human capital approach be abandoned. Rather, he anticipated that it would become part of a new 'theory of credentialism'.

11 H.G. Shaffer, 'A critique of the concept of human capital' in M. Blaug (ed.), *Economics of Education: Selected Readings* (Harmondsworth, Middx, Penguin, 1968); N.W. Chamberlin, 'Some further thoughts on the concept of human capital' in G.G. Somers and W.D. Woods (eds), *Cost Benefit Analysis of Manpower Policies*; K.E. Boulding, 'Man as commodity' in I. Berg (ed.), *Human Resources and Economic Welfare* (New York, Columbia University Press, 1972).

12 Note J. Vaisey with K. Norris and J. Sheehan, *The Political Economy of Education* (London, Duckworth, 1972), especially pp. 29–30.

13 Ibid., pp. 30–1. The dual consumption–investment nature of education, training, health care, and the like has plagued human capital theory from its inception, and is probably the principal source of Marshall's many doubts concerning the human capital concept. Note J. Wiseman, 'Cost–benefit analysis in education' in R.A. Wykstra (ed.), *Human Capital Formation and Manpower Development*.

14 M. Blaug, 'The empirical status of human capital theory: a slightly jaundiced survey', p. 832. Many, if not most, of the British economists who have used human capital theory were in educational economics. For a brief review of the ways in which human capital theory was applied to education in Britain during the 1960s, see

M. Woodhall, *Economic Aspects of Education: A Review of Research in Britain* (Slough, National Foundation for Educational Research, 1972). Note also M. Blaug (ed.), *Economics of Education: Selected Readings*, Vols. I and II (Harmondsworth, Middx, Penguin, 1968 and 1969). See, as well, J. Vaisey, *The Economics of Education* (London, Faber, 1962).

15 B.O. Pettman and B. Showler, 'Government vocational training schemes in Great Britain', *International Journal of Social Economics*, **1**, 2 (1974), 184–8.

16 B. Stein, *Work and Welfare in Britain and the USA* (London, Macmillan, 1976), pp. 65–6.

17 B.O. Pettman and B. Showler, 'Government vocational training schemes in Great Britain', p. 186.

18 Department of Employment, *Training for the Future: a Plan for Discussion* (London, HMSO, 1972); Training Services Agency, *A Five Year Plan* (London, HMSO, 1974); Manpower Services Commission/Training Services Division, *TOPS Review, 1978*, 1978; N.J. Adnett, 'Manpower training in the United Kingdom: some aspects of the government's role', *International Journal of Social Economics*, **4**, 2 (1977); B.O. Pettman and B. Showler, 'Government vocational training schemes in Great Britain'; F. Livesey, 'The operations of Government Training Centres', *Bulletin of the Oxford University Institute of Economics and Statistics*, **32** (1970); B. Stein, *Work and Welfare in Britain and the USA*, pp. 67–70; B.O. Pettman (ed.), *Training and Retraining: A Basis for the Future* (London, Transcripta Books, 1973), especially Parts 2, 4, and 6; B.O. Pettman (ed.), *Government Involvement in Training* (Bradford, MCB Publications, 1978), Parts 1 and 2.

19 B. Stein, *Work and Welfare in Britain and the USA*, pp. 65–6.

20 A.P. Thirlwall, 'Government manpower policies in Great Britain: their rationale and benefits'.

21 J. Corina, 'Planning and the British labour market: incomes and manpower policy, 1965–70' in J. Hayward and M. Watson (eds), *Planning, Politics and Public Policy: The British, French and Italian Experience*, p. 194. At times, the rationale for manpower policies has been explicitly counter-cyclical, as in the case of the Training Service Agency's support for extra training facilities, especially those geared to young people, from 1976–7 onwards; see J.J. Hughes, 'Training for what', *Industrial Relations Journal*, **9**, 3 (1978); also Manpower Services Commission, *Annual Report, 1977–78*, p. 19.

22 B. Stein, *Work and Welfare in Britain and the USA*, pp. 67–70.

23 Ibid., pp. 70–9; Manpower Services Commission, *Annual Reports* for the years 1975–6, 1976–7 and 1977–8.

24 J.J. Hughes, *Cost–Benefit Aspects of Manpower Retraining*, Department of Employment and Productivity, Manpower Paper No. 2 (London, HMSO, 1970); see also K. Hartley, 'The economics of training: theory and evidence', *European Training*, **1**, 2 (1972). Despite the paucity of work in the economics of training before 1972, by mid-decade economic terminology had become standard in policy discussions regarding training; see, for example, S. Mukherjee for the Manpower Services Commission, *There's Work to be Done* (London, HMSO, 1974), Sections 1 and 9.

25 J.J. Hughes, *Cost–Benefit Aspects of Manpower Retraining*, p. 37.

26 See, for example, M. Blaug, M.H. Peston, A. Ziderman, 'The utilisation of qualified manpower in industry' in OECD, *Policy Conference on Highly Qualified Manpower* (Paris, OECD, 1966) and M. Blaug, M.H. Peston and A. Ziderman, *The Utilisation of Educated Manpower in Industry: A Preliminary Report* (London, Oliver and Boyd, 1967).

27 The following account has benefited from an examination of government records on the cost–benefit analysis of GTC training, held, first, by the Department of Employment and, subsequently, by the Training Services Agency, later the Training Services Division, of the Manpower Services Commission.

28 G.H. Mooney, *The Valuation of Human Life*, p. 52.

29 R.F. Fowler, *Duration of Unemployment on the Register of Wholly Unemployed*, Studies in Official Statistics, Research Series No. 1 (London, HMSO, 1968).

30 D.I. MacKay, 'After the "shake-out"', *Oxford Economic Papers*, **24**, 1 (1972).

Notes for Chapter 6

1 Surveys of cost–benefit and cost-effectiveness analysis in the British public sector published in the early to mid-1970s did not contain references to CBA in the health field. See J.N.Wolfe, *Cost Benefit and Cost Effectiveness: Studies and Analysis*, and T. Newton, *Cost–Benefit Analysis in Administration*. It was in the more specialist literature that information about CBA in the health field first appeared. See M. Perlman (ed.), *The Economics of Health and Medical Care: Proceedings of a Conferernce held by the International Economic Association at Tokyo* (London, Macmillan, 1974) and M.M. Hauser (ed.), *The Economics of Medical Care* (London, George Allen and Unwin, 1972). For econometric studies of the National Health Service and a review of the state of the literature in health economics in the late 1960s see: M.S. Feldstein, *Economic Analysis for Health Service Efficiency: Econometric Studies of the British National Health Service* (Amsterdam, North-Holland, 1967), especially the bibliography.

2 G. Teeling-Smith, 'The economics of screening' in C.R. Hart (ed.), *Screening in General Practice* (Edinburgh, Churchill Livingstone, 1975), p. 31, and A. Williams, 'The cost benefit approach', *British Medical Bulletin*, **30**, 3 (1974), 253. In the late 1960s and early 1970s the economic interpretation of allocation gained wider currency within the health service. See, for example, A.L. Cochrane, *Effectiveness and Efficiency: Random Reflections on Health Services* (London, The Nuffield Provincial Hospitals Trust, 1972), especially Chapters 8 and 9.

3 Even in America this is a consideration. In 1965 Klarman explained the lack of economists working in the health field in the United States by observing that the area does not conform to the market model. See H.E. Klarman, *The Economics of Health* (New York, Columbia University Press, 1965), pp. 10–11.

4 Economists often refer to the process whereby doctors assess the needs of their patients as rationing, but have frequently found themselves unable to explicate it. See M. Cooper, 'Economics of need: the experience of the British health service' in M. Perlman (ed.), *The Economics of Health and Medical Care*, pp. 96–101.

5 A. Williams, '"Need" as a demand concept (with special reference to health)' in A.J. Culyer (ed.), *Economic Policies and Social Goals*, p. 69.

6 See N. Glass, 'Cost benefit analysis and health services', *Health Trends*, **5**, 3 (1973), 51 and A. Williams, '"Need" as a demand concept', in A.J. Culyer (ed.), *Economic Policies and Social Goals*, p. 66.

7 R. Boguslaw, *The New Utopians: A Study of System Design and Social Change* (Englewood Cliffs, N.J., Prentice-Hall, 1965), pp. 15, 56–8, 75–8.

8 B. Abel-Smith, *Value for Money in Health Services* (London, Heinemann, 1976), p. 122.

9 M.S. Levitt, 'Problems of efficiency' in M.M. Hauser (ed.), *The Economics*

of Medical Care, including the discussion by A.J. Culyer.

10 G. Teeling-Smith, 'A cost-benefit approach to medical care' in M.M. Hauser (ed.), *The Economics of Medical Care*.

11 Ibid., p. 148.

12 Interview, Economic Adviser, Department of Health and Social Security, London, 15 September 1976.

13 A. Williams, 'Measuring the effectiveness of health care systems' in M. Perlman (ed.), *The Economics of Health and Medical Care*, p. 374.

14 N. Glass, 'Cost benefit analysis and health services', p. 53. See also B.C. Weisbrod, 'Research in health economics: a survey', *International Journal of Health Services*, **5**, 4 (1975), 655–6.

15 G. Teeling-Smith, 'The economics of screening' in M.M. Hauser (ed.), *The Economics of Health Care*, p. 31.

16 J.A. Roberts, 'Economic evaluation of health care: a survey', *British Journal of Preventive and Social Medicine*, **28**, 3 (1974), 211 and D.J. Reynolds, 'The cost of road accidents'.

17 J.A. Roberts, 'Economic evaluation of health care', pp. 212–13 and A. Williams, 'The cost–benefit approach', p. 253.

18 A. Williams, 'The cost–benefit approach', p. 254 and N. Glass, 'Cost–benefit analysis and health services', p. 52.

19 G. Teeling-Smith, 'The economics of screening', p. 31.

20 J.D. Pole, 'Economic aspects of screening for disease' in *Screening in Medical Care: Reviewing the Evidence* (London, Oxford University Press for the Nuffield Provincial Hospitals Trust, 1968), p. 141.

21 Department of Health and Social Security, *Prevention and Health: Everybody's Business: A Reassessment of Public and Personal Health* (London, HMSO, 1976), pp. 72–3.

22 Ibid., Chapter V, and First Report from the Expenditure Committee, *Preventive Medicine*, Vol. I, H.C. 169-i, Session 1976–77, pp. xli–lxxiii.

23 DHSS, *Prevention and Health: Everybody's Business*, Chapter VI. See also J.M.G. Wilson, 'Some principles of early diagnosis and detection' in G. Teeling-Smith (ed.), *Surveillance and Early Diagnosis in General Practice* (London, Office of Health Economics, 1966); G. Teeling-Smith, 'The economics of screening'; and H.P. Ferrer, *Screening for Health: Theory and Practice* (London, Butterworths, 1968), Chapter 2.

24 A.J. Culyer, 'The economics of health' in R.M. Grant and G.K. Shaw (eds), *Current Issues in Economic Policy* (Oxford, Philip Alan, 1975), pp. 169–71. The possibilities for rationalization inherent in screening were sketched in C. Hart, 'The history of screening' in C.R. Hart (ed.), *Screening in General Practice*.

25 DHSS, *Prevention and Health: Everybody's Business*, p. 80.

26 H.C. 169-i, Session 1976–77, pp. lxiii–lxvii.

27 DHSS, *Prevention and Health: Everybody's Business*, pp. 27–30; Department of Health and Social Security, *Prevention and Health, Reducing the Risk: Safer Pregnancy and Childbirth* (London, HMSO, 1977), pp. 9, 12.

28 DHSS, *Prevention and Health, Reducing the Risk*, p. 10.

29 Ibid., Chapter II.

30 T. McKeown, 'Human malformations: introduction', *British Medical Bulletin*, **32**, 1 (1976), 1.

31 Ibid., p. 2; malformations deriving from single genes are rare. See also, C.O. Carter, 'Genetics of common single malformations', *British Medical Bulletin*, **32**, 1 (1976).

32 R.W. Smithells, 'Environmental teratogens of man', *British Medical*

Bulletin, **32**, 1 (1976).

33 T. McKeown, 'Human malformations: introduction', p. 2. See also I. Leck, 'Descriptive epidemiology of common malformations (excluding central nervous system defects)', *British Medical Bulletin*, **32**, 1 (1976).

34 J. MacVicar, 'Antenatal detection of fetal abnormality – physical methods', *British Medical Bulletin*, **32**, 1 (1976).

35 K.M. Laurence, 'Prenatal diagnosis of chromosome disorders', *British Medical Bulletin*, **32**, 1 (1976).

36 C.O. Carter, 'Genetics of common single malformations', p. 21. See also G.D. Stark, *Spina Bifida: Problems and Management* (Oxford, Blackwell Scientific Publishing, 1977) and L.E. Sever, 'Epidemiologic aspects of neural tube defects' in B.F. Crandall and M.A. Brazier (eds), *Prevention of Neural Tube Defects: The Role of Alpha-Feto Protein* (New York, Academic Press, 1978).

37 UK Collaborative Study on Alpha-fetoprotein in relation to Neural-tube Defects, 'Maternal serum alpha-fetoprotein measurement in antenatal screening for anencephaly and spina bifida in early pregnancy', *The Lancet*, **1**, 8026 (1977), 1324 (hereafter referred to as UK Collaborative Study).

38 Sub-Committee Secretariat, Joint Standing Sub-Committee on Screening in Medical Care, Department of Health and Social Security, 'Economic consequences for the public sector of a spina bifida screening programme', April 1976.

39 Ibid. The selective surgical policy introduced in 1971 is reviewed in J. Lorber, 'Ethical concepts in the treatment of myelmeningocele' in C.A. Swinyard (ed.), *Decision Making and the Defective Newborn: Proceedings of a Conference on Spina Bifida and Ethics* (Springfield, Ill., C. Thomas, 1978).

40 S.C. Rogers and J.A.C. Weatherall, *Anencephalus, Spina Bifida and Congenital Hydrocephalus: England and Wales, 1964–1972*, Office of Population, Censuses and Surveys, Studies on Medical and Population Subjects, No. 32 (London, HMSO, 1976), p. 9. The figure for spina bifida incidence excludes encephalacele.

41 Ibid., pp. 7, 9–10, 18–27.

42 D.J.H. Brock, 'Prenatal diagnosis – chemical methods', *British Medical Bulletin*, **32**, 1 (1976).

43 D.J.H. Brock and R.G. Sutcliffe, 'Alpha-fetoprotein in the antenatal diagnosis of anencephaly and spina bifida', *The Lancet*, **2**, 7770 (1972); D.J.H. Brock, A.E. Bolton and J.M. Monaghan, 'Prenatal diagnosis of anencephaly through maternal serum – alphafetoprotein measurement', *The Lancet*, **2**, 7835 (1973); D.J.H. Brock, A.E. Bolton and J.B. Scrimgeour, 'Prenatal diagnosis of spina bifida and anencephaly through maternal plasma – alpha-fetoprotein measurement', *The Lancet*, **1**, 7861 (1974); D.J.H. Brock, J.B. Scrimgeour and M.M. Nelson, 'Amniotic fluid alphafetoprotein measurements in the early prenatal diagnosis of central nervous system disorders', *Clinical Genetics*, **7**, 2 (1975).

44 UK Collaborative Study.

45 Interview, civil servants, Department of Health and Social Security, London, 11 August 1977.

46 Ibid.

47 H.C. 169-i, Session 1976–77, p. xv.

48 Ibid.

49 Ibid. As the government noted in its response to the Sub-Committee's Report, it had turned its attention to the subject of prevention before the publication of the Sub-Committee's recommendations. See, for example, Department of Health and Social Security, *Priorities for Health and Personal Social Services in England, A Consultative Document* (London, HMSO, 1976), pp. 20–2 and DHSS, *Prevention and Health: Everybody's Business*. For the government's

response see Department of Health and Social Security, Department of Education and Science, Scottish Office, Welsh Office, *Prevention and Health*, Cmnd. 7047 (1977). Note, in addition, Department of Health and Social Security, *Priorities in the Health and Social Services, The Way Forward* (London, HMSO, 1977), pp. 8–9.

50 Note, First Report from the Expenditure Committee, *Preventive Medicine*, Volume III, Minutes of Evidence, Appendices and Index, H.C. 169-iii, Session 1976–77, pp. 611–13.

51 Ibid., p. 347.

52 Interview, civil servants, 11 August 1977; interview, Senior Medical Officer, Department of Health and Social Security, London, 26 November 1976.

53 J.D. Pole, 'Programmes, priorities and budgets', *British Journal of Preventive and Social Medicine*, **28**, 3 (1974).

54 Civil Service Commission, *Economists: Posts in Government* (London, HMSO, 1976), p. 17. For a concise description of the organizational structure of DHSS in this period and the place of the EAO within it, see Expenditure Committee (General Sub-Committee), *Developments in the Civil Service since the Fulton Report*, Minutes of Evidence, H.C. 368-xi, Session 1975–76, especially pp. 335–51.

55 H.C. 368-xi, Session 1975–76, pp. 336, 338, 343; see also 'Functions of the medical staff of the Department of Health and Social Security', *Health Trends*, **8**, 3 (1976).

56 Interview, Economic Adviser, DHSS, London 15 September 1976.

57 Z. Stein, M. Sussex and A.V. Guterman, 'Screening programme for prevention of Down's syndrome', *The Lancet*, **1**, 7798 (1973).

58 Ibid., p. 308.

59 World Health Organization, Technical Report Series No. 497, *Genetic Disorders: Prevention, Treatment and Rehabilitation* (Geneva, World Health Organization, 1972), and A. Milunsky, *The Prenatal Diagnosis of Hereditary Disorders* (Springfield, Ill., C.C. Thomas, 1973).

60 'Economic aspects of the prevention of Down's syndrome (Mongolism)', International Institute for Applied Systems Analysis Research Report, Schloss Laxenburg, Austria, March 1975.

61 Ibid., p. 203.

62 Ibid., p. 205.

63 Ibid., p. 214.

64 Ibid., comments of discussants.

65 Ibid.

66 Ibid., p. 215.

67 S. Hagard and F.A. Carter, 'Preventing the birth of infants with Down's syndrome: a cost–benefit analysis', *British Medical Journal*, **1**, 6012 (1976).

68 S. Hagard, F. Carter and R.G. Milne, 'Screnning for spina bifida cystica: a cost–benefit analysis', *British Journal of Preventive and Social Medicine*, **30**, 1 (1976).

69 'Economic consequences for the public sector of a spina bifida screening programme'.

70 Ibid.

71 Ibid.

72 Ibid.

73 Ibid.

74 UK Collaborative Study, p. 1323.

75 Interview, civil servants, DHSS, London 11 August 1977.

76 Department of Health and Social Security, Draft Health Circular, 1977.

77 'Prenatal screening for spina bifida', *The Lancet*, **1**, 8056 (1978) and 'Neural-tube defects', *The Lancet*, **1**, 8059 (1978).

78 Ibid. and S. Yanchinski, 'Doctors split on screening pregnant women to detect spina bifida babies', *New Scientist*, 12 January 1978.

79 About a third in the mid-seventies.

80 DHSS, Draft Health Circular.

81 See, for example, D.J.H. Brock *et al.*, 'Maternal plasma alpha-feto protein screening for fetal neural tube defects', *British Journal of Obstetrics and Gynaecology*, **85**, 8 (1978).

82 'Prenatal screening for spina bifida'.

83 Ibid.

84 See especially editorials and correspondence in *The Lancet* during 1978. Some of the specific references are cited below.

85 S. Macintyre, 'To have or have not – promotion and prevention of childbirth in gynaecological work' in M. Stacey (ed.), *The Sociology of the NHS, Sociological Review Monograph*, 22 (1976).

86 Y.B. Gordon *et al.*, 'Fetal wastage as a result of an alpha-fetoprotein screening programme', *The Lancet*, **1**, 8066 (1978); 'Neural tube defects', *The Lancet*, **1**, 8061 (1978); 'Screening for spina bifida', *The Lancet*, **1**, 8067 (1978); 'Screening for neural tube defects', *The Lancet*, **1**, 8069 (1978); 'Fetal wastage as a result of an alpha-fetoprotein screening programme', *The Lancet*, **1**, 8070 (1978); 'Screening for neural tube defects', *The Lancet*, **2**, 8085 (1978).

87 'Ethical problems of screening for neural tube defects', *The Lancet*, **2**, 8081 (1978); 'Ethical problems of screening for neural tube defects', *The Lancet*, **2**, 8083 (1978); 'Ethical problems of screening for neural tube defects', *The Lancet*, **2**, 8088 (1978).

88 Second Report of the UK Collaborative Study on Alpha-fetoprotein in Relation to Neural-tube Defects, 'Amniotic-fluid alpha-fetoprotein measurement in antenatal diagnosis of anencephaly and open spina bifida in early pregnancy', *The Lancet*, **2**, 8144 (1979). See also, Third Report of the UK Collaborative Study, 'Survival of infants with open spina bifida in relation to maternal serum alpha-fetoprotein level', *British Journal of Obstetrics and Gynaecology*, **89**, 1 (1982); Fourth Report of the UK Collaborative Study, 'Estimating an individual's risk of having a fetus with open spina bifida and the value of repeat alpha-fetoprotein testing', *Journal of Epidemiology and Community Health*, **36**, 2 (1982); and M.A. Ferguson-Smith (ed.), 'Early prenatal diagnosis', *British Medical Bulletin*, **39**, 4 (1983).

89 For example, I.W. Chubb *et al.*, 'Acetylcholinesterase in human amniotic fluid: an index of fetal neural development?', *The Lancet*, **1**, 8118 (1979); A.D. Smith *et al.*, 'Amniotic-fluid acetylcholinesterase as a possible diagnostic test for neural-tube defects in early pregnancy?', *The Lancet*, **1**, 8118 (1979); Report of the Collaborative Acetylcholinesterase Study, 'Amniotic fluid acetylcholinesterase electrophoresis as a secondary test in the diagnosis of anencephaly and open spina bifida in early pregnancy', *The Lancet*, **2**, 8242 (1981).

90 Report to the Medical Research Council by their Working Party on Amniocentesis, 'An assessment of the hazards of amniocentesis', *British Journal of Obstetrics and Gynaecology*, **85**, Supplement No. 2 (1978).

91 The National Institute of Child Health and Human Development Study Group, National Registry for Amniocentesis Study Group, 'Midtrimester amniocentesis for prenatal diagnosis: safety and accuracy', *Journal of the American Medical Association*, **236**, 13 (1976); N.E. Simpson *et al.*, 'Prenatal diagnosis of genetic disease in Canada: report of a collaborative study', *Canadian Medical*

Association Journal, **115**, 8 (1976).

92 Working Group on Screening for Neural Tube Defects of the Standing Medical Advisory Committee, Department of Health and Social Security, *Report*, July 1979.

93 Department of Health and Social Security, Health Notice, 'Health service development: report of the Working Group on Screening for Neural Tube Defects', HN (79) 116, December 1979.

94 For example, J.R. Owens *et al.*, '19-year incidence of neural tube defects in area under constant surveillance', *The Lancet*, **2**, 8254 (1981).

95 R.W. Smithells *et al.*, 'Possible prevention of neural tube defects by periconceptual vitamin supplementation', *The Lancet*, **1**, 8164 (1980) and R.W. Smithells *et al.*, 'Further evidence of vitamin supplementation for prevention of neural tube defect recurrences', *The Lancet*, **1**, 8332 (1983).

96 G.H. Mooney, *The Valuation of Human Life*, p. 36.

97 S. Hagard *et al.*, 'Screening for spina bifida cystica: a cost–benefit analysis', p. 50.

98 Culyer has made this point with reference to another screening study. A.J. Culyer, *Need and the National Health Service* (London, Martin Robertson, 1976), p. 68.

Notes for Chapter 7

1 K.R. Minogue, *The Liberal Mind* (London, Methuen, 1963), p. 22.

2 Ibid., pp. 42–3.

3 S.E. Rhoads, 'Economists and policy analysis', *Public Administration Review*, **38**, 2 (1978), 114. Note also R.L. Schott, 'The professions and government: engineering as a case in point' and F.C. Mosher, 'Professions in public service' in the same issue.

4 On the generality of Neoclassical theory see D. Winch, 'Marginalism and the boundaries of economic science' in R.D. Collison Black, A.W. Coats and Craufurd D.W. Goodwin (eds), *The Marginal Revolution in Economics* (Durham, N.C., Duke University Press, 1973), especially pp. 63–4, 68–9. Note also H.A. Simon's remarks concerning rationality as the main export commodity of economics in 'Rationality as process and as product of thought', *American Economic Review, Papers and Proceedings*, May 1978, espeically pp. 1–2.

5 In this connection, see R.A. Solo, 'Neoclassical economics in perspective', *Journal of Economic Issues*, IX, 4 (1975), 637–9; E. Rotwein, 'Empiricism and economic method: several views considered', *Journal of Economic Issues*, VII, 3 (1973); L.A. Boland, 'Conventionalism and economic theory', *Philosophy of Science*, **37**, 2 (1970); L.A. Boland, 'Testability in economic science', *South African Journal of Economics*, **45**, 1 (1977); T.C. Koopmans, 'Economics among the sciences', *American Economic Review*, **69**, 1 (1979), Section VI; W. Leontief, 'Theoretical assumptions and non-observed fact', *American Economic Review*, LXI, 1 (1971); R.L. Basmann, 'Modern logic and the suppositious weakness of the empirical foundations of economic science', *Schweizerishe Zeitschrift für Volkswirtschaft und Statistik*, III, 2 (1975).

6 In this regard, it should be noted that even certain methodologists accept as correct a broad eclecticism in the choice of assumptions, hypotheses and so on. Note E. Rotwein's discussion of Bronfenbrenner in 'Empiricism and economic method', pp. 366–8, 375.

7 Note P. Self, *Econocrats and the Policy Process*, Chapter 4.

8 Note P. Winch, *The Idea of a Social Science* (London, Routledge and Kegan

Paul, 1958), pp. 54–5.

9 A. Rapoport (ed.), *Carl von Clauswitz, On War* (Harmondsworth, Middx, Penguin, 1978), Editor's Introduction, pp. 66–80. The quotation comes from p. 80.

10 T.C. Koopmans, 'Economics among the sciences', p. 7 and Section VII; J. Morley English, 'Economic concepts to disturb the engineer', *Engineering Economist*, **19**, 3 (1974).

11 *The Leitch Committee Report*, Chapters 25 and 27.

12 J.R. Hicks, 'The scope and status of welfare economics', p. 307.

13 C.B. Macpherson, *Democratic Theory: Essays in Retrieval* (Oxford, Clarendon Press, 1973), p. 188.

14 Ibid., pp. 189–90.

15 K.R. Minogue, *The Liberal Mind*, p. 107.

16 T. Parsons, *The Structure of Social Action*, Vol. I, Chapter IV; the quotation is from p. 148.

17 Ibid., p. 133. See also, C.B. Macpherson, *Democratic Theory*, p. 192 and Essay III.

18 I.M.D. Little, *A Critique of Welfare Economics* (London, Oxford University Press, 1973).

19 Note, by analogy, Solo's remarks about Hicks's approach to the theory of monopolistic competition in R.A. Solo, 'Neoclassical economics in perspective', pp. 632–4.

20 J.R. Hicks, 'The scope and status of welfare economics'.

21 Ibid., p. 325.

22 R.H. Day, 'Orthodox economists and existential economics', *Journal of Economic Issues*, IX, 2 (1975).

Index